HOBBIT
VIRTUES

ALSO BY CHRISTOPHER A. SNYDER:

Gatsby's Oxford (2019)

The Making of Middle-earth: A New Look Inside the World of J.R.R. Tolkien (2013)

The Britons (2003)

The World of King Arthur (2000)

An Age of Tyrants: Britain and the Britons, A.D. 400-600 (1998)

HOBBIT VIRTUES

Rediscovering Virtue Ethics Through J. R. R. Tolkien's

The Hobbit and *The Lord of the Rings*

CHRISTOPHER A. SNYDER

PEGASUS BOOKS
NEW YORK LONDON

HOBBIT VIRTUES

Pegasus Books, Ltd.
148 W 37th Street, 13th Floor
New York, NY 10018

First Pegasus Books cloth edition August 2020

Interior design by Maria Fernandez

Every effort has been made to obtain permissions for excerpts in the proceeding text.
Please contact Claiborne Hancock at Pegasus Books with any queries or concerns.

ISBN: 978-1-64313-410-9

10 9 8 7 6 5 4 3 2 1

Printed in the United States of America
Distributed by Simon & Schuster
www.pegasusbooks.us

Dedicated to the One

and to the Flame Imperishable

CONTENTS

"I would claim, if I did not think it presumptuous in one so ill-instructed, to have as one object the elucidation of truth, and the encouragement of good morals in this real world, by the ancient device of exemplifying them in unfamiliar embodiments. . . ."

—J. R. R. Tolkien,
Letters, 194 (September 1954)

Author's Note

This book draws primarily on J. R. R. Tolkien's *The Hobbit* and *The Lord of the Rings* (abbreviated in the notes as *LOTR*). In most cases I follow Tolkien's spelling and capitalization in these two works; for example, he usually capitalizes when he is speaking of the "Races" of Middle-earth (Hobbits, Dwarves, Elves, Men, etc.) but not when he is referring to a specific member or number of that grouping. His use of the terms "Race" and "Men" are both problematic today (more on this in chapter nine).

As this book was going to press (May 2020) millions of people were suffering from a global pandemic. In the midst of this darkness there were innumerable acts of moral and physical courage and selflessness. I wish to thank those who are giving us help and hope.

PREFACE

Love thy neighbor.

These three words from the "Love Commandment" seem, on their face, to be quite simple. They are Jesus's restatement of the Golden Rule, and thus have great antiquity in both the Greek and Jewish (Leviticus 19:18) traditions; similar commandments can be found in Hinduism, Confucianism, and Buddhism as well. This is also political advice, one rabbi's challenge to those living in a multicultural world—ancient Judea under Roman rule, where several languages were spoken and many religions observed. Jesus's followers knew, however, that loving one's neighbor was much harder than loving family or friends. How could a Jewish peasant love a Roman soldier or a Greek tax collector?

Respecting one's neighbor, let alone loving him or her, remains a challenge to modern Americans and those living in other Western democracies. The 2016 U.S. presidential election, the Syrian and Latin American refugee crises, and Brexit voting and rhetoric all revealed deep fissures between neighbors who found that, even when they spoke the same language, they could not understand or sympathize with each other. Civil discourse gave way too often to violence, protest, and abusive online taunts and insults. How do we protect such democratic hallmarks as free speech and freedom of assembly when the body politic is suspicious of one another, holds divergent worldviews, and discards civility?

It begins, I suggest here, with talking, finding a common language that reaches across party lines, cultures, and religions. That language can be—indeed, may have to be—what philosophers call *virtue ethics*, laws or principles that guide moral action both privately and (most importantly for this book) publicly. For thousands of years and across many continents, human beings living in society held up such principles as truthfulness, courage, and self-sacrifice to be essential for stable, peaceful communities that included more than just family members and often different cultures and religions. There is no scholarly consensus on where or how virtue ethics originated. But whether one was obeying the laws of an all-powerful god, employed reason to select moral virtues, or ascribed all behaviors to inheritance and evolutionary biology, these principles had a nearly universal attractiveness and effectiveness. Though many philosophers may have lost confidence in these principles in the wake of the last century's two world wars, the average citizen, in even war-torn lands, did not. What war and terrorism could not destroy, however, is now under a perhaps even more serious assault: a worldwide method of communication that has been co-opted to promote the egotistical, narcissistic, and prejudicial tendencies within us all—for fame and profit and power. How can we possibly redirect such technology for the common good?

It begins, I argue in this book, with the Philosopher and the Hobbit.

It is noteworthy that, a thousand years ago, Jewish, Persian, and Arab scholars spent great efforts studying and translating Aristotle's ethical writings, and that their work determined much of the curriculum of the first universities in Europe. Aristotle was simply "the Philosopher" for the great minds and teachers of the Middle Ages. Aristotle argued, principally in the *Nicomachean Ethics* (edited by his son Nicomachus) and the *Eudemian Ethics* (edited by his friend Eudemus), that virtues (*aretai*) are rational states (*hexeis*), or a stable disposition, in a person's soul. They involve choosing how to act in a difficult situation and continuing to choose the correct action to the point of it becoming a habit, thus developing a character that we might term "virtuous." We seek virtue, according to Aristotle, because we seek a final good that is happiness (*eudaimonia*), or living well and doing well. Those who achieve this are "blessed" (*makarios*).

Subsequent ages did not discard Aristotle's teachings on ethics (as they did for much of his writings on astronomy) but rather debated some and added others to his great list of moral virtues (see Appendix A). Moreover, one can read the *Nicomachean Ethics* side-by-side with Confucius's *Analects* and see that there is much agreement regarding right conduct in a civil society, even though these seminal thinkers of the West and the East developed their philosophies independently. Nor are Hinduism, Taoism, Buddhism, and other ancient Eastern religions and philosophies strangers to the language of virtue ethics. Indeed, C. S. Lewis called his matrix of overlapping religious laws "the Tao" (see Appendix C). Both Lewis and his friend and Oxford colleague J. R. R. Tolkien, however, saw a great rift growing between the language of early 20th-century philosophers, artists, and poets and that of their predecessors. It is an intellectual schism that must be healed if we are to rediscover the wisdom of these ancient ethical traditions of the East and the West.

That brings us to the Hobbit. When Professor Tolkien first discovered the Hobbit Bilbo Baggins living in his cozy hole in the ground, he was simply a little creature about to embark on a great adventure involving Wizards, Dwarves, Elves, and dragons.

Bilbo was the humble protagonist of a tale told to the professor's children, what Tolkien and Lewis would call a "fairy-story." Much wisdom can be found in such children's tales and fables. When the bedtime story evolved into a novel, Tolkien found that this Hobbit and his companions could also be literary devices for displaying vices and virtues, indeed even developing a distinctive "Hobbit philosophy" by the end of the book. The immediate popularity of *The Hobbit* (1937) led to his friends, fans, and publisher to clamor for "more Hobbit tales." The novel's ultimate sequel, *The Lord of the Rings*, gave Tolkien an opportunity to further explore uniquely Hobbit virtues, this time necessary to prevent a war for the domination of Middle-earth (whose mythology he had begun in the trenches of the First World War and continued during the Second). *The Lord of the Rings* proved even more successful, a worldwide popularity that has only increased since its original serial publication in 1954–55.[1]

Why have so many readers from so many cultural, political, and religious backgrounds responded so positively to Tolkien's writings? And why were Peter Jackson's film adaptations of *The Lord of the Rings* (2001–03) so popular among viewers and even critics? The answer lies beyond the artistic or technical skills of Tolkien and Jackson, as great as they are (the former was not a professional novelist when he wrote *The Hobbit*, the latter had never made a blockbuster or award-winning film before *The Fellowship of the Ring*). I would suggest that, in addition to being great stories (fairy-stories), the novels and films resonate with so many people because they feature characters who display widely recognizable and respected virtues: courage, humility, self-sacrifice, wisdom, and friendship, for example. And while it is not unusual in "fantasy" novels and films to see kings and warriors displaying such virtues, Tolkien's great contribution was the creation of Hobbits, little creatures capable of heroic virtue. Most of us may not be able to see ourselves as warriors, Wizards, or kings, but we can relate to the diminutive Hobbits with their mundane habits and lifestyle.

I have written this book to tease out some of these virtues from Tolkien's literary figures and use them as vehicles for discussing the history and continuing relevance of said virtue.[2] Tolkien was a devout Catholic and a professional medievalist, and thus it should not surprise us to see many of these Middle-earth virtues in the Gospels and in the writings of Church Fathers like Augustine and Aquinas. He was also born during the reign of Queen Victoria, fought to defend England and democratic values in the First World War, and died at the height of Watergate and the Vietnam War. The German Catholic philosopher Josef Pieper (1904–97), inspired by his own reading of Plato and Aquinas, called for a return to the tradition of moral virtues as a way to keep open the dialog between generations.[3] The rapidity of change in cultural trends and of technological innovation, even greater now than in Tolkien's lifetime, makes finding a common language ever more important.

Many readers and critics have also seen the influences of classical philosophy, Greco-Roman and Norse mythology, and secular Arthurian romance on Tolkien's writing, while others have seen consistencies between his thought and Eastern philosophy and religions.[4] I have previously written about the ways that history and archaeology can give us insights into Tolkien's intellectual world.[5] Here, I want to especially bring us back to Aristotelian virtue ethics, a major influence on thinkers from Aquinas to Kant and, through the Catholic catechism, Tolkien himself. Aristotle argued that virtue was a Golden Mean that must be sought between extremes of vice, and yet today the algorithms of social media and mass advertising push us *toward* extremes, whether of our political positions or our spending habits.[6]

The present work is not primarily literary criticism or even a book about Tolkien. It is, rather, a call to use Tolkien (and other writers) as guides to rediscover the ancient language of virtue ethics, and an argument for why this language is so crucial for us today if we want to sustain democracy and civil society. While these virtues may privately help one become a better person, they are essential for us small and flawed creatures to communicate and get along with each other. If we are to save Hobbiton—a place that values good food, stories told by fireside, and fellowship—from the political machinations of the Big Folk, we must come out of our holes and arm ourselves with these virtues.

"We probably do not use the *word* 'virtue' often, if at all, but of course it does not follow from this that we do not recognize virtues and vices," writes historian of philosophy Julia Annas. "When we read Aristotle on the virtues or Epicurus on pleasure, it certainly seems that we understand what is said unforcedly, that we know how to use, and extend the use of, these very concepts."[7] I am not suggesting that virtue ethics are the solution to the world's problems, nor that they can by themselves lead to personal salvation. It is simply a language, and languages help us talk to one another. It is also an ancient and nearly lost language that may help prevent us from falling completely into a state of naked self-interest, from bestiality. Animals can love their mates, their children, maybe even those who feed them; loving one's neighbor is a command to humans to live up to their uniquely human potential. We should not be too proud, however, to look to the smallest among us for example. There is much we can learn from Hobbits.

Tending Your Garden

In the darkly satirical novel *Candide* (1759), written by the *philosophe* Voltaire, the young hero goes on a quest in part to discover the meaning of life. After many misadventures, he and a group of friends find themselves forming a community on a small farm near Istanbul. When at the end of the novel Candide contemplates the simple but honest lifestyle of his Turkish neighbors, he offers to his companions the following words of wisdom: "We must take care of our own garden."

J. R. R. Tolkien (1892–1973) shares little in common with the urbane world-traveler Voltaire. Yet, with his Hobbits, Tolkien seems to suggest that cultivating gardens is important, even noble, if not entirely sufficient. It is a particularly English virtue to garden, even if it is only a tiny patch of green. Tolkien was himself born in Bloemfontein, South Africa, but spent much of his childhood in the rural English Midlands. He came to idolize the small farms, rolling hills, rivers, and forests of western England and Wales, reinforced by his country walks in Oxfordshire, where he lived, as a student and as a professor, for most of his life. From these experiences he constructed the Shire, that part of Middle-earth inhabited by Hobbits. Growing things in the Shire, and the living and intelligent trees in the forests of Middle-earth, are at the very heart of the "secondary world" Tolkien created through words and images. In the drawings and paintings that he made to accompany *The Hobbit*, trees and other flora play a prominent part.

Hobbits are small and burrow holes in the ground, like rabbits (a not coincidental similarity). They enjoy a close friendship with the earth, according to Tolkien.[1] Bilbo Baggins, hero of *The Hobbit*, is very proud of his garden and bequeaths it to his young cousin Frodo Baggins, hero of *The Lord of the Rings*. Both well-to-do Hobbits, however, have gardeners who do much of the work for them: Gaffer Gamgee and his son Samwise. The Gaffer and Sam are themselves philosophers, though of a much humbler stature than Voltaire. The Gaffer dispenses life advice through folksy maxims, while his son has a romantic and adventurous heart, clumsily composing poetry. "You are a new people and a new world to me," exclaims Faramir, the noble captain of Gondor, when he first meets Frodo and Sam. "Your land must be a realm of peace and content, and there must gardeners be in high honour." Yes, gardeners are greatly honored in the Shire, confirms Frodo.[2]

Tolkien seems to be having a bit of fun here, satirizing the English love of gardening, embedded class distinctions, and the folksy advice given by farmers and craftsmen. Yet there is some serious philosophy in all this Hobbit talk. Hearth and home, creature comforts, food and family—these are very important things to Hobbits, as they were to Tolkien and his Oxford friends, especially those of the group Tolkien and Lewis called the Inklings. "Human grandeur is a very dangerous thing," warns Doctor Pangloss in *Candide*, and indeed most Hobbits avoid ostentatious displays of wealth and getting involved in the politics and wars of the Big Folk. But this contentedness is not enough, and the isolation of the Hobbits is not sufficient to provide them with security. Bilbo has some "Tookish blood," a desire for adventure buried deep inside him, and he needs a little push from the Wizard Gandalf to leave the security of his home to go on an adventure where he will face great malice, violent greed, and ultimately a great war. Sam desires "a nice little hole" in the Shire "with a bit of garden of my own," and the Elf-queen Galadriel gives Sam the gift of a small box filled with earth from her orchard, promising him that if he makes it back to the Shire, the soil from Lothlórien will make his own little garden without equal in Middle-earth.[3] Frodo must make great sacrifices of comfort and prosperity to prevent all of Middle-earth from falling into tyranny and slavery. Even with the great tyrant Sauron defeated, Frodo and his friends return to a Shire devastated by industry and the lesser tyranny of "Sharkey" and his thugs. While Sam the gardener uses Galadriel's gift to restore the Shire to a "good green and pleasant land," Frodo's war wounds will not heal and allow him peace and domesticity. Thus it was for many of England's returning soldiers in 1919.

Readers of *Candide* and of Tolkien's fiction will of course recognize that the garden is heavily symbolic. It recalls the Garden of Eden in Genesis, fruitful yet susceptible to serpents and sin. "We got to get ourselves back to the Garden," sing Crosby, Stills, and Nash in the Joni Mitchell–penned song "Woodstock." *Can* we get back to that Edenic state, through our own efforts? C. S. Lewis, in his book *The Four Loves*, begins his discussion of charity with a parable about a garden:

> . . . a garden will not fence and weed itself. . . . A garden is a good thing . . . [but] it will remain a garden, as distinct from a wilderness,

only if someone does these things to it. Its real glory is of quite a different kind. The very fact that it needs constant weeding and pruning bears witness to that glory. It teems with life. It glows with colour and smells like heaven and puts forward at every hour of a summer day beauties which man never could have created and could not even, on his own resources, have imagined. . . . When God planted a garden He set a man over it and set the man under Himself. When He planted the garden of our nature and caused the flowering, fruiting loves to grow there, He set our will to "dress" them. . . . [Man's] laborious—and largely negative—services are indispensable. If they were needed when the garden was still Paradisal, how much more now when the soil has gone sour and the worst weeds seem to thrive on it best?[4]

Tolkien was very fond of Oxford's Botanic Garden, which sits between Lewis's college (Magdalen) and his own (Merton), and there it is said grew his favorite tree. Both men could gaze out the windows of their offices upon their own college's gardens. Addison's Walk, which winds along the willow-lined River Cherwell between Magdalen and the Botanic Garden, was the location of the famous late-night conversation between the two English professors that led, in part, to Lewis's conversion to Christianity. As Tolkien read aloud most of *The Lord of the Rings* to Lewis and the other Inklings, Lewis would have recognized and appreciated the many appearances of gardens and gardeners in the novel, and of course the importance of trees to Tolkien's whole legendarium.

Cultivating one's garden can also be seen as tending to our individual souls, cultivating virtues through reason and discipline. Voltaire and Tolkien may both have had in mind the advice given by Socrates in Plato's *Republic*: the ideal (or at least stable) state requires citizens who have their own affairs in order, who govern their passions and then, and only then, are equipped to govern others. Tyrants, argue Plato and Aristotle, are men whose selfish urges dictate most of their actions, men who rule arbitrarily, capable *sometimes* of helping *some* people succeed but who ultimately lead to political instability, corruption, and a lack of social and economic justice. Middle-earth's Master of Lake-town, Saruman/Sharkey, Morgoth, and Sauron are all tyrants in this philosophical sense, and Gandalf and Galadriel fear that they too would rule this way if they were given the power of the One Ring. Faramir and Aragorn are similarly wary of political power without self-control, and the one figure in Middle-earth who has mastered his "inner-regime"—Tom Bombadil—wants no part of war and politics. [5]

Hobbits are to be found somewhere between the tyrants and the Wise. Their small stature keeps them from having aspirations of political grandeur, yet they can only resist the One Ring, not master it. Gandalf is drawn to the Hobbits because they seemingly possess qualities or virtues seldom seen in the great cities and realms of the West. It is hard to surprise a Wizard, but neither Saruman the White nor Gandalf the Grey fully comprehend the capabilities of Hobbits. No power in the world knows everything about Hobbits, confesses Gandalf. "Among the Wise I am the only one who goes in for hobbit-lore: an obscure branch of knowledge, but full of surprises." [6] Virtue ethics, a branch of moral philosophy, fell out of favor among philosophers as the Great War and bloody revolutions challenged the positivism and progress of Western society. Deontology (following the rules and doing one's duty at all costs) and consequentialism (especially utilitarianism and hedonism) at first filled this intellectual void, but at the turn of the 21st century, virtue ethics was beginning to make a comeback. Tolkien—whose life spanned from Victorian optimism to the existential crises of the 1960s and early '70s—responded to these vicissitudes in philosophy and ideology through his Middle-earth writings, though often in subtle ways that many readers have overlooked.

While in *The Hobbit* Tolkien presents to us these halflings as a satirical mirror, poking fun at our bourgeois concerns and at the English character, in the Prologue to *The Lord of the Rings* he stresses that these "remarkable people" are "relatives of ours," but they "lived quietly" in Middle-earth and "seemed of very little importance" to their neighbors, the Elves and the Dwarves.[7] They "love peace and quiet and good tilled earth" and do not understand machines more complicated than mills, looms, and hand tools. They do not study magic but possess from heredity certain skills—most notably quickness and the ability to escape being seen. The Shire is a tiny nation of farmers and gardeners, brewers of beer and cultivators of pipe-weed. Hobbits are not a war-like people and never fought among themselves, are slow to quarrel, and do not hunt living things for sport. They are clannish, lovers of genealogy, and follow the law (The Rules) through free will because they are "both ancient and just." This despite having very little formal government: no king, only an elected mayor and a hereditary Thain (military captain), the latter mostly an honorary title.

We learn from the Prologue of *The Lord of the Rings* that growing food and eating it occupies most of a Hobbit's time. Smoking pipes and blowing smoke-rings consumes a fair share of that time as well, and they admire poetry, music, and riddle-making. They love parties and giving gifts to others on their own birthdays. At the emotional climax of *The Hobbit*, the dying Dwarf king, Thorin Oakenshield, asks Bilbo (whom he once described as "descendant of rats!") for forgiveness and praises Hobbit virtues:

"There is more in you of good than you know, child of the kindly West. Some courage, and some wisdom, blended in good measure. If more of us valued food and cheer and song above hoarded gold, it would be a merrier world."[8]

The words of a dying king should be taken seriously. Is Tolkien here presenting us with a "Hobbit philosophy" to be ranked among those of the Wise? Consider Thorin's choice of words: *good, kindly, courage, wisdom, valued*. These are terms one can find in the ethics of Plato, Aristotle, Confucius, and many other philosophers and religious teachers. That Thorin says that Bilbo has some courage and some wisdom blended in good measure is a significant nod toward Aristotle and the Golden Mean. That food and cheer and song are to be valued above gold, however, suggests that Aristotle's Good Life (*eudaimon*) lived in the free community (*polis*) should include epicurean and aesthetic delights as well.

How do we identify the Good? How does one display courage and wisdom? How do we discern the balance, or good measure, of these virtues? How does one develop "character" or prove one's worth? Are there limits to when, where, and how much food and cheer and song we can enjoy? These questions are answered, in part, by Tolkien when he tackled the more ambitious literary project of *The Lord of the Rings*. Newly introduced Hobbits—Frodo, Sam, Peregrin "Pippin" Took, and Meriadoc "Merry" Brandybuck—become vehicles for Tolkien to explore in greater depth the virtues listed by Thorin and to add others, most notably fellowship, love, and self-sacrifice. We will examine each of these "Hobbit virtues" in chapters two through eight of the present book. Gandalf also returns in *The Lord of the Rings* to act as mentor and spiritual guide for the younger Hobbits, and we see through many adventures that Wizards, Elves, Dwarves, and Men are also capable of virtue as well as vice. This will be explored in chapter nine.

"Is virtue [*aretê*] teachable?" Socrates is asked at the outset of Plato's dialog *Meno*, "or is it rather acquired by practice? Or . . . does it come to men by nature . . . ?" Aristotle, in the *Nicomachean Ethics,* argued that in order to be "virtuous" one must learn, practice, and habituate virtues. We find this in many ancient ethical systems, and moral teachers like Jesus often used agrarian imagery and parables: plowing soil, planting seeds, growing and cultivating. The Confucian sage Mencius (ca. 372–289 B.C.) stressed that one must cultivate *jen* (humaneness) and *yi* (rightness) as the farmer cultivates grain, while the Chinese general, governor, and philosopher Wang Yangming (1472–1529) taught the concept of moral self-cultivation through practicing a tradition that has been transmitted (*chuanxi*).[9] The Psalms and Proverbs are replete with examples of moral cultivation: those who delight in the law of the Lord "are like trees / planted by streams of water, / which yield their fruit in its season / and their leaves do not wither" (Psalm 1); "Whoever sows injustice will reap calamity" (Psalms 22); "A capable wife . . . considers a field and buys it; / with the fruit of her hands she plants a vineyard" (Proverbs 31). The Romans were so proud of their agrarian roots that the farming life permeated their poetry and philosophy. Horace, in the *Odes,* recommends the cultivation of tranquility and contentment, while Virgil, in Book Two of the *Georgics,* praises the simple country life in contrast with the corruption of the city. In Zen Buddhism, creating a garden—even a dry landscape of rocks and sand—is to create a space of simple beauty where one can meditate on truth and meaning.

When the dying Thorin first describes Hobbit philosophy to Bilbo, we also hear an echo of one of the oldest literary texts ever preserved, *The Epic of Gilgamesh* (ca. 2000 BC). The Sumerian hero-king Gilgamesh, who has just lost his close friend Enkidu to death, seeks wisdom from an unlikely source—an ale-wife:

> "Thou, Gilgamesh, let full be thy belly,
> Make thou merry by day and by night.
> Of each day make thou a feast of rejoicing,
> Day and night dance thou and play!
> . . . For this is the task of mankind!"[10]

In Mordor, Sam is tempted by the One Ring; it offers him the chance to be, like Gilgamesh, a heroic warrior and a mighty king. He turns all this down for a garden:

> In that hour of trial it was the love of his master [Frodo] that helped most to hold him firm. . . . The one small garden of a free gardener was all his need and due, not a garden swollen to a realm; his own hands to use, not the hands of others to command.[11]

To grow food and brew ale, to feast and dance and play, to love and to enjoy fellowship—these are Hobbit virtues, and we humans should recognize them as well. Many cultures perform these virtues at weddings, birthdays, anniversaries, coming of age ceremonies, and on religious holidays. We are, at these celebratory times, fulfilling the "task of mankind" and are most Hobbit-like. Let us return to these virtues—seeing ourselves at our best and happiest—to make the world a merrier place.

HUMILITY

The first thing one notices about Hobbits is that they are small, about half the size of a grown human. "They are inclined to be fat in the stomach," writes Tolkien, have curly hair (on their heads and feet) but no beards, possess "good-natured faces, and laugh deep fruity laughs (especially after dinner, which they have twice a day when they can get it)."[1] While this is partly a description of the professor himself, it also draws on characteristics of medieval dwarves and goblins as well as creatures from Victorian and Edwardian children's literature. The composite is nevertheless memorable and unique. These "halflings" are hardly the stuff of heroic adventure tales, and yet Bilbo Baggins grows in moral stature throughout his first adventure, while staying grounded—"close to his roots," we might say—and demonstrating the virtue of humility, a virtue as elusive in our world today as are Hobbits themselves.

The Anglo-French words "humility" and "human" both derive from the Latin root *humus*, "earth or ground." To be human is to be from the earth in many cosmologies, including God's creation of Adam from the dust and ashes of the Garden in Genesis. [2] The Latin word *humilitas* (adj. *humilis*) can denote "lowness, small stature, or insignificance," and was applied to the lower social order of the Roman Empire: the *humiliores*, as distinct from the *honestiores* (persons of high status and property). Under Roman imperial law *humiliores* were subject to crucifixion, torture, and corporal punishment. As we saw in the last chapter, Hobbits are definitely creatures "of the earth" and are virtually unknown outside the Shire, while Bilbo is constantly being likened to small animals and threatened with bodily harm.

The Romans were not the only ancient people to see humility as a negative characteristic. In early heroic literature like *The Epic of Gilgamesh* and *The Iliad*, heroes are often semidivine and always aristocratic. They boast of their strength and political power, while the *humiliores* are rarely if ever seen. Gilgamesh exhausts the resources of his people by taking their husbands and sons into his army, their wives into his palace to cook and make cloth, and their daughters into his harem. [3] Agamemnon, Achilles, Hector, and Odysseus—princes all—are given to boasting and taunts, and after hearing the caustic soldier Thersites call for the Greeks to abandon Agamemnon and return home, Odysseus unleashes his wrath upon the hunchback:

> ". . . Thersites! . . . Keep quiet.
> Who are *you* to wrangle with kings . . . ?
> Stop your babbling, mouthing the names of kings. . . ."
> And he cracked the scepter across his back and shoulders.

The rascal doubled over, tears streaking his face
and a bloody welt bulged up between his blades.[4]

Homer depicts Odysseus literally beating a commoner with the scepter of royal power, and the poet says, of the rest of the Greek soldiers, "Their morale was low but the men laughed now, / good hearty laughter. . . ."[5]

In these heroic cultures it is the warrior and his culture that generate most virtues, including the pursuit of wealth and honor. Aristotle argued that proper pride (*megalopsychia*, "high-mindedness") is necessary for a man to reach for great and lofty things.[6] Roman generals like Pompey and Caesar idolized Alexander the Great, the Macedonian prince (taught by Aristotle), whose great conquests included the wealth of Asian cities, the daughters of Persian and Afghan kings, and the accumulation of royal and divine titles. While ancient Athenians and Romans prized modesty and moderation, their leaders seldom practiced these virtues and certainly had no desire to be seen as meek or humble.

When and where does humility as a virtue arise? Humility or meekness (הוונע, *anavah*) appears in the Torah as a quality beloved by the Lord—"God opposes the proud but gives grace to the humble" (Proverbs 3:34)—and embodied by Moses— "For Moses was a man exceeding meek above all men that dwelt upon earth" (Numbers 12:3). Given that Moses was a prince of great strength, *meek* here clearly does not mean *weak*. In *The Bhagavad Gita*, the Hindu virtue *amanitvam* denotes a lack of pride or arrogance, and Gandhi saw it is an essential starting point for the practice of other virtues and the pursuit of truth. In Taoism, humility is not a word but a phrase meaning roughly "not to dare to be first in the world," and, along with compassion and frugality, is one of the Three Treasures (virtues) possessed by those who follow the Tao. Similarly, in Buddhism humility is essential to the path of Enlightenment.

But it is in early Christianity, in Jesus and the early martyrs, that humility becomes a radical virtue confronting the worldly and violent tendencies of Roman culture. In the Sermon on the Mount, Jesus addresses a crowd of people living in the margins, the commoners of Judea (*am ha'aretz*), who had their political liberties taken by a series of Hellenistic and Roman imperialists beginning with Alexander's conquest of the Persian Empire. The cruelest of these overlords instituted punishments like crucifixion, and after the brief Maccabean respite, Jewish authorities were forced into a policy of appeasement with the Romans. The Herodian dynasty of puppet princes, and the Roman-appointed High Priest, benefitted in wealth and status from their alliance with Rome. While Jesus did not advocate a violent overthrow of imperial rule, as some feared (and the Zealots sought), he did in the Beatitudes directly challenge the worldly ambitions of contemporary Hellenistic and Roman culture:

Blessed (Μακάριοι) are the poor in spirit (πτωχοὶ τῷ πνεύματι), for theirs is the kingdom of heaven.

Blessed are those who mourn, for they will be comforted.

Blessed are the meek (πραεῖς), for they shall inherit the earth.

Blessed are those who hunger and thirst for righteousness, for they will be filled.

Blessed are the merciful, for they will have mercy.

Blessed are the pure in heart, for they will see God.

Blessed are the peacemakers, for they will be called the children of
God.

Blessed are those who are persecuted for righteousness' sake, for theirs
is the kingdom of heaven.

Blessed are you when people revile you and persecute you and utter all
kinds of evil against you falsely on my account. Rejoice and be glad
for your reward is great in heaven. . . . [7]

He also instructed his followers to "turn the other cheek," to not meet violence
with violence, and to love their enemies. The rabbi, in true humility, washed the feet
of his disciples; the Prince of Peace stood in stark contrast with the princes of violence
and conquest in the ancient world. To surrender to the authorities of Rome and the
Sanhedrin, to surrender his life as a sacrificial lamb, was a radical display of love and
humility that few could have predicted. He called on his followers to do the same,
and as Christianity spread from Judea to the great cities of Asia Minor, Greece, and
Italy, these new "Christians" (first called so in Syria) embraced martyrdom as the
ultimate virtue rather than perform the pagan sacrifices ordered by Roman governors
and emperors.

For three hundred years the sporadic but sometimes spectacular persecution of
Christians produced saints (*sancti*) who held up this model of humility preached by
Jesus. But the conversion of the Emperor Constantine the Great in 312 began an accom-
modation between Christians (now legal) and Roman authorities. Constantine and his
imperial successors were no pacifists. Similarly, the Christian conversion of Germanic
and Celtic barbarians living on the borders of Rome, whose warlords conquered and

inherited most of the Western Roman Empire in the fifth and sixth centuries, was only successful because it convinced these new kings that they could rule (and make war) with God's assistance in the manner of Joshua, Saul, and David. The difference between these heroic societies and that of Homeric Greece was that the church now served as a check to their most violent instincts—or at least it tried.

The European Middle Ages was, in large part, a thousand years of trying to figure out the seemingly contradictory impositions of church and state. Augustine had argued in his monumental *The City of God* that, for all its great military and imperial ambitions, the Roman Empire fell just like all of its successors because of misplaced loyalties. Citizenship in the City of God depended on the condition of one's soul, not the amount of wealth or power one accumulated. "The way to Christ is first through humility, second through humility, third through humility," he wrote. [8] While Augustine was one of the first to articulate a theory of Just War, he believed that law, education, and the moral discipline of the monastic orders were more important in keeping peace and order in the City of Man. The early monasteries strove to replicate the City of God on earth, and humility was an important and much-practiced discipline. Later, the mendicant friars practiced humbling themselves through poverty and begging. The Dominican friar Thomas Aquinas defined a humble person as a *homo acclinis*, "one inclined to the lowest place." [9] He agreed with Aristotle, however, that one must avoid both overestimating *and* underestimating one's own powers. [10]

It was only with the formalization and standardization of chivalry, beginning ca. 1100 that rulers could argue that they were producing "soldiers of Christ" capable of moral discipline while waging just war. Orders like the Knights Templar strove for that ideal balance between Christian virtues and pagan/heroic military prowess. That they and other knights more often fell short of the ideal should not obscure the unique attempt at resolving this tension within Christendom.

C. S. Lewis argued, more from literary examples than historical ones, that the medieval knight was perhaps the boldest and most difficult experiment in curbing human tendencies.[11] Chivalry places a "double-demand on . . . human nature," wrote Lewis. "The knight is a man of blood and iron . . . [but] he is also a demure . . . guest in hall, a gentle, modest, unobtrusive man." Thus could Sir Thomas Malory describe Sir Launcelot as both the mightiest of Arthur's knights and also "the meekest man that ever ate in hall among ladies."[12]

When Lewis and Tolkien first became friends in the late 1920s they bonded over reading (in the original language) Old Norse tales of gods engaged in incessant warfare and heroes who slew dragons and strove for Valhalla in a vast and cold northern landscape. These northern European warrior-heroes—Beowulf, Cú Chulainn, Roland—were motivated by vengeance as much as honor, and boasted of their deeds. In this they differed little from Gilgamesh, Achilles, and Odysseus. Theirs was also a doomed world: "heathen, noble, and hopeless," as Tolkien once described it.[13] How did these two medieval scholars move from pagan mythology and violent Norse sagas to producing the humble Hobbit and child-heroes of Narnia? Why did two devoutly Christian authors choose to populate their invented worlds with so many deities, heroes, and beasts plucked straight from the pagan (at least in origin) tales of the Greeks and the Romans, the Anglo-Saxons and the Norse, the Welsh and the Finnish?

I would argue that Bilbo Baggins is such a compelling and effective guide through Middle-earth precisely because he is humble like us—neither saint nor demigod, but a small being, obsessed with creature comforts, who finds himself on an unexpected adventure in the company of Dwarves, Elves, and dragons inspired by the literature Professor Tolkien loved and taught: *Beowulf,* the *Nibelungenlied,* the *Eddas,* and *Sir Gawain and the Green Knight.* Bilbo is a meek or humble creature who, when pressed, acts with bravery and cunning to defend his friends. But even with an Elvish blade and a magic ring, he is no warrior.[14] He is of the earth and longs to return to his Hobbit hole. He is also on occasion "humbled," or made aware of the limitations of his power and abilities. He is brave when facing the dragon Smaug, but the cloak of invisibility that comes from wearing the Ring makes him a bit vain and careless with his riddling answers to Smaug's questions. Ultimately, they reveal the Hobbit's connections to Lake Town and Smaug embarks on a flight of terror and revenge. "Never laugh at live dragons," Bilbo chastises himself, and he is indeed partly complicit in the death and destruction that follows.[15]

Frodo and Sam start out like Bilbo: they love the Shire, enjoy the comfort of a hot bath and the pleasures of ale and pipeweed. Frodo begins his journey out of a sense of responsibility to fix what Bilbo has unknowingly done: brought the Ring of Power into the Shire. "Frodo undertook his quest out of love—to save the world he knew from disaster at his own expense, if he could," wrote Tolkien in a 1963 letter, "and also in complete humility, acknowledging that he was wholly inadequate to the task."[16] Frodo makes a promise to Gandalf, and Sam likewise promises to accompany his master. Both Hobbits are completely untested as warriors, and along with Merry and Pippin they fail in their first adventure against the Barrow-wights. With weapons from the barrows (and Bilbo's sword, Sting) all four Hobbits grow in ferocity and skills, first at Khazad-Dûm and later in Gondor and Mordor. "Very few characters in literature capture the humble person's disposition as successfully as Tolkien's heroic hobbit, Sam Gamgee," writes philosopher Craig Boyd.[17] Whereas Frodo starts his quest already possessing a good deal of humility, Sam demonstrates perhaps the greatest growth in this virtue. And, as Boyd points out, Sam exemplifies the medieval theological principle of being worthy of heroic virtue *because* he does not seek to be a hero in the first place.

Frodo becomes a pacifist when he returns to the Shire, while his three companions take up arms to defend their home. But whether one refuses to fight or chooses to fight only in defense of family and community, humility can be practiced as a virtue and displayed by those who we would not see as lowly or meek. Aragorn and Faramir both display great humility while being skilled but reluctant warriors. They do not boast of their martial deeds, nor do they patronize the halflings. Gandalf and Galadriel display humility in rejecting the Ring when it is offered to them, and neither figure glorifies warfare.[18] "In Tolkien's work there is no pompous boasting over such deaths," writes Ralph C. Wood, "nor is there any glory to be found in heroic defeat. War is a miserable business . . . not the noble ideal that ancient pagans and many modern Christians have made it."[19]

We, on the other hand, have somehow returned to the Homeric model of boasting and of humiliating our foes, and we do not hesitate to shy away from power. Whether in the political arena or that of sports, it is the loud and brash figure, the one constantly calling attention to themselves and their accomplishments, that we are unabashedly drawn to. The philosopher Friedrich Nietzsche (1844–1900) bemoaned the weakness and pacifism he saw in Christianity, calling the "will to power" a man's driving force—the highest man is he who determines all values and directs all wills.[20] This *Übermensch* should not hesitate to grasp power and dominate the weak, should not apologize for his victories. Adolf Hitler and other fascists of the mid-20th century were drawn to this aspect of Nietzsche's writings, appropriating the parts they found most appealing and combining them with notions of racial superiority.

It is not an exaggeration to say that we now seem closer to Nietzsche than to the humility embraced by the early Christian martyrs or even that idealized in chivalry. Nationalism is once again being used as an excuse for embracing the will to power in American political discourse as much as in other nations that we see as antidemocratic. Humility is thus, in our day as in Jesus's, a radical virtue confronting the worldly and violent tendencies of our culture. We should return to upholding the virtue of humility, but we must not mistake it for weakness. It is, on the contrary, the first step on the path to moral strength. Humility is why Bilbo and Frodo could bear the Ring for so long without being overthrown by its evil. It was a self-awareness and an inner strength—walking in the true light of who you are, to paraphrase Aquinas—and it prepared them to find the courage they would need on their long and perilous journeys.

COURAGE

On September 11, 2001, nineteen men who were members of the radical group al-Qaeda boarded airplanes in Boston, New York, and Washington, DC, took control of the cockpits (by cutting the throats of the pilots with box-cutters), and flew three of those planes into the World Trade Center towers and the Pentagon, resulting in the death of nearly 3,000 men, women, and children. On the fourth plane, a struggle between the terrorists and a small group of passengers resulted in the plane crashing in Pennsylvania, killing all on board. In the hours and days that followed, first responders—police, paramedics, firefighters—worked tirelessly to save the lives of survivors in New York and Washington.

In October 2012, in Pakistan, a fourteen-year-old girl named Malala Yousafzai, who had spoken out against the oppression of the extremist Taliban in her small village, was on a school bus on the way home from school. A masked gunman boarded the bus and asked, "Who is Malala?" then shot her on the left side of her head. She woke up ten days later in a hospital in Birmingham, England, and spent several months undergoing surgery and rehabilitation. As soon as she was able, she returned to speaking out against the mistreatment of women and children in tyrannical regimes throughout the world. She started the Malala Fund and, in December 2014, won the Nobel Peace Prize, becoming the youngest ever Nobel laureate.

When discussing these traumatic events, emotions wax and language seems to fail us. How do we apply virtue terms like bravery, courage, and heroism? Many of the 9/11 terrorists and the gunman who shot Malala were trained soldiers, while Malala and most of the first responders in New York and Washington were not. Soldiers are, throughout most of history, the "heroes" of literature, whether of West or East. Yet, while it is not cowardice that motivates terrorists and jihadists, the virtue of courage was more truly demonstrated by Malala and the first responders on 9/11. They are the heroes of these stories.

In wartime, it is not hard to find examples of men and women who have demonstrated great courage through risking their lives to save others, be they fellow soldiers or civilians.[1] There are, of course, also examples of cowardice and cruelty in war. But in times of peace we have struggled to define precisely words like bravery, courage, and heroism. Without precision, such powerful words can become meaningless.[2] Do we expect soldiers, police officers, and firefighters to embody courage because of the nature of their jobs? Do we respect them for it or take it for granted? How can a person without the physical attributes and training of these professionals demonstrate courage? We might be able easily to identify cowardice, but what makes someone a hero?[3] The English word *courage* derives from the Romance languages, with the common root *cor*, or "heart," leading to its original Middle English usage to convey spiritedness and even wrath.[4] We still convey this in the expression "stout-hearted." But Tolkien was notoriously suspicious of words derived from the Romance languages and turned elsewhere for inspiration for courage and other Middle-earth virtues.

Before delving into that, however, it might help to go back to the ancient Greeks for some precision about what *we* mean by courage. For Homer, courage (*ênoreê*) is almost entirely a male and martial virtue, exhibited mainly on the battlefield and inspired (often divinely) by the love of glory and battle comrades.[5] Alasdair MacIntyre points out that, in heroic societies, courage often serves to strengthen bonds of friendship and community.[6] Later, Greek philosophers broadened their investigation of this virtue and differentiated between *physical* and *moral* courage.[7] Physical courage is usually related to the threat of great physical harm or death, while moral courage is the virtue needed to defend ideas or principles that are unpopular or ridiculed. The latter can have great consequences (e.g., being fired or losing a friend), and sometimes a threat can require both physical and moral courage (e.g., Socrates being executed by the state for defending his philosophical methods and truths).[8] For Plato, courage (*andreia*) is wisdom about what is to be feared, the virtue of the spirited part (*thumoeides*) of the tripartite soul that controls the appetites; the auxiliaries of his ideal *polis* possess great physical courage.[9] Aristotle similarly believes that all people are subject to passions, and how they reason and respond to these passions determines virtue or vice and, ultimately, one's character. Courage, for him, is the ability to pursue the Good through the difficult and the dangerous. Both the Greek term Plato and Aristotle use, *andreia*, and its Latin equivalent, *virtus*, indicate that courage for the ancient Greeks and Romans was literally a "manly" virtue (*andros* and *vir* being the Greek and Latin words, respectively, for *man*), and for the typical Roman the aim of courage was *gloria*, or "honor." A rare classical female example of this type of courage was that of Lucretia, who, according to Livy, took her own life to regain her honor after being raped, but only after exhorting her family to avenge her. Romans were attracted to Stoicism in part because of the emphasis it placed on courage and self-control.

Courage is a classical virtue because it is the rational and appropriate response to fear, while cowardice and recklessness are the extreme responses or vices. To be without fear is to be irrational or mad, and both the Greeks and the Romans typically attributed the reckless bravery of barbarians to their lack of reason.[10] "Aristotle argued that it is not the fearless person who is courageous," writes Jamie Carlin Watson, "but the one who acts appropriately in the face of fear, especially the fear of death."[11] With Hobbits, Tolkien does not give us fearless warriors, but rather small heroes who overcome their fears through unexpected demonstrations of both physical and moral courage.

The Courage of Hobbits

As we have seen, Bilbo Baggins is praised at the end of *The Hobbit* with having *some* courage and *some* wisdom, blended in just the right measure. At the beginning of the book it is not at all clear that Bilbo has either of these virtues. Gandalf may see these qualities within Bilbo, but the Dwarves and his neighbors do not. "Bilbo is remarkable for his unremarkability," remarks Laura Garcia, his only obvious virtues being those of hospitality and geniality.[12] Once out of the Shire it does not take Bilbo long to demonstrate that he is nimble and clever, but at what point in the story does Tolkien's narrator tell us that Bilbo is courageous? He experiences fear frequently and reacts variously by shrieking like a teakettle, melting like jelly, closing his eyes, and wishing that he were back in his cozy hobbit hole with a nice supper! He also runs and hides from danger, such as we might expect from a burglar rather than a warrior.

Bilbo "plucked up courage" to try to pick the pockets of the trolls, but was caught immediately and the whole episode would have ended poorly for him and the Dwarves had Gandalf not showed up in the nick of time.[13] In the Misty Mountains Bilbo showed no courage during the goblin attack and very little facing Gollum, though he summoned some strength to leap—invisible and in the dark—over the miserable creature before running off. The Ring similarly aided him during his fight with the spiders of Mirkwood, though he "plucked up some courage" again to throw stones and taunt them before fighting them while invisible with his elvish dagger, Sting.[14]

While these martial episodes certainly made Bilbo bolder and more confident, it was not until he entered the Lonely Mountain and faced the dragon Smaug that Bilbo truly demonstrates courage. As Bilbo crawls through a tunnel filling with heat and vapor, toward a growing red glow and monstrous noise, Tolkien stops his narration to describe what was happening in Bilbo's psyche or soul:

> It was the bravest thing he ever did. The tremendous things that happened afterwards were as nothing compared to it. He fought the real battle in the tunnel alone, before he ever saw the vast danger that lay in wait.[15]

Not one for much "psychological introspection" in his novels, Tolkien wants his readers to pause here and try to feel what Bilbo was experiencing. The fear of the unknown, crawling in the dark *toward* great danger, choosing to face a terrible monster he had no hope of defeating—this, for the little Hobbit, was Bilbo's great moment of heroic courage. While Bard the bowman is the one who ultimately slays the dragon, and Bilbo is knocked unconscious before the climactic battle really begins, in *The Hobbit,* Tolkien seems more interested in exploring the kind of courage that a small, insignificant creature can muster in the face of both psychological fear and enormous physical danger than he is in lengthy heroic war narrative. Heroes, writes Andrew Michael Flescher, "are, in a very important sense, *ordinary*. They have non-heroic roots. They possess flaws. . . . Heroes represent the best of humanity within the domain of mortal limitation."[16] Bilbo fits this description of a hero: flawed, but doing his very best to act in the service of others within his physical limitations as a Hobbit. He even has the courage to return to the Dwarves after he has given the Arkenstone to the Elvenking—courage to face the consequences of his actions—in part because he promised to wake up Bombur![17]

In *The Lord of the Rings*, we begin again in the Shire where most Hobbits have little interest in the affairs of Dwarves and Elves and dragons. The exceptions are Frodo Baggins and Samwise Gamgee. Frodo walks mysteriously in the woods under starlight while his neighbors whisper that he is cavorting with Elves. Sam dreams of meeting Elves and going on the kind of adventures he has heard Bilbo recite, but his father and others are skeptical. Sam is crazy about the stories of the old days, complains Gaffer Gamgee, "and he listens to Mr. Bilbo's tales. . . . *'Elves and dragons!'* I says to him. *'Cabbages and potatoes are better for me and you.'"*[18] With the knowledge about the true nature of the Ring provided by Gandalf, Frodo makes the courageous decision to remove it from the Shire and to follow the path of Bilbo as an exile, "a flight from danger into danger, drawing it after me."[19] Sam, on the other hand, is at first motivated by his fear of the Wizard and his desire to see Elves. For both, their courage grows incrementally, from facing the possible wrath of Farmer Maggot to the mortal dangers of Old Man Willow, the Barrow-wights, and the Black Riders, which they faced in fellowship with the Hobbits Merry and Pippin.

Though not trained as soldiers, all four Hobbits are eventually forced to fight the goblins, orcs, and trolls, which the Enemy has called into his service. Beginning in the mines of Moria, armed with proper weapons, the *thumos* of the Shire-folk is wakened. "Suddenly, and to his own surprise, Frodo felt a hot wrath blaze up in his heart. 'The Shire!' he cried," as he stabbed the cave-troll.[20] Sam fells an orc and a "fire was smouldering in his brown eyes." Merry and Pippin need a bit of the draught of Treebeard to awaken their fighting spirits, but both eventually enter military service with contrasting formal oaths to Théoden and Denethor, respectively. "Filled suddenly with love for this old man, [Merry] knelt on one knee, and took [Théoden's] hand and kissed it."[21] Offering his sword to the king, Merry becomes esquire of Rohan: "As a father you shall be to me," he exclaims to Théoden. Pippin, on the other hand, filled with both guilt over the death of Boromir and fear of his cold father, offers fealty to Denethor with his sword: "Little service, no doubt, will so great a lord of Men think to find in a hobbit . . . yet such as it is, I will offer it, in payment of my debt."[22] Both Hobbits fight valiantly in the defense of Minas Tirith—Merry fighting the Witch-king himself—and Tolkien chooses most often to have us view the great battles through their Hobbit eyes.

The path to Mordor provides many different kinds of danger for Frodo and Sam. Frodo offers at the Council of Elrond to take the Ring to Mordor because it has to be destroyed and yet none of the assembled warriors or the Wise volunteer. "'I will take the Ring,' he says, 'though I do not know the way.'"[23] As Aeschylus writes in *Prometheus Bound*, "I have not courage, yet needs must I pluck courage from manifest necessity." Sam immediately volunteers to accompany Frodo and is willing to be "drownded" rather than to be left behind at Amon Hen. Together they move bravely toward Mordor, toward dangers known and unknown, facing an attack from Gollum, the horror of the Dead Marshes, and the Rangers from Gondor. Sam fought valiantly against Sheelob and, facing a tower full of orcs at Cirith Ungol, "flung the Quest and all his decisions away, and fear and doubt with them," to rush to Frodo's rescue. He may slay many orcs before he falls, Sam realized, without any song sung about "Samwise the Strong."[24] As it turned out he had to face only one of the orc captors in battle, but Tolkien takes us through a long narrative journey of Sam courageously facing his doubts and fears as he climbs the tower.

Reunited and free, Frodo and Sam must still make their way across the vale of Gorgoroth and through the gathering armies of Mordor before they reach Mount Doom. Frodo, burdened with the horrible power of the Ring, suffers from fears and malicious visions in addition to hunger, thirst, and physical pain as they move across the plain and up the mountain. Sam summons enough strength and courage for them both in his most heroic moment of the whole quest:

> "Come, Mr. Frodo!" he cried. "I can't carry it for you, but I can carry you and it as well. So up you get! Come on, Mr. Frodo dear! Sam will give you a ride. . . ."
>
> As Frodo clung upon his back, [. . .] Sam staggered to his feet; and then to his amazement [. . .] some gift of final strength was given to

him, Sam lifted Frodo with no more difficulty than if he were carrying a hobbit-child. . . .[25]

This scene is one of the most important moments in the book and one of the most arresting in Peter Jackson's film, *The Return of the King*. Courage, strength, and love all come together in this heroic moment for Samwise the Hobbit. For many, this moment of toil and tears is redolent of imagery from the Passion of the Christ, in particular of Simon of Cyrene helping Jesus carry the cross along the Via Dolorosa. Tolkien likely would have had this image in his mind along with that of the battlefield rescue of soldiers at the Western Front, as he remarks in a 1956 letter about the heroism of the English privates and batmen (servants to the English army officers) he knew during the First World War, as his chief inspiration for Sam.[26]

Tolkien's Theory of Courage

Modern philosophy has struggled with the virtue of courage.[27] For Immanuel Kant (1724–1804) and his followers, courage was an important part of doing one's duty. For existentialists, courage is often equated with the "authenticity" in which one takes responsibility for the meaning and direction of one's life and faces the anxiety of the age. Unsurprisingly, Tolkien turned instead to ancient and medieval examples of courage as inspiration for his fiction. We would expect him to agree on this virtue with Aquinas, who, interpreting Aristotle and Macrobius, thought courage had three parts: confidence, perseverance, and freedom from anxiety.[28] But there is a peculiar type of *pagan* courage that Tolkien admired in the Anglo-Saxons, a Heroic Age virtue he thought particular to the barbarians of early medieval Europe. It is demonstrated in the words and acts of the old warrior Beorhtwold as he prepares to die fighting against Viking invaders next to his lord, Beorhtnoth, at the Battle of Maldon in AD 991:

> *Hige sceal þē heardra,*   *heorte þē cēnre,*
> *mōd sceal þē māre,*   *þē ūre mægen lytlað.*
> Will shall be the sterner, heart the bolder,
> Spirit the greater, as our strength lessens.

These words are, for Tolkien, "an exaltation of undefeated will," "made for a man's last and hopeless days."[29] He saw this type of courage in many young British soldiers who went "over the top" of the trenches during the First World War. Both Sam and Frodo exhibit this virtue as they walk through the perilous landscape of Mordor and make their way up Mount Doom.

Tolkien first explored this "theory of courage" in his landmark critical essay of 1936, "*Beowulf*: The Monsters and the Critics." Here he declares this "the great contribution of early Northern literature," the "creed of unyielding will" illustrated by the attitude of Odin, Thor, and the other deities of Asgard marching to their doom and defeat at Ragnarök.[30] Tolkien quotes the literary critic W.P. Ker in describing the Northern gods as having "an exultant extravagance in their warfare," "on the right side, though not on the side that wins," choosing heroic men as their allies in this war, this "absolute resistance, perfect because without hope."[31]

Tolkien's Rohirrim, or Riders of Rohan, embody elements of Anglo-Saxon, Gothic, and Norse cultures. Their courage, however, lies nearer to what Aristotle would deem "reckless" or "irrational" behavior in battle. They often need to be motivated by glory and honor (Éowyn), their battle frenzy manifest in poetic joy (Éomer).[32] For the courage of Men like Beren, Aragorn, and Faramir, however, Tolkien turns to the military virtues of chivalric literature. The courage of Count Roland in *Chanson de Roland* is very much of the Beowulf variety, and perhaps even more reckless, but his companion Oliver makes rational assessments of martial danger and advises Roland accordingly. Similarly, Lancelot is driven by passion to rescue his love Guinevere in Chrétien de Troyes's *Lancelot, or The Knight of the Cart*, while Gawain makes calm and clear decisions about the path he takes in both the French romance and in *Sir Gawain and the Green Knight* (which Tolkien translated). The courage to battle monsters is displayed by Arthur and many of his knights in the medieval Welsh prose romances like *Culhwch and Olwen*.

Fighting the Long Defeat

There is a darkness and pessimism in much of Tolkien's Middle-earth writings that often gets overlooked. Galadriel speaks of the Elves "fighting the long defeat," and throughout *The Lord of the Rings* there is the underlying sorrow of the Elves leaving Middle-earth in increasing numbers. Frodo, Bilbo, Gandalf, and Galadriel all depart on the White Ship, never to return to Middle-earth, in a scene at the end of the novel that many have interpreted as symbolic of death (though Tolkien denied this interpretation). It is perhaps significant that the only fully Arthurian work that Tolkien wrote was *The*

Fall of Arthur, an alliterative retelling of the sundering of the Round Table, the death of Sir Gawain, and the defeat of King Arthur. If Arthur is to return from Avalon and restore Camelot, we do not know it, for Tolkien left the poem unfinished.[33]

In his *Beowulf* essay, Tolkien not only describes the cold, dark tone of the Anglo-Saxon heroic poem, he goes so far as creating his own Old English proverb to capture the pessimism of the pagan Northern world:

> *lif is læne: eal scæceð leoht and lif somod*
> Life is fleeting: all departs, light and life together.[34]

Both *Beowulf* and "The Battle of Maldon" illustrate, in Tolkien's words, "man at war with the hostile world, and his inevitable overthrow in Time." The "lofty tone and high seriousness" of *Beowulf* comes not from the hero's superhuman strength fighting Grendel and the dragon, but rather from his courage in the face of inevitable death: "He is a man," writes Tolkien, "and that for him and many is sufficient tragedy. . . . [M]an, each man and all men, and all their works shall die."[35] While the mood of these early medieval poems is like a shadow of despair hovering over their action, still, observes Tolkien, the "worth of defeated valour in this world is deeply felt." Tolkien found in his reading of medieval Celtic and Germanic literature "a dauntless human courage in the face of unremitting hostility, whether human or natural."[36]

The small community, small government world of the early Middle Ages appealed to both Tolkien and C. S. Lewis. The only time Tolkien wrote specifically about his personal political beliefs, he claimed that he leaned toward anarchy ("philosophically understood as abolition of control"), or "unconstitutional Monarchy," and that he distrusted anyone who used the words "State" or "Government" to refer to people rather than abstracts.[37] The vice or virtue was not in the system, in other words, but in the individual. Lewis makes this point in *Mere Christianity*:

> . . . nothing but the courage and unselfishness of individuals is ever going to make any system work properly. It is easy enough to remove the particular kinds of graft or bullying that go on under the present system: but as long as men are twisters or bullies they will find some new way of carrying on the old game under the new system. You cannot make men good by law: and without good men you cannot have a good society.[38]

Tolkien and Lewis do not provide political solutions for Middle-earth or Narnia by creating new types of government: They focus rather on the ethical behavior of governors of different types of political systems in their invented worlds. Courage is a necessary virtue in these worlds—think of Lucy and Peter as much as Éowyn and Aragorn—necessary in personal *and* in political terms. For both authors, however, even heroic courage does not guarantee success. "Tolkien's protagonists are heroes not because of their successes, which are often limited," writes John Garth, "but because of their courage and tenacity in trying."[39]

Finding courage faced with great danger, and having the tenacity to keep moving, to keep fighting even when there seemingly is no hope of victory—these are virtues that Tolkien gave to the Hobbits Bilbo, Frodo, and Sam. Almost no one thought Hobbits capable of such courage, but Tolkien's own experiences in the war with the common soldier, many plucked from small English villages, showed him what the humblest creatures are capable of. The average reader of Tolkien may not be able to see themselves in warrior princes like Aragorn and Legolas, but finding courage in unexpected places—Merry and Pippin and Éowyn included—gives one hope that we too might be able to rise to the occasion and persevere in our struggles, even if we do not get to fully enjoy the victory.

FELLOWSHIP

The pioneering American author and editor Lilian Whiting (1847–1942) once wrote, "To be rich in friends is to be poor in nothing."[1] The saying may be the inspiration for the angel Clarence's advice to George in the movie *It's a Wonderful Life* (1946)—"Remember no man is a failure who has friends"—but it is an ancient sentiment that crosses many cultures.[2] Proverbs 18:24 touts the importance of having a "friend who sticks closer than a brother," and Jesus ups the ante even more: "Greater love has no one than this, that he lay down his life for his friends" (John 15:13). J. R. R. Tolkien wrote powerfully about friendship in his fiction, and many have seen this as a reflection of the important friendships he had in school in Birmingham and later as both a student and a professor at Oxford. But rather than offer prosaic descriptions of *friendship*, Tolkien stressed *fellowship* as a slightly different and perhaps even more powerful concept. I would argue that it is, indeed, a particularly (though not exclusively) Hobbit virtue, and that had he spent the bulk of his life in a different environment, Tolkien's fellowships would have been broader and more inclusive.

Friendship is certainly viewed as a virtue in most traditions. Plato examines both love (*erôs*) and friendship (*philia*) in two of his Socratic dialogs, the *Lysis* and the *Symposium*. Fellowship (*koinonia*), which first appears in the pre-Socratic tradition with the meanings of both "association" and "participation," appears in *The Republic* while Socrates is discussing communal rights and duties, and, as *koinonia* exists among Plato's Forms, it represents the perfection of relationship.[3] When Aristotle discusses different kinds of friendship in the *Nicomachean Ethics*, the *Eudemian Ethics*, the *Rhetoric*, and the *Politics*, he employs the term *philia* to describe both "friendliness" (as a quality) and "friendship."[4] He states that *philia* is the motive of society itself since "*philia* is the pursuit of a common social life"—that society depends on friendship and that friendship is necessary for justice.[5] *Philia* is one of his twelve moral virtues in the *Nicomachean Ethics*, where in Book VIII Aristotle distinguishes three objects that are loved or lovable (*philóton*): the good, the pleasant, and the useful.[6] All but the first kind are "incidental" friendships to Aristotle, who defined the perfect friendship as enduring, "the friendship of men who are good and alike in virtue."[7] In the *Politics*, Aristotle discusses "political friendship" (*politike philia*) and defines the *polis* as a "community" (*koinonia*) that has some functions or interests in common.[8] The Roman Stoic philosopher Seneca believed that God gave man two things to distinguish him from animals—reason and fellowship (*consortio*)—and that it is fellowship that has given man dominion over animals.[9] "Remove fellowship and you will destroy the unity of mankind on which our life depends."

It is not until we get to Christian theologians that we see the concept of fellowship elevated above other kinds of associations. The word *koinonia* appears about twenty times in the Bible, mostly in the Epistles of the New Testament. While the Septuagint uses the Greek term to describe all kinds of associations and alliances, Paul uses *koinonia* in the sense of "participation in" the suffering of Jesus.[10] John uses *koinonia* to connect Christians to one another as well as to God:

> That which we have seen and heard we proclaim also to you, so that you too may have fellowship with us; and indeed our fellowship is with the Father and with his Son Jesus Christ. . . . If we say we have fellowship with him while we walk in darkness, we lie and do not practice the truth. But if we walk in the light, as he is in the light, we have fellowship with one another, and the blood of Jesus his Son cleanses us from all sin.[11]

For early Christians, the Twelve Disciples formed a fellowship that continued to meet and hold communion after the Crucifixion in order to preserve their connection to Christ. They encouraged the new Christian communities spreading throughout the Roman world to do the same and to help one another live virtuously. "The Old and New Testaments and Clement [of Alexandria] all warn against relationships which would endanger the moral integrity of the person," observes Mary Carita O'Brien. "Sin and righteousness cannot have *koinonia*."[12]

Aristotle had stated that friends see another self in their friend, wish to live together (if possible), and that their friendship does not achieve an external good but *is itself the good*.[13] Thomas Aquinas picked up Aristotle's views on friendship as nonutilitarian and goes even further, arguing that love of a friend (*amor amicitiae*) involves the constant presence of the friend in one's thoughts. [14] "... [F]riendship, as understood by Aristotle and Aquinas is not an inevitable part of any recognizably human life," writes John Casey. "It *is* an ethical and cultural ideal ... [and] has a very good claim to be considered part of the good life for man." [15] Friendship and fellowship in their highest sense are thus not inevitable social behaviors of animals, but human virtues which must be pursued, understood, and cultivated.

The young J. R. R. Tolkien would have studied the concepts of *koinonia* and *amor amicitiae* in his classical education at King Edward's School in Birmingham as well as in his catechetical lessons with Father Francis at the Birmingham Oratory. But it was in two unique fellowships—the T.C.B.S. and the Inklings—that he would have direct experience with the true power and intimacy of a group of like-minded friends. These fellowships were tested by love and loss, by war and professional rivalry. For Tolkien, friendship and fellowship were *both* important, though not without challenges, and his friendship with C. S. Lewis was the *sine qua non* for the fellowships in *The Hobbit* and *The Lord of the Rings* to be published and inspire millions.

The T.C.B.S. and the Inklings

Tolkien attended the all-boys day-school King Edward's in Birmingham (his father's old school) from 1900 to 1911. [16] Since Tolkien had been forbidden by his guardian Father Francis from having a relationship with his fellow lodger Edith Bratt (also an orphan, with whom he had recently fallen in love), "he came to associate male company with much that was good in life," writes his biographer Humphrey Carpenter. [17]

Early in 1910, after passing the Oxford entrance exam, Tolkien was named "Librarian" at the school (a title bestowed on select senior boys) and invited some of his friends to join him for clandestine "teas" in the library that consisted of smuggled-in foods and robust conversation. These "Tea Club" meetings migrated to the Tea Room at Barrow's department store on Corporation Street where, in a semiprivate compartment, Tolkien would meet with a set group of school friends that included Christopher Wiseman, Rob Gilson (the schoolmaster's son), and Geoffrey Bache Smith. Soon the group adopted the moniker "the Tea Club and Barrovian Society," or T.C.B.S.

While most members of the T.C.B.S. enjoyed school sports (especially rugby), what really united this group of young men was their passion for debate and love of untrendy, pre-modern art and literature. All were more or less well-versed in Greek and Latin and appreciated Anglo-Saxon poetry, Norse mythology, and Pre-Raphaelite art. They rejected the cynicism of the day. "All four were bright, idealistic, and a tad prudish," write biographers Philip and Carol Zaleski, and were "perfectly fitted for each other. . . . Within the T.C.B.S. Tolkien came into his own . . . finding his voice in the loud, exuberant, sometimes boorish thrust-and-parry of male camaraderie. . . ."[18] It was, he would write in a 1916 letter to Smith, "Friendship to the Nth Power."[19]

It was perhaps Rob Gilson who coined that description, for the letter was written by Tolkien in response to receiving the news of Gilson's death on the first day of the Battle of the Somme. All four T.C.B.S. stalwarts, along with other close friends, had by then entered the war: Wiseman joining the British navy at Scapa Flow, the other three as army officers in France. The T.C.B.S. had continued to meet sporadically after Tolkien and Smith went off to Oxford and Wiseman and Gilson to Cambridge. At a December 1914 meeting at Wiseman's home (dubbed "The Council of London"), debate had fired

Tolkien's ambition to write poetry, especially about the faerie realm, "a beginner at the very least of large things." The T.C.B.S., Tolkien wrote to Smith, was "granted some spark of fire . . . that was destined to kindle a new light, or . . . rekindle an old light in the world . . . destined to testify for God and Truth in a more direct way even than by laying down its several lives in this war. . . ."[20] By the time the armistice was declared in November 1918, Tolkien and Wiseman were the sole survivors of the T.C.B.S.

Much has been written about Tolkien's subsequent friendship with C. S. Lewis and his newfound Oxford fellowship, the Inklings.[21] It will suffice to say here that much of what brought the T.C.B.S. members together was the same for the Inklings. Tolkien and Lewis were colleagues in the English faculty at Oxford when they first met in May 1926. They both appreciated ancient languages and poetry with meter, and soon they started meeting with other Oxford dons to translate Old Norse literature under Tolkien's tutelage. In 1931, together they joined a new Oxford club created by undergraduate Edward Tangye Lean called the Inklings, and they liked the name so much that they kept it as they resurrected the name for the twice a week gatherings of their own friends and colleagues at the Eagle and Child pub (or "the Bird and Baby," as they liked to call it) on Tuesday mornings and in college rooms (usually Lewis's Magdalen digs) on Thursday evenings. Sometime Inklings included Lewis's old friends Owen Barfield and medievalist Nevill Coghill, his brother, Warnie (Maj. Warren Lewis), doctor R. E. Havard, Tolkien's son Christopher, Shakespeare and Pope scholar H. V. "Hugo" Dyson, and Oxford University Press editor and esoteric writer Charles Williams.

Whether gathered indoors drinking beer around a fire or taking long country walks in the Oxfordshire wilds, the Inklings were often engaged in "excited talk about what we had been reading the week before," remembered Coghill, "disputing and quoting" amid "thunderous disagreements and agreements."[22] It is clear that both Tolkien and Lewis cherished these gatherings and saw the group as a fellowship that would form a model for their "walking, talking, eating" fellowships in Middle-earth and Narnia. Tolkien described the Inklings variously as a "literary club of practicing poets," an occasion for "colloguing" (a suitably archaic word for conversing secretly or conspiring), "the Lewis séance," "the brotherhood," and "the undetermined and unelected circle of friends who gathered about C.S.L."[23] As for "C.S.L.," he dedicated his first book of theology, *The Problem of Pain* (1940), to the Inklings, confessing to Dom Bede Griffiths:

> What I owe to them all is incalculable. Dyson and Tolkien were the immediate human causes of my own conversion. Is any pleasure on earth as great as a circle of Christian friends by a good fire?[24]

While Christianity was an important commonality for the group, another bond for many of the Inklings was that they had survived combat service in the First World War and German air raids in the Second. Food (and beer) shortages during and after the Second World War led them to share resources and, at least on one occasion, celebrate together the gift of a canned ham sent to Lewis by one of his American admirers. The formal thank you letter Lewis sent to their benefactor survives as an Inklings version of the Declaration of Independence, with signatories C. S. Lewis, W. H. Lewis, H. V. Dyson, Lord David Cecil, Colin Hardie, R. E. Havard, Christopher Tolkien, and J. R. R. Tolkien:

. . . we have a small informal literary club which meets in my rooms every Thursday for beer and talk, and—in happier times—for an occasional dinner. And last night, having your ham to dine off, we had a meal which eight members attended. . . . [I]n various colleges we got two bottles of burgundy and two of port . . . fish and a savoury: and we had a . . . banquet rarely met with . . . [in] five years or more.[25]

In the Company of Dwarves

When we first meet him in *The Hobbit*, Bilbo Baggins lives alone, in comfort but seemingly without close friends. Gandalf disturbs all this by inviting the Dwarves to Bilbo's home, where they immediately challenge his congenial hospitality by raiding his larder. When Bilbo first agrees to join their fellowship it is a contractual arrangement, but despite their cultural differences Bilbo at last starts to see the Dwarves as friends. He rescues them, burgles for them, and shares their hardships on the long quest. When he is given the opportunity to remain safely with the Elves of Mirkwood and be honored by them, he turns down the Elvenking's offer: "Thank you very much I am sure. . . . But I don't want to leave my friends like this, after all we have gone through together."[26] When Thorin learns that Bilbo has given the Arkenstone to Bard and the Elves, he orders Bilbo to depart, "no friendship of mine goes with him." The other Dwarves felt shame and pity at his going, and Bilbo bids them farewell: "We may meet again as friends."[27]

After the Battle of the Five Armies, the dying Thorin calls Bilbo to him to say his final farewell, adding, "I wish to part in friendship from you, and I take back my words and deeds at the Gate."[28] After Thorin's death Bilbo departed with the friendship of the surviving Dwarves, expressed in mutual offerings of hospitality. "If ever you visit us again," said Balin, "the feast shall indeed be splendid!"[29] If you are passing my way, replied Bilbo, "[t]ea is at four; but you are welcome at any time!" When he returns to Bag End Bilbo finds that he has been presumed dead and many of his belongings were being auctioned off. "It is true that for ever after he remained an elf-friend, and had the honour of dwarves," but "he was no longer quite respectable" among the inhabitants of Hobbiton.[30]

The Fellowship of the Ring

The only Hobbits who were impressed with Bilbo's tales of adventure were his nephews and nieces on the Took side of the family, his cousin Frodo Baggins, and his gardener's son, Samwise. This younger generation of Hobbits formed a fellowship of sorts that reached from Hobbiton to Buckland, and included Pippin Took, Merry Brandybuck, Fredegar "Fatty" Bulger, and Folco Boffin. They frequented the local pub (the Green Dragon!) together, dined together, sang songs, and took country walks—all popular Inkling activities. In Bree, the Hobbits are joined by "Strider," the name Aragorn bore as a ranger of the North. "A hunted man sometimes wearies of distrust and longs for friendship," he shares when he first meets Frodo, offering to be his guide.[31]

Tolkien originally conceived of *The Lord of the Rings* as one novel but was convinced by his publisher to release it serially, as a trilogy. Hence, he needed to create titles for these three parts, and for the first, he came up with, in August of 1953, *The Fellowship of the Ring*. This title fit well, he remarked to his editor, because the last chapter of the first volume was titled "The Breaking of the Fellowship."[32] The Fellowship refers to the nine companions who set out from Rivendell on December 25 with the mission of destroying the One Ring in Mordor: Frodo the Ring-bearer, followed, in order of their volunteering (or being chosen by Elrond to accompany Frodo), by Sam, Merry, Pippin, Gandalf, Legolas, Gimli, Aragorn, and Boromir. As for Merry's and Pippin's participation, Gandalf advises Elrond that in this matter it might be better to trust rather in their friendship with Frodo than to the Hobbits' wisdom.[33] In addition to calling this a fellowship Tolkien uses the synonyms "the Company of the Ring," "the Companions of the Ring," "the Nine Walkers," or simply "the Company."

When the Company leaves Rivendell no charge is put upon them by Elrond, as Head of the Council, other than that on the Ring-bearer. The others are to go "as free companions," states Elrond, but the further they go in each others' company the harder it will be to withdraw. The first of the Company to fall on the quest is Gandalf, while fighting the Balrog in Moria: "he saved us, and he fell," Frodo tells Celeborn and Galadriel. "Yet hope remains while all the Company is true," responds the Lady.[34] Boromir does *not* remain true and tries to take the Ring from Frodo in the chapter Tolkien labels "The Breaking of the Fellowship." When Boromir subsequently dies fighting the Uruk-hai, Legolas insists that the first act is to lay to rest and honor their fallen comrade. Aragorn then chooses, quite remarkably, to follow the orcs who have captured Merry and Pippin rather than to go to Minas Tirith or follow Frodo and Sam to Mordor: "The Company has played its part. Yet we that remain cannot forsake our companions while we have strength left."[35] Thus does Aragorn choose to honor fellowship, even more than his vow to destroy the Ring, and Legolas and Gimli follow his lead in this. While this path does not lead him to rescue the two Hobbits, Aragorn's virtuous act does set into motion several events—finding Gandalf the White, meeting Éomer and Éowyn, providing aid and counsel to Théoden—that ultimately *do* aid both Frodo and Gondor.

The Company is reunited in Ithilien after the Ring is destroyed amid the fragrant trees and the feasts celebrating the fall of Sauron. It is a thoroughly medieval celebration, with princes and minstrels, thrones and pavilions, much laughter and tears of joy. Even many days after the crowning of Aragorn in Minas Tirith, the four Hobbits remained, "for Aragorn was loth for the fellowship to be dissolved."[36] "The Companions of the Ring dwelt together in a fair house with Gandalf," until arrival of the Elves and the wedding of Aragorn Elfstone and Arwen Even-star, and traveled together to Rohan and Fangorn. But there, in a chapter titled "Many Partings," Legolas and Gimli said their farewells: "Here then at last comes the ending of the Fellowship of the Ring," declares Aragorn, "I fear that we shall not all be gathered together ever again."[37] They would not, for Frodo and Gandalf were accorded passage with the Elves on the White Ship, the last to leave Middle-earth. "Well, here at last, dear friends, on the shores of the Sea, comes the end of our fellowship in Middle-earth," declares Gandalf to Sam, Merry, and Pippin. "Go in peace! I will not say: do not weep; for not all tears are an evil."[38]

The Knights of the Round Table

Tolkien was not only himself a member of a famous fellowship of writers; he was a scholar of medieval fellowships and a fellow of a medieval college. It is to the

Middle Ages that we should expect to find important models for his Middle-earth fellowships, especially to the most renowned of all medieval fellowships: the Knights of the Round Table.

For better or worse the European Middle Ages was dominated by the corporation, or body of people, as opposed to individualism and individual rights. Hence there were many types of medieval fellowships. Monastic houses where communities of male and female contemplatives lived, often in isolation, date to the 4th century AD, and were followed by cathedral chapters and mendicant houses (Franciscan and Dominican) in towns. These, in turn, inspired the medieval universities (Bologna, Paris, Oxford, Cambridge) where students and teachers lived in communities, often inside walled colleges built by or in imitation of the monastic houses. By the late Middle Ages craft guilds controlled the regulation of production and exchange in the medieval towns, while in the countryside daily life was regulated by the manor. Military fellowships gave rise to feudalism and chivalry, followed by chivalric orders like the Knights Templar and confraternities like the Knights of the Garter and the Order of the Star.

The origins of medieval military fellowships Tolkien knew quite well. The Latin term *comitatus* was used to describe both cavalry units in the late Roman army and the warband that followed barbarian chieftains who operated on (and often inside) the imperial frontier. The historian Tacitus (AD 55–117) was the first to use the term *comitatus* to describe the relationship between a Germanic chieftain and his retainers who took an oath to serve him. Roman emperors sometimes surrounded themselves with a bodyguard recruited from barbarian nations, and eventually Germanic warlords were competing with emperors and their comitatensian troops (heavy cavalry) for rule of much of Europe. The most successful warlords established royal courts where they feasted heavily armed retainers, bestowing titles and treasures to the most faithful. The courts that most intrigued Tolkien, however, were those that mixed early medieval history and oral legend: those of Hrothgar and Beowulf, Arthur and Alfred, the Nibelungs and the Æsir.

The knight is the successor to the early medieval mounted warrior, and from the 11th century on these armored killing machines dominated warfare in Europe and the Middle East. Medieval bards and poets gave us an idealized picture of the *chevalier errant* ("wandering knight") and the *preux chevalier* ("gallant knight"), but their descriptions are often echoed in the writings of the chroniclers and historians.[39] In other words, life began imitating art, and chivalric fellowships appeared throughout Christendom in imitation of those ascribed to Arthur and Charlemagne. Tolkien had mixed feelings about the Arthurian tradition. In a 1951 letter to editor Milton Waldman, he remarked that he had created his own narrative for Middle-earth rather than attempt a retelling of the Arthurian legend because it contained too much of the Celtic fantastical, courtly French, and Christian elements.[40] And yet, not only did he produce a scholarly edition of *Sir Gawain and the Green Knight* (1925) but he even attempted in the 1930s his own epic Arthurian poem, the unfinished (but posthumously published) *The Fall of Arthur* (2013). Tolkien was so attracted to the story of Arthur's departure for the healing Isle of Avalon that the theme (and name Avallónë) appears much in his Middle-earth writings.[41]

While Tolkien would have been intimately familiar with most of the medieval sources of the Arthurian story, his and Lewis's image of Arthur's fellowship would most likely have derived from Sir Thomas Malory's prose epic, *Morte D'Arthur* (1485). Here King Arthur gathers the best knights in the world to his Round Table for feasting and telling of tales. Many of these men are kings and princes with their own lands, but they choose freely to give up these external goods to be in fellowship with Arthur and with each other. Yes, it is an honor to be a Knight of the Round Table and, yes, Arthur regularly bestows lands and titles on his knights, but in the medieval French romances and in Malory the best knights hardly ever return to their own lands. So does Aragorn bestow lands and titles on Faramir and other lords and so does he keep the members of the Fellowship of the Ring at his court as long as he can, reminding Pippin that he is a Knight of Gondor and must return when bidden. Éomer likewise reminds Merry that he is "Holdwine of the Mark," a name derived from the Anglo-Saxon *hold-wine*, "loyal friend."[42] Through the adventure of the Ring the Hobbit fellowship was expanded to include those of the other "Races" of Middle-earth, but even its highest members—Gandalf and Aragorn—come to embrace many Hobbit virtues.

C. S. Lewis on Friendship and Fellowship

J. R. R. Tolkien and C. S. Lewis often met, apart from Inklings gatherings, on Monday mornings throughout the 1930s and '40s. It was often "one of the pleasantest spots of the week," wrote Lewis. "Sometimes we talk English school politics, sometimes we criticize one another's poems; other days we drift into theology or 'the state of the nation': rarely we fly no higher than bawdy and 'puns.'"[43] As we have already seen, Tolkien was instrumental to Lewis's conversion to Christianity and Lewis was largely responsible for Tolkien seeking to publish *The Hobbit* and *The Lord of the Rings*. Both confess this in private letters, but after Lewis died in November

1963, Tolkien was clearly shaken. Like an old tree gradually losing its leaves, "this feels like an axe-blow near the roots," he wrote to his daughter, Priscilla, just days after Lewis's funeral.[44] "Very sad that we should have been so separated in the last years; but our time of close communion endured in memory for both of us." As the months passed, however, many people sought to discover elements in Tolkien's fiction that may have been influenced by Lewis, and this became a major irritant to Tolkien. "We were separated first by the sudden apparition of Charles Williams" (in 1939), wrote Tolkien to his son Michael, "and then by [Lewis's] marriage," to Joy Davidman (in 1956), which apparently Lewis did not disclose to Tolkien or other Inklings for some time.[45] Nevertheless, Tolkien described Lewis as "a great man," "honest, brave, intellectual—a scholar, a poet, and a philosopher—and a lover, at least after a long pilgrimage, of Our Lord."[46]

We do not have explicit commentary from Lewis on his friendship with Tolkien, but he does leave us clues in his somewhat dated but oft profound work, *The Four Loves* (1960). Written toward the end of his life and when he attended very few Inklings meetings, Lewis remarks that while Eros is necessarily between two lovers,

> . . .two, far from being the necessary number for Friendship, is not even the best. . . . In each of my friends there is something that only some other friend can fully bring out. By myself I am not large enough to call the whole man into activity: I want other lights than my own to show all his facets. Now that Charles is dead, I shall never again see Ronald's reaction to a specifically Caroline joke. Far from having more of Ronald, having him "to myself" now that Charles is away, I have less of Ronald.[47]

While it is not certain here that Lewis is specifically referring to Charles Williams and John Ronald Tolkien, it at least shows his expansive view of friendship. Fellowship is a greater good for Lewis because it also makes friendships stronger. "He is lucky beyond desert to be in such company," continues Lewis, "when the whole group is together, each bringing out all that is best, wisest, or funniest in all the others. These are the golden sessions. . . ."[48]

We settle too often for simple associations, fraternities and sororities of all sorts, and seldom aspire to the riches of these "golden sessions." Friends should make us better people, not just share in our obsessions and indulgences. Plato realized that he was being used by his student and companion, Dionysius II of Syracuse, and the "wolf-love and want of fellowship" between himself and the tyrant led Plato to flee Sicily and return to Athens to found the Academy.[49] In the Martin Scorsese film *The Wolf of Wall Street* (2013), stockbroker and con man Jordan Belfort (Leonardo DiCaprio) indulges every carnal pleasure while surrounding himself with animalistic cronies who adore his unbridled greed; he ultimately betrays his wife and his associates to cut a better deal with the FBI. Scorsese's film leaves us feeling that all human beings are tempted by greed and avarice, that we are all in danger of becoming wolves and that those we love and surround ourselves with will betray or abandon us at the first sign of weakness.

But something deep within us longs for true fellowship, to have companions like Sam and Merry and Pippin who would fight monstrous evil and follow us into the fires of Mordor to support us in doing the right thing. The food and ale and songs we share together do not define the fellowship—they are the rewards of doing battle together, side by side, against evil. We may not be called to face orcs and dark lords and dragons, but we can, as friends, help each other to identify orcish and dragonish behavior whenever and wherever it appears. It is important to note that orcs cannot experience fellowship, that dragons and tyrants are not capable of the sharing and selflessness required by friendship. Hobbits, on the other hand, have the capacity not just to experience fellowship with other Hobbits, but to form deep friendships with Men and Dwarves and Elves. Hobbits can overcome the natural suspicion of those who look different, whose culture and ways are different. Not all Hobbits have broad and inclusive worldviews, for many are comfortable just staying at home; but Bilbo Baggins shows us that it is worth the risk to venture beyond our comfortable holes.

Good Cheer:

Food, Drink, and Laughter

We live in a world where science and technology have made farming safer and more efficient, where we no longer need to drink beer or wine because the water is unsafe. Yet this is a world where obesity and hunger coexist—sometimes in the same place—where famine and disease attack the people of tyrants who live in gilded palaces, where medicine created to relieve pain destroys the lives of thousands, and where plastic islands and polluted rivers carry on the legacy of our technological sophistication. Can it be a virtue to eat and drink like a Hobbit? Is wholesome, uncontrollable laughter appropriate for our times?

I would argue, along with Professor Tolkien, that the appreciation of food and drink and jokes shared in fellowship—in other words, "good cheer"—are appropriate in any age. We have seen that the Hobbits are primarily farmers and gardeners and brewers—why would it be improper for them to celebrate the fruits of their labors? But true appreciation of food and drink requires participation in—or at least knowledge about—growing and harvesting, cooking and brewing. Most of us are divorced from these processes, a luxury few could afford in the ancient and medieval worlds. We live in cities and expect our food to be grown, prepared, and delivered to us. In America, there is a deep and growing divide between urban and rural populations, between white collar workers and laborers, and it colors our culture and our politics. Where that happens in Middle-earth we see the towers of Wizards fall, the machines of industry and war destroyed, the cities susceptible to decadence and decay. Tolkien took a stand next to trees and growing things, felt most comfortable fighting side by side with farmers and laborers, and avoided cars and machines whenever he could. He enjoyed good food and good ale shared with friends, and an occasional pipe and glass of gin. In Oxford he found a balance between the necessary agrarian world and a town that could provide such conveniences as libraries, bookstores, and pubs. It was for him and for C. S. Lewis the good life (*eudaimonia*) that Aristotle saw as the necessary trajectory for civilized life.

Epicureans, Hedonists, and Teetotalers

Most people in the ancient world spent little time worrying about enjoying food and drinking too much. The energy expended on hunting, farming, and preparing meals left them with little time or resources to overindulge. In the ancient city-state, however, there were some who lived lives independent of food production. Skilled workers, professional soldiers, artists, and writers could enjoy the fruits of those who labored outside the city walls, the farmers and slaves who fed them in return for military and legal protections. This was especially true of the Greek *polis* and its successor, the Roman *civitas*. It was the Greeks and the Romans who gave us philosophers and poets who theorized about growing and consuming food and drink, and who left us written and visual praise of the grape and of bread and circus.

Plato took up the subject of food and drink in many of his dialogues, and it seems that his teacher Socrates was also particularly interested in the subject. In Plato's *Symposium*, the drunken politician Alcibiades praises Socrates's ability to abstain from most pleasures of the flesh, or at least to practice moderation, for such pleasures have less appeal to him than do ideas and argument. According to Xenephon, Socrates was wont to point out at these *symposia* (banquets) when eating habits seemed to betray irregularities in character. At one banquet, he picked on a young man who was eating too much fish (an Athenian obsession), calling him an *opsophagus*. As classicist James Davidson points out in his wonderful history of desires in ancient Athens, *Courtesans & Fishcakes*, Socrates was not saying that eating fish was in itself wrong, but that eating too much "relish" (*opson*)—be it seafood or meat—in proportion to the staple (*sitos*), which was usually bread, creates the vice of *opsophagia* which "inverts the dietary hierarchy and allows simple sustenance to be diverted into pleasure."[1]

Plato seems to be assigning a hedonist position to Socrates in the *Protagoras*, where he proposes that the only good is pleasure.[2] The two major hedonistic theories in the ancient world were those of the Cyrenaics and those of the Epicureans.[3] Aristippus of Cyrene, founder of the Cyrenaics, was an associate of Socrates's who, in Xenophon's *Memorabilia*, rejects Socrates's argument that living a life of pleasure will make him enslaved to stronger people who can delay their gratification for the sake of further ends. He will avoid such people and retain his freedom, replies Aristippus, by "rejecting social ties and traveling in many countries, with commitments to none."[4] Aristippus "enjoyed pleasure from what was present, and did not laboriously chase after the enjoyment of what was not present."[5] Bilbo Baggins is close to being a Cyrenaic in this regard, but Gandalf's guidance and Bilbo's love for Frodo keep him tied to his community while he is off on adventure and prevent him ultimately from keeping the Ring.

The philosophy of the Athenian Epicurus (341–270 BC), briefly a student at the Academy, included the goal of happiness, which resulted, he argued, from the absence of physical and mental pain. A strict materialist, Epicurus rejected Plato's Theory of Forms and argued that the gods were not interested in the pleasures and pains of mortals, who were captive to their anxieties, especially fear of death. Eliminating such fears would leave people free to enjoy physical pleasures as well as friendship (*philia*) and altruism. Though Epicureanism was much later associated particularly with the enjoyment of fine food, Epicurus himself was content with little and strived to achieve self-sufficiency, believing "the greatest benefit of self-sufficiency is freedom."[6]

Aristotle's argument for moderation leads him to reject the excesses of food and alcohol consumption. "Men are called gourmets or gourmands or drunkards in accordance with the form of intake in which they are susceptible to unreasonable overindulgence," he writes in the *Eudemian Ethics*.[7] Aristotle produced a treatise *On Drunkenness* (surviving only in fragments) and addressed the issue in the *Problemata* (a work attributed to him but assembled by his peripatetic school over a long period of time), which consists of a series of questions on observing the behavior of the intoxicated.

The ancient Greeks drank wine exclusively, and not only filtered it but always diluted it with water. Only barbarians drink undiluted wine, thought the Greeks, and both Philip of Macedon and his son Alexander the Great were criticized for this practice and their frequent drunkenness. Greeks produced sweet wines and dry wines, dark red, white, and amber. They drank locally produced table wines, aged wines, and valued distinctive vintages from Thasos, Chios, Lesbos, and Cyprus. The wine trade dictated economies and wars, and the youthful god of wine, Dionysius (Bacchus), presided over Greek drama. Dionysius was thought to have invented wine and tried to instruct mortals on how to drink, as in this story from the *Life of Aesop*:

> When Dionysius invented wine, he mixed three cups of wine and showed human beings how they ought to make use of drinking. The first one, he said, was for pleasure, the second for good cheer, and the third for carelessness. For this reason, master, drink the cup of pleasure and that of good cheer, but yield the cup of carelessness to the young. [8]

Homer's writings are full of depictions of feasting gods and mortals, but they are far from the earliest evidence of the enjoyment of food and drink in the ancient world. The so-called "Venus figurines," dating back to the late Stone Age, are hard to interpret but seem to suggest a widespread linking of fatness with fertility (and perhaps female beauty) in Europe and Asia. [9] Ancient Egypt had similar depictions—large belly and sagging breasts—of *male* gods and pharaohs representing fertility. In ancient Egypt and Mesopotamia beer was the daily drink for most, while wine was the preserve of the rich and powerful. Beer was likely invented by the Sumerians but improved by the

Egyptians, who celebrated how beer saved humanity from the bloodlust of the goddess Sekhmet with the Tekh Festival, or "The Festival of Drunkenness," first observed in the Middle Kingdom period (2040–1782 BC). The story of Joseph's Egyptian service in Genesis makes it clear that to "eat the fat of the land" is to enjoy God's beneficence. In ancient (and modern) Judaism, four cups of wine were to be drunk during the Passover meal, and observance of Simchat Torah includes parading of the Torah around the synagogue accompanied by drinking, singing, and dancing. On Purim, the obligation according to the Talmud is to "*levasumei* [drink] to make oneself fragrant with wine . . . until one cannot tell the difference between '*arur Haman*' [cursed be Haman] and '*barukh Mordekhai*' [blessed be Mordecai]."[10]

Nevertheless, most ancient civilizations developed an antipathy to overindulgence and castigated and ridiculed those whose appetites led to obesity and habitual drunkenness.[11] Prohibitions against consuming too much alcohol existed in Egyptian law while Hammurabi's Code was more interested in the regulation of beer sales.[12] The Hebrew Bible, particularly the priestly Leviticus, dictates rules for what can and cannot be eaten by the Israelite and what grain and flesh should be sacrificed to the Lord. Notably all fat and blood belong to God and should not be consumed by humans according to the laws of *kasruth*, while gluttony and drunkenness are acts of disobedience and social evils to be purged from the community.[13] Most of the major world religions have similar prohibitions or agree with Aristotle that moderation (if not abstention) should govern man's relationship with food and alcohol. The Quran defines foods that are *halal* ("permitted") and those that are *haram* ("forbidden")—the latter including carrion, blood, and pork—and the obligation of fasting during the month of Ramadan. Though alcohol is also considered *haram* by Muslims, many interpret that to mean drunkenness rather than complete abstinence.[14] The Third Precept of Buddhism encourages followers to avoid all sensory excesses, including gluttony, while the Fifth Precept warns that alcohol and other intoxicants cloud the mind and thus are an obstacle to understanding. The Hindu *Tirukkural* warns against overeating and several Vedas prohibit alcohol, but moderation in drinking is more common among Hindus.

In early Christianity there are mixed messages on food and drink. Jesus, though himself quite capable, does not insist on fasting; he takes his meals with tax collectors, sinners, and those who are ritually unclean; he performs miracles with bread, fish, and wine; and he is accused at least once of being "a glutton and a drunkard" by his enemies (Luke 7:34). This last instance is the only time gluttony is mentioned in the New Testament, though Paul warns in his letters against allowing the "belly" to rule.[15] It was not until the 4th century that Christianity developed an ascetic tradition like that of John the Baptist and the Essenes. The monks and nuns of the desert fought against all temptations of the flesh seeking to imitate Jesus's forty days in the wilderness. Early medieval monastic authors like John Cassian (360–430) and Aldhelm of Malmesbury (639–709) even argued that the sin first committed by Adam and Eve in eating the forbidden fruit was gluttony, not pride, as most theologians read this episode in Genesis.

The monasteries of the Middle Ages were not just sites for spiritual battles against desires of the flesh, they were also places where agricultural fields were farmed, food of all sorts was produced, and where both wine and beer were to be found. Beer was the everyday drink, and monks often operated their own breweries. Wine was needed for the Eucharist, of course, but vintage wine was also kept for special occasions and aristocratic visitors. Medieval penitential manuals record type and amount of food and drink to be withheld because of a confessed sin or a period of fasting and abstinence for the monk or nun. Some members of the laity were given abstinence from food and drink as penance as well. Such were the habits of the First and Second Estate; the medieval peasantry, on the other hand, hardly needed to abstain from luxuries—meat, wine, and food surplus were for them quite rare.

From the Ancient Symposium to the Medieval Feast

Both Plato and Xenophon, as we have seen, chose to write about the symposium as the arena where their teacher Socrates displayed his philosophical habit. The symposium took place in the men's room (*andrōn*) of the Athenian townhouse, with several couches arrayed in a squared circle on a raised floor, two guests to a coach. After eating, the tables were removed and a libation of unmixed wine was made for the god, after which diluted wine was mixed in a large krater before being poured into individual decorated cups of various sizes. The symposiarch, or president of the banquet, would decide the ratio of water to wine (five parts water to two parts wine was considered reasonable).[16] Songs to the god, poetry, and music provided by flute-girls filled the room. Davidson points out that sometimes guests drank from the same mixing bowl or shared a cup, a sign of intimacy and commensality practiced frequently by the Spartans.[17] In comedies like Aristophanes's *Wasps*, the wine-lover (*philopōtes*) is a man of character, a gentleman (*agathon*) who, if he cannot prevent overindulgence by his comrades, can at least mollify any personal hurt or property damage with a fable or a good joke.

While symposia and banquets were mostly aristocratic gatherings, the ancient and medieval worlds also had the more democratic tavern. Athens and Byzantium had *kapeleia* on every corner selling cheap wine, Roman towns were filled with *popinae* for plebeian pleasure, and the medieval "public house" could provide space for both comfort and conflict. The St. Scholastica Day Riot in Oxford in 1355 began when a student complained about the quality of wine being served at a tavern and threw a pot at the landlord's head. Townsmen and students alike armed themselves and the riot turned into battle in which sixty-two students were slain. In *The Canterbury Tales* Chaucer shows that taverns, like private feasts, could also be the location for songs and storytelling. Both churches and *taberna* were established all along the greatest medieval pilgrimage routes, including *el camino de Santiago* ("The Way of St. James"), the road from the French Pyrenees to Santiago de Compostela in northwestern Spain.

The Feast of Fools and Carnival were two church-sanctioned occasions for feasting and revelry in the medieval world. The former arose in 12th-century France when, on January 1 (the Day of Circumcision), low-ranking subdeacons and choirboys were given control of the liturgy, resulting in gloriously semi-pagan songs about feasting and drinking making their way into churches and similar activities spilling out into the streets. "While the liturgical Feast of Fools struggled for survival inside the churches," writes Max Harris, "unrelated festivities of bourgeois confraternities of fools outside the churches burgeoned. Dressed in motley costumes with ass's ears, secular fools had their own distinct traditions of parades, comic performances, and mimicry."[18] *Carnival* (literally "a farewell to flesh"), extending nearly from Epiphany to *Mardi Gras* ("Fat Tuesday"), was an occasion for colorful feasts, costume parades and balls, and athletic competitions throughout medieval Christendom. Such celebrations included consuming the last stores of rich food and drink before the beginning of Lent, reconciling pagan agricultural festivities with the church calendar.

Carnival has, of course, survived in much of Europe, the Caribbean, and Latin America, as well in French-Catholic communities in the United States like New Orleans, Louisiana, and Mobile, Alabama. Some modern European nations—especially Italy and Spain—need no religious occasion to celebrate food, drink, and fellowship and rival Hobbits in their almost continual consumption of (and obsession with) good food and drink.[19] Tolkien, though no fan of French cuisine, would have enjoyed an occasional dinner at High Table at his or his colleagues' college, and that too could be a gastronomic marathon of sherry, a three- or four-course meal accompanied by two wines, a dessert table with fortified wines and sweets, and finally whisky or brandy back in the Senior Common Room followed by coffee. Lewis planned his long walks in the countryside, often in the company of Tolkien or other Inklings, around good pubs and country inns to be reached at the end of a long day's march. Extending their weary feet to the fireplace, lighting their ubiquitous pipes, the Oxford dons could easily be mistaken for a company of Middle-earth travelers about to tell tales from the heroic past.

How Many Meals does a Hobbit Really Need?

Tolkien tells us that Hobbits generally are "inclined to be fat in the stomach," with "well-fed faces" and mouths apt for laughter and eating and drinking, which they did "often and heartily"—six meals a day including two dinners whenever they can get them.[20] Hobbits are brewers of beer and cultivators of pipe-weed, indeed were the first in Middle-earth to smoke this herb in pipes.[21] Bilbo stocked his pantry with tea and coffee (in addition to various pies, tarts, and cakes) and his cellar with ale and red wine. We are not told where Bilbo could procure tea and coffee and wine in Middle-earth, though the Wood-elves of Mirkwood had barrels of wine from their southern kin and the vineyards of Men.[22] The younger Hobbits also enjoyed the mead given to them by the Elves and the Ent-draught brewed by Treebeard.

The Hobbit begins with an unexpected party: Gandalf and thirteen Dwarves show up at Bilbo's house for afternoon tea and stay well past dinner. The Dwarves, like carousers at a Greek symposium, eat and drink everything in Bilbo's kitchen and pantry and joke about destroying his plates and cutlery while singing a washing-up song. The behavior of the Dwarves tests Bilbo's conventional Hobbit hospitality, but he is drawn into their adventure when harp and drum, flutes and fiddles are brought out and the Dwarves sing a haunting song about their ancient home and treasure. Bilbo forgets all else and is swept away to distant lands, and his heart is enchanted by the description of jewels and gold crafted by Dwarvish hands.

Food and drink play an important role throughout Bilbo's first adventure. He survives the attempt of the trolls to have a feast of roast Dwarves and "burrahobbit," and is given temporary refuge by Elrond at the Last Homely House. "Mind Bilbo doesn't eat all the cakes!" tease the Elves of Rivendell. "He is too fat to get through key-holes yet!"[23] Bilbo would remark much later in Rivendell, at the Council of Elrond: "Elves may thrive on speech alone, and Dwarves endure great weariness; but I am only an old hobbit, and I miss my meal at noon."[24] They did not find the hospitality of the Elves when they encountered the stone-giants and goblins in the Misty Mountains. There too Bilbo had a memorable encounter with a most bloodthirsty creature: Gollum, the miserable, slimy thing that eats goblins who stray into his dark abode. Not only does he threaten to eat Bilbo, but several of the riddles he *and* Bilbo employed in their contest included reference to food and eating: eggs, fish, teeth. "Gollum was really hungry," remarks the narrator, and these riddles were making him even hungrier. "Is it nice, my preciousss?" he asked himself, looking at Bilbo. "Is it juicy? Is it scrumptiously crunchable?"[25]

In *The Lord of the Rings* we find out that Gollum was once Sméagol, one of the River-folk, who were close relations to Hobbits. Gollum is, in many ways, a twisted mirror image of a Hobbit—dark and slimy, inhospitable and treacherous, living in an underground abode far from comfortable—similar to the way orcs and goblins are twisted versions of Elves. Where Bilbo and Frodo show hospitality and generosity with their food and drink, Gollum eats sentient beings and lures Frodo into the bloodthirsty clutches of Sheelob. Gollum, Sheelob, and Ungoliant (the monstrous spider that also appears in *The Silmarillion*) are offered as warnings to what can happen if obsession with food and drink go too far.

After Bilbo survives Gollum's treachery and is reunited with Gandalf and the Dwarves, the company is hosted in the strange house of Beorn the skin-changer. Tolkien's own drawing of Beorn's house makes it clear that it is a mead-hall, a common royal abode among Celtic and Germanic chieftains of the early Middle Ages. Beorn keeps giant bees for their honey and beeswax and provides the company with bowls of mead and a great feast with the help of strange animal servants who can walk on their hind legs and carry torches and plates. In Mirkwood they encounter what Yeats would call "trooping fairies," a mysterious party of feasting Elves "eating and drinking and laughing merrily," whose revelry disappears whenever Bilbo and the Dwarves draw near.[26] At the Elvenking's court the butler and chief of the guards help themselves to the heady new wine from Dorwinion—while Bilbo helps himself to the keys—and more tipsy Elves visiting the cellar enabled the Dwarves' escape packed in barrels.

Like *The Hobbit*, *The Fellowship of the Ring* begins with a party, this time a "long-expected party" that Bilbo was hosting for most of the Shire. Celebrating his own "eleventy-first" birthday, it was to be "a party of special magnificence," complete with an open-air kitchen, cooks drafted from every inn and eating-house for miles, Dwarf-made toys as presents for the children, three formal meals, and Gandalf's fireworks.

Frodo also, we are told, liked to throw parties with meals where "it snowed food and rained drink, as hobbits say." [27] His last dinner party at Bag End was a gathering of young Hobbits who were in high spirits helping Frodo finish off his wine, the last of the Old Winyards. [28] On their last day before leaving Bag End, Sam came up from the cellar wiping his mouth: "He had been saying farewell to the beer-barrel in the cellar." [29] The Hobbits in *The Fellowship* enjoy the food and hospitality of a succession of increasingly grand hosts: mugs of beer with Farmer Maggot (whose mushrooms a young Frodo had pilfered), supper and singing with Tom Bombadil and Goldberry, Lord Elrond's great feast, the magical refreshments of Galdriel and Celeborn. Butterbur's ale at the Prancing Pony in Bree leads to Pippin's storytelling and Frodo's singing and dancing—and unwanted attention—and the bowls of cool water in the House of Bombadil "went to their hearts like wine and set free their voices." [30] Miruvor, the cordial of Imladris, revives the Hobbits' hearts and fills their limbs with vigor when they are nearly buried by the snows of Caradhras. [31]

At their departure from Lórien the Fellowship are given many gifts by the Elves, but perhaps the most important of these is *lembas*:

The food was mostly in the form of very thin cakes, made of a meal that was baked a light brown on the outside, and inside was the color of cream. . . . "We call it *lembas* or waybread, and it is more strengthening than any food made by Men. . . . Eat little at a time, and only at need. For these things are given to serve you when all else fails. The cakes will keep sweet for many days, if they are unbroken and left in their leaf-wrappings. . . ."[32]

Lembas has associations both with hardtack (the biscuit eaten by soldiers and sailors as far back as ancient Rome) and with the bread of the Eucharist, known in Catholicism as *viaticum*, "for the way." *Lembas* sustains Frodo and Sam all the way to Mordor, and Frodo thinks it will do Gollum some good. When Frodo offers Gollum food in the Dead Marshes, however, a strange greenish light appears in Gollum's eyes, but he chokes on the waybread, tasting only dust and ashes, preferring raw fish and rabbit.[33] To his dismay Sam cooks the rabbits that Gollum fetches, making a stew lacking only fresh herbs and taters. All Hobbits can cook, writes Tolkien, learning the art from a very early age, but Sam was an especially good cook and carried his pans and implements with him on the journey to Mordor. As for Gollum: "He doesn't eat grasses or roots, no precious . . . Sméagol won't grub for roots and carrotses and—taters. . . ."[34]

The starving and treacherous Gollum brings Frodo and Sam to the lair of the great spider Sheelob, "grown fat with endless brooding on her feasts"—the blood of Elves and Men and orcs—for "all living things were her food, and her vomit darkness."[35] She "lusted for sweeter meat" than the orcs she had been trapping, and Gollum, who long ago "bowed and worshipped her," now brought her two Hobbits, just as Sauron had long been sending prisoners to sate her unquenchable thirst for blood.[36] As Sam battles Sheelob we have the confrontation of two sides of appetite—one who grows vegetables, cooks with herbs, and appreciates flavor, the other a creature of constant lust whose gluttony is never satisfied despite the blood she consumes from her living victims. If Tolkien is in agreement here with the Old Testament laws of *kasruth*, the vitality of blood belongs solely to the Lord and is thus *treyf* (forbidden food), yet Sheelob claims it for her own and is worshipped and feared by Gollum, the anti-Sam.

Laughter

When we first meet the Elves of Middle-earth, they are singing a comedic song in Rivendell as Bilbo and the Dwarves pass by. "So they laughed and sang in the trees; and pretty fair nonsense I daresay you think it," remarks *The Hobbit*'s narrator. "Not that they would care; they would only laugh all the more if you told them."[37] Laughter plays an important role in *The Lord of the Rings*. Frodo's adventure begins amid the laughter and cheer of Bilbo's party, and he manages to maintain that disposition (mostly) all the way to Bree. Being wounded by a Morgul blade on Weathertop, however, requires healing by Elvish arts, accompanied by the good cheer of Bilbo and the younger Hobbits in Rivendell. Similarly, his great suffering under the power of the Ring and from Gollum's biting off his finger at the Crack of Doom also require healing, and this is wrought by the great laughter of Gandalf at their reunion. "'A great shadow has departed,' said Gandalf, and then he laughed, and the sound was like music . . . and [the] thought came to Sam that he had not heard laughter, the pure sound of merriment, for days upon days without count."[38] The apparent tragedy for Middle-earth has here been turned—by what Tolkien terms a *euchatastrophe*—into a comedy.

The legal scholar Frank Buckley developed a taxonomy of comedy, positing four social virtues—integrity, moderation, fortitude, and temperance—and three charismatic virtues of comedy—grace, taste, and learning.[39] Like Aristotle's taxonomy, each of these "comic virtues" has corresponding "comic vices" of insufficiency and of excess. "Fortitude is a principal comic virtue," argues Buckley, "since one of the best ways to protect oneself from being laughed at is to laugh in the face of adversity."[40] Bilbo is laughed at by the Dwarves in the beginning of *The Hobbit*, which prompts him to go on their dangerous quest to prove that he is no coward. On the journey with the Dwarves he proves to be a source of humor—not the butt of jokes—by employing riddles, gallows humor, ridiculous taunts, etc. He even finds strength in comedy facing the giant spiders and Smaug. It is significant that Bilbo and Gandalf share a laugh—and tobacco—in the book's closing words.

The Bird and Baby:
Balancing the Divine and the Profane

> I know [of] no more pleasant sound than arriving at the B. and B. and hearing a roar, and knowing that one can plunge in.[41]

As we have seen, Tolkien enjoyed the company of his Oxford friends on long country walks and gatherings in pubs and college dining halls. Several of the pubs that Tolkien and the Inklings frequented in Oxford—the Lamb and Flag, the White Horse, the King's Arms—are still in operation (some have been since the late Middle Ages). But no Oxford pub is more famous for its association with the Inklings than the Eagle and Child on St. Giles Street, nicknamed by the Inklings "the Bird and Baby" from the sign that once hung above its entrance. Sometime in the early 1930s the Inklings meeting every Tuesday morning in the Eagle and Child, a gathering lent to not-so-serious storytelling, conversation, and laughter, became an established routine.[42] More formal gatherings took place on Thursday evenings in the college rooms of one of the group's members, most often in C. S. Lewis's rooms at Magdalen College. On both occasions tea, ale, and pipe were the accompaniments to the jokes, storytelling, and readings of early drafts of *The Lord of the Rings*.

The Inklings gatherings at the Bird and Baby and other pubs was a reconstructing of the distinctly Oxford collegiate fellowship. A fellow of an Oxbridge college enjoys, among other privileges, the company of other scholars at tea in the Senior Common Room, meals at High Table in a formal dining hall, and often dessert wines and spirits in a smaller room after dinner. Oxbridge colleges also have their own bars, but these are more the domain of the undergrads. Despite these luxuries dons sometimes do not care for the company of the fellows of their own college—Tolkien did not when he was at Pembroke—and thus meetings at a pub or in the private rooms of other dons provided less formal spaces for fellowship with more frank and noisy discussion.

In a 1944 letter, Tolkien complained to his son Christopher that the *Daily Telegraph* described his friend C. S. Lewis, whom Tolkien usually called Jack or C.S.L., as the "'Ascetic Mr. Lewis'—!!! I ask you! [Lewis] put away three pints in a very short session we had this morning, and said he was 'going short for Lent.'"[43] In a 1948 letter addressed to Lewis, Tolkien admits to the "malicious delight" he gets from seeing Hugo Dyson "slightly heated with alcohol" and showing off in front of the other Inklings.[44] Davidson asks whether "commensality (the fellowship of the table) . . . emphasizing *companionship*," as in the breaking of bread together and sharing of fine wine and port in Oxford collegiate life, is not in fact more akin to the Eucharist than to "alcoholic" behavior.[45] Lewis's brother, Warnie, did suffer from alcoholism and was hospitalized on several occasions, and one should not ignore genetic predisposition and the toll alcohol can take on individuals and their families. It is, of course, never a good idea to mix drinking and driving (most of the Inklings lived within walking distance). But "good cheer" was very much part of the world of Tolkien, as it was in his sub-creation, and he did not see the enjoyment of food and drink as in conflict with his Catholic and Thomistic values.

As much as Hobbits enjoy their six meals a day, ale, and pipeweed, both *The Hobbit* and *The Lord of the Rings* are about the periods and circumstances when we must go without these creature comforts. The two books also show that such hard-won products of the land are best enjoyed in fellowship, in moderation, and best of all as part of community celebrations like birthdays, weddings, reunions, and coronations. Every year for seventeen years after Bilbo's disappearance from his own party, Frodo would toast his cousin on their combined birthdays, September 22. Every year on January 3, J. R. R. Tolkien's birthday, fans around the world raise a glass and make a simple toast: "To the Professor."

Telling Stories and Singing Songs

I n human history, there has never been a time with more people on the planet sharing more stories more quickly and efficiently with one another than at this moment. The advent of the internet, social media, and smartphones gave our species the means to communicate with words, pictures, and video across nations and cultures and thousands of miles almost instantaneously. Nearly every *Homo sapiens* has the ability to be a storyteller and to reach millions with their message. The question is, how are we using this technology? Are we telling better stories because of digital media?

Every person can sing a song, recite a poem, or tell a story. One need not be a trained singer or professional poet to do so. In making storytelling a Hobbit virtue, Tolkien may be suggesting that we should all indulge in this activity, on occasion, to make for a merrier world.

The Greatest Stories Ever Told

We begin with a problem of definitions. Folklore, folktales, fables, fairy tales (or fairy-stories), myths, romance, fantasy—we throw these words around, often interchangeably, and use them imprecisely. Academics are of little help, for anthropologists, ethnologists, folklorists, and philologists each have their own disciplinary definitions, and often there is no agreement *within* the discipline.[1] For the purposes of this chapter, it might be helpful to think of storytelling as a very ancient practice that started entirely through oral performance, with professionals (be they painters or poets or priests) coming later.[2] Storytelling can exist side by side with written literature, even interact with it, and may be accompanied by music, but it is not owned by specialists: it is a virtue only if all people can participate in the activity. That we can propose it as a virtue means that we must at the outset contradict popular contemporary use of the term *story* to mean "a fabrication or lie." For Tolkien saw both myth and fairy-stories as meaning the opposite: They are vehicles for carrying truth.

The earliest evidence of storytelling is probably the cave art of the Upper Paleolithic, some examples dating to more than 35,000 years ago. In sites ranging from Indonesia to Australia, Romania to France, Spain to Brazil, there are surviving examples of paintings of a variety of animals and humans arranged in scenes occasionally evoking a narrative.[3] While the lions and rhinos of Chauvet Cave, in southeastern France, are perhaps the most sophisticated example of this Ice Age art, and those of nearby Lascaux the most numerous, hunting and dancing are depicted in a painting at Serra da Capivarra, Piauí, Brazil (28,000–6,000 BC).[4] Who knows how long hominins (including Neanderthals) have been telling stories, but when narrative writing by *Homo sapiens* first emerges in

Egypt and Mesopotamia in the third millennium BC, we begin to see the important role storytelling played. In the *Epic of Gilgamesh* (ca. 2150–1400 BC), the Egyptian Westcar Papyrus (ca. 2000–1300 BC), the Vedas (second millennium BC), *The Iliad* and *The Odyssey* (8th century BC), we have not only stories but also storytellers within the story. Homer gives us, for example, Demodocus, the blind bard who appears at the court of the Phaeacian King Alcinous in *The Odyssey*. *The Odyssey* is structured such that the story of the Trojan War is retold in episodes by several characters, including Odysseus himself. Homer's original audience knew the story of the Trojan War, but the way Homer structures the retelling (as well as his drawing of its characters) makes it so compelling and enduring.

In ancient Greece, there is no clear distinction between myth and fable, and the three words—μύθος, λόγος, and αινος—are used almost interchangeably. Myth writers like Homer and Hesiod were succeeded by the fabulist Aesop (ca. 620–564 BC) and by the dramatists of the sixth and fifth centuries BC. Aesop, who was believed by ancient writers to have been a slave from Samos, wrote short, simple, and unadorned fables (λόγοι) whose brevity and clarity of message made them easy to memorize.[5] Aesop's stories are the quintessential examples of the Greek fable, defined by the Greek rhetorician Theon (2nd century BC) as a fictitious narration, usually involving speaking animals or inanimate objects, that illustrates a general principle or lesson.[6] The Roman rhetorician Quintilian (AD 35–100) writes of teachers of literature: "Their pupils should learn to paraphrase Aesop's fables [*fabellas*], the natural successors of the fairy stories of the nursery [*fabulis nutricularum*]."[7] Euripides writes, in his tragedy *Heracles* (c. 423 BC): "Console [your children] with stories, / those sweet thieves of wretched make-believe."[8] Writers like Dio Chrysostom and Strabo agree that myths and fabulous stories are told to children to comfort them and by women to distract each other from their labors.[9] The political historian Thucydides even warns against the prose chroniclers, and he may have had in mind Herodotus, "Father of History," whose ethnographic inquiries, or researches (*historiae*), often consisted of strange stories he heard from locals on his travels throughout the Greek and Persian territories.

Plato famously had a problem with the make-believe of the poets and playwrights and has Socrates in his dialogues often attacking poets while simultaneously reworking Aesopic fables and creating his own myths and allegories. In Plato's *Ion*, Socrates questions whether the prize-winning *rhapsode* (a professional reciter of poetry) is capable of understanding and interpreting Homer as well as delivering moving performances of Homeric poetry (line 531a7), or whether he is just a divinely inspired transmitter, "an airy thing, winged and holy" (534b3–4). In Book II of the *Republic* Socrates argues that parents fill their children's heads with fictitious tales at a very early age, just as children begin character development (377b11), when they should be reciting only myths that encourage true virtue (378d7–e3). "There is an old quarrel between philosophy and poetry" continues Socrates in Book X (line 607b5–6), suggesting that poets can only imitate created things and should be banished from the ideal state because they are chiefly responsible for the popularity of these fabrications. In both *Gorgias* and *Phaedrus* Socrates makes a similar attack on rhetors, arguing that they often artfully and effectively mislead their audiences.[10] On the other hand, in the *Republic*, Plato also gives us the story of the Ring of Gyges (2:359a–2:360d), which has the power to turn its wearer invisible, and the Allegory of the Cave (7:514a–7:517a); the former undoubtedly influenced Tolkien's depiction of the One Ring, while the latter is utilized by Lewis in both *The Chronicles of Narnia* and his apologetics.

Storytelling has both secular and religious functions in the Bible, in ancient Sanskrit texts, in Buddhism, and in Taoism and Confucianism.[11] Jesus, of course, frequently uses the parable (παραβολή, *parabolē*) as part of his teaching, according to the Gospel writers, and parables can be found throughout the history of Judaism as well as in the Quran. The parable is literally a "comparison," usually taking the form of a short story, that conveys an ethical or religious principle. Unlike fables, parables operate in the mundane or realistic realm rather than the fantastic. Most of the major religions of the world utilize multiple types of narrative—cosmological myths, laws, battle accounts, religious poetry, parables, sayings, etc.—to convey religious truths collected over centuries or even millennia. In most cases the biography of the founder is presented as historical drama. Tolkien practiced most of these forms in his fiction, especially in his posthumously published *Silmarillion*.

Bards and Poets

It is worth noting that although Tolkien aspired to be a poet and spent most of his professional life studying and teaching poetry, professional bards and poets rarely appear in his Middle-earth writings. The bard can be found in nearly every ancient society, often achieving high status and sometimes performing priestly duties. Ancient Greece's Heroic Age had its *aoidos* (ἀοιδός), who sang both epic and lyric verse accompanied by the lyre. Homer and Hesiod are the most famous poets of epic and myth in the Greek Dark Age, while the Archaic period bears the name the Lyric Age from the war poetry of Archilochus and Tyrtaeus and the choral lyric of Sappho (accompanied by music and dance). By the Greek Classical Age the term *rhapsode* came to be used for professionals who performed Homeric and other verse in Greek cities.[12] Greek dramatists, of course, also told stories in verse, a tradition inherited by the Romans (nearly all Roman plays were based on Greek stories) as well as that of the "inspired poet" (*vates*). In the Late Roman Republic and the Augustan Age the epic poetic tradition was continued by Virgil and the lyric by Catullus, Horace, and Ovid.

Greek and Roman writers also described the poets and storytellers of the barbarian world. They were especially fascinated with the Celtic peoples, and ascribed to them the triad of bard, *vates*, and Druid: the bard to recite the history/genealogy of the tribe, the *vates* to channel prophecy from the gods, and the priestly Druid to interpret all of this and advise the king. The Druids were all but destroyed by the Romans (surviving only in Ireland) but bards continued the roles of storyteller, singer, and genealogist in early medieval Ireland, Scotland, Wales, and Brittany. The Germanic peoples had bards performing similar roles, including the *scop* of Anglo-Saxon England and the *skáld* of the Norse courts. It was the barbarian bardic tradition that most interested Tolkien—*Beowulf*, the Old Norse *Eddas* and *Sagas*, the Breton *lais*—but he also appreciated the romances and alliterative verse of the High Middle Ages that incorporated many of the earlier (often pagan) stories. All this verse was aristocratic, meant primarily for the courts of kings, barons, and bishops.[13]

Tolkien wrote both lyric and alliterative verse in the style of ancient and medieval poets. Yet, despite his great admiration for the skill of these professional poets and singers, Tolkien chose for his novels to focus on the storytelling and verse-making of seemingly unremarkable Hobbits, warrior Men, and mostly unseen Elves. In doing so he makes storytelling an accessible virtue, not solely for the pleasure of the rich and powerful.

Hobbit Tales

The narrative style Tolkien chooses to begin *The Hobbit* with is very much that of the storyteller: "In a hole in the ground there lived a hobbit." Then follows vivid descriptions of both the Hobbit and his hole. It is Tolkien's version of "Once upon a time," and the tone is appropriate for a story told to children. This is, of course, because it *was* a story told to children, *his* children, long before it became a book. His authorial voice remains that of a narrator of a children's book until we get to the standoff between the Dwarves and Bard and the Elves at the Lonely Mountain, when the story gets darker and the narrative style resembles that of Old Norse sagas.[14] The book ends with a return to the Shire and the return of the folksy and humorous narrator.

Internal instances of and references to storytelling and songs in *The Hobbit* are numerous. Bilbo recalls that when he was young, Gandalf used to visit the Shire and tell "such wonderful tales" about "dragons and goblins and giants and the rescue of princesses and the unexpected luck of widows' sons" at parties.[15] In other words, Gandalf and the Hobbits shared a love of fairy tales. After the Dwarves are well-fed they bring out their instruments, including Thorin's beautiful golden harp, and begin playing music so "sweet that Bilbo forgot everything else, and was swept away into dark lands under strange moons."[16] As the fire died they begin singing songs about "the deep places of their ancient homes,"

Far over the misty mountains cold
To dungeons deep and caverns old
We must away ere break of day
To seek the pale enchanted gold.[17]

Again, the music and the lyrics about dragons and gold has a magical effect on Bilbo, until "something Tookish woke up inside him, and he wished to go and see the great mountains, and hear the pine-trees and the waterfalls, and explore the caves, and wear a sword instead of a walking stick."[18] Thorin then rehearses the tale of his grandfather's mighty halls full of armor and treasure, seized by the dragon Smaug, and of the ruin of the city of Dale.

Thorin's company rides off merrily with Bilbo and Gandalf, telling stories and singing songs between meals. When the party enters Rivendell a song bursts like laughter from the trees as the Elves greet the travelers, poking fun at the eating habits of Hobbits and of Dwarves' beards. The "pretty fair nonsense" and foolishness of the singing Elves contrasts with the seriousness of their master, Lord Elrond, who tells Gandalf and Thorin the stories of their swords, Orcrist and Glamdring, ancient blades made in Gondolin. "I wish I had time to tell you even a few of the tales or one or two of the songs that they heard" in the House of Elrond, says the narrator.[19] The goblins who surprise the party in the mountain caves also sing "or croak" a song, mechanical and violent, as they whip their prisoners. It is full of monosyllabic noise and a great contrast to the merrymaking of the Elves.

When Bilbo encounters Gollum deep within the mountain he suggests a riddle game. Both the Anglo-Saxons and the Norse had riddle traditions, and Tolkien knew these sources well, even inventing two Old English riddles and publishing them as a new philological discovery![20] It is interesting that Bilbo employs riddles both with Gollum and with Smaug, as if deceptive narrative is most appropriate in dealing with monstrous opponents.

Tolkien adopts a different narrator voice for the Prologue of *The Lord of the Rings*. "This book is largely concerned with Hobbits," he writes, "and from its pages a reader may discover much of their character and a little of their history."[21] He then makes reference to the Red Book of Westmarch, the earliest chapters of which, assures the narrator, were published as *The Hobbit*. This academic façade has precedent in medieval chronicles and romances and is an effective literary conceit allowing the professor here to answer the requests of readers and publisher for more information about Hobbits. It is effective in setting up the adventure tale that follows, though *that* unfolds slowly after much more "hobbit talk" in chapters one through three of the *Fellowship*. The first scene in chapter one takes place at the Ivy Bush, an inn in the Shire, where several Hobbits are telling tales and rumors about "the history and character of Mr. Bilbo Baggins" and his cousin Frodo Baggins, whose joint birthdays were about to be celebrated at "a party of special magnificence."[22] This technique works well as an introduction of Frodo as well as Samwise Gamgee, whose father Gaffer Gamgee says is crazy about stories of the old days and Bilbo's adventure tales.[23]

At the long-expected party Gandalf entertains the Hobbit children with fireworks and Bilbo makes a formal speech. He refers to "ancient history"—his arrival by barrel in Esgaroth—and the confused party guests fear that "a song or some poetry was now imminent," but "he did not sing or recite," he merely announced that he was leaving, and then literally vanished in front of them.[24] As Bilbo takes his leave of Gandalf, accompanied by two Dwarves, he sings a song of his own making—"The Road Goes Ever On and On"—and makes his way in the dark on his long secretive journey. The talk of Bilbo's second disappearance from the Shire lasted for more than a year, and Frodo was left to defend the treasures of Bag End (including its cellar and pantry). As the years passed there were rumors of strange things happening outside the Shire, including the departure of the Elves from Middle-earth, strange Dwarves from faraway lands seeking refuge in the West, and whispers of the return of "the Enemy" to Mordor.[25]

When Gandalf finally returns to Hobbiton, he tells Frodo that he has discovered the true story about the Ring, of its origins and how both Gollum and Bilbo came to possess it. Gandalf's many stories in chapter two, "Shadows of the Past," serve to situate his wisdom and prepare Frodo for his role as Ring-bearer. Sam is drawn into the adventure because he can't help eavesdropping on Gandalf's tales, and when he and Frodo leave Hobbiton with Pippin, Sam is filled with desire to see the Elves while Frodo sings Bilbo's walking-songs. "With most hobbits it is a supper-song or a bed-song; but these hobbits hummed a walking-song."[26] Soon enough they are answered by a song from a troop of High Elves, "O Elbereth! Gilthoniel!" Their leader, Gildor Inglorion, hails Frodo as "Elf-friend" and allows the Hobbits to join them on their march and in their feast. "Now is the time for speech and merriment!" declares Gildor, and the three Hobbits are each enthralled by the food and drink and starlight that seemed to surround the Elves. "Well, sir, if I could grow apples like that, I would call myself a gardener," remembers Sam years later. "But it was the singing that went to my heart . . ."[27]

Stories from Gildor and from Farmer Maggot provide the Hobbits with some information about the Black Riders that are pursuing them, and at Crickhollow Frodo's company enjoys a brief respite to enjoy food, beer, and one of Bilbo's bath-songs while they bathe.[28] Merry and Pippin sing a "dwarf-song" and then venture into the Old Forest where Frodo attempts another song before Merry and Pippin are captured by Old Man Willow.[29] They are freed by the ever-singing Tom Bombadil. "I know the tune for him," he assures the Hobbits, and then sings them back to his house for dinner:

> *Hey! Come derry dol! Hop along, my hearties!*
> *Hobbits! Ponies all! We are fond of parties.*
> *Now let the fun begin! Let us sing together!*[30]

His lady Goldberry, the Riverman's daughter, joins in the singing and her radiance inspires Frodo to recite extemporaneously before all eat and drink in fellowship in the House of Bombadil. For Tom, almost everything is expressed in terms of song: Old Man Willow is "a mighty singer," he fell in love with Goldberry because of her singing in the rushes, he chases away nightmares and Barrow-wights by singing. When rain delays the Hobbits' departure, Tom tells them many long tales and remarkable stories about the Old Forest, often accompanied by singing and dancing, and about the Barrow-downs with their unquiet graves of fallen kings.[31] "His songs are stronger songs" than the cold incantations of the Barrow-wights, and he breaks their dark spell with his merry singing.

At the Prancing Pony in Bree, Pippin gives a comic account of Bilbo's birthday party, and Frodo, unwisely, sings and capers to Bilbo's song "The Cat and the Fiddle," Tolkien's satire of the Mother Goose nursery rhyme "Hey Diddle Diddle."[32] There Butterbur gives Gandalf's letter to Frodo, and in a postscript the Wizard offers a few lines of verse (*All that is gold does not glitter, / Not all those who wander are lost* . . .) to help him identify Strider as Aragorn.[33] Their new Ranger companion displays his knowledge of lore and verse on the journey to Rivendell, chanting the tale of Tinúviel and prompting Sam to remember a poem about the Elvenking Gil-galad and to sing an old tune with his own lyrics about Old Tom and a troll.[34]

Once in Rivendell and healing from the wound he received on Weathertop, Frodo is immersed in an atmosphere of song and verse. "Here you will hear many songs and tales," Gandalf tells Frodo before reuniting him with Bilbo, who has been composing songs and working on his book.[35] Aragorn helps Bilbo with his verses and Frodo is treated to all manner of music in Rivendell, including Bilbo's long song about the mariner Eärendil and the Elves' song to Elbereth. But it is story that takes center stage in Rivendell, and at the Council of Elrond we get many: Glóin's account of the fatal return of the Dwarves to Moria and Sauron's interest in Bilbo's ring, Elrond's tale of Sauron and the Rings of Power, Boromir's account of the fall of Osgiliath, Faramir's dream (in verse!) about Isildur's Bane, Bilbo's poem about Aragorn and the true story about how he came to possess the Ring, and Gandalf's long tale about Gollum and the treason of Sauron. Each story provides bits of information needed to make the all-important decision: what to do with the One Ring.

Bilbo sends the Companions of the Ring off on their long journey with a song that pays homage to the past and to the future:

> *I sit beside the fire and think*
> *of people long ago,*
> *and people who will see a world*
> *that I shall never know.*[36]

Gimli sings a song of the faded glory of the Dwarvish city in Moria, Legolas sings of the Elf-maid Nimrodel when the Company enters Lothlórien, Frodo and Sam join the Elves in singing laments for the fallen Gandalf, and Galadriel herself sings a parting song for the Company as they head out from Lórien. Both Aragorn and Legolas compose songs for the funeral of Boromir, but the songs all but cease with the breaking of the Fellowship. The Rohirrim sing stern songs as they march into battle, and Éomer, with the lust of battle upon him, laughs at despair as he recites his fell staves on Pellenor Fields. [37]

When Aragorn, Legolas, and Gimli first encounter the Riders of Rohan, Éomer is astonished by the old tales about the Lady in the Golden Wood seemingly coming true. "These are indeed strange days," he remarks. "Dreams and legends spring to life out of the grass." [38] Hobbits are to Éomer only "a little people in old songs and children's tales out of the North. Do we walk in legends or on the green earth in the daylight?" Aragorn answers that a man may do both, "For not we but those who come after will make the legends of our time." And as for the green earth, it too is a "mighty matter of legend." Treebeard recites to Merry and Pippin the old lists of the peoples and creatures in Middle-earth, chants verse about his adventures, and sings a song about the Entwives, while all the Ents join in a martial song as they march on Isengard. [39] Aragorn recalls the songs of the Rohirrim, and Gandalf the White sings a song about Galadriel to break the spell in Meduseld. Gandalf also recites some of the Rhymes of Lore to Pippin as they speed to Minas Tirith, teaching him about the origins of the *palantiri*. [40] Gollum is able to compose rhymes about his hard life—and catching fish!—and recall the story of the battle at the Dead Marshes. [41] And even on the sinister stairs of Cirith Ungol, Frodo and Sam are able to bring some light by discussing the adventure tales they heard growing up in the Shire, and how their own adventure will be told in future tales. [42] Because Galadriel had given Frodo the vial containing the light of Eärendil, Sam remarks that they are still part of the ancient tale of the Silmarils: "Don't the great tales never end?"

After their victory at Minas Tirith, the Men of the West compose poetry and songs of different types: an unnamed bard of Rohan composes an elegy for the fallen warriors, while at Cormallen Men cheer "with many voices and many tongues" a praise-song for the Hobbits. [43] In victory Legolas composes songs to the sea and even a great eagle cries out above the city, "Sing all ye people!"—and the people did. [44] Then, of course, there was the matter of finishing Bilbo's adventure book and Frodo adding tales of his own, which he does, leaving the last pages for Sam to finish—appropriately so, for Sam has proven to be a warrior-poet as well as a gardener. Sam puts his hands behind his back when he "speaks poetry"—like his rhyme of the Oliphaunt—and he draws courage as he sings, composing words to old tunes. He is, for Tolkien, the Hobbit whose unsophisticated love of tales and poetry shows that all readers can aspire to this virtue.

Writing Fairy Stories

This long litany of examples of songs, poems, and storytelling in *The Hobbit* and *The Lord of the Rings*, beyond giving him an arena to practice his own poetry, shows that Tolkien felt these things to be crucial to living the Good Life. Poems and stories can convey virtues in a community while the acts of composition and performance can themselves be virtuous. ". . . the morality of *The Lord of the Rings* is better described as traditional and communal," writes Ralph C. Wood. "It is sustained by the various companies of hobbits and men and elves who narratively transmit their virtues by way of familial lore . . ."[45]

As we have seen, the Western philosophic tradition was somewhat hostile to myths and fairy stories. Cicero compares an account "to the merest fairy-story [*tota commenticia*], hardly worthy of old wives at work by lamplight."[46] The wonder tales told by Apuleius (born ca. AD 125) in his *Metamorphoses, or The Golden Ass*, were originally told for the entertainment of adults (some are quite risqué), while *True Stories* by the Sophist Lucian (2nd century AD) is a collection of outrageous first-person adventure tales, a genre for whose origins he blames the trickster Odysseus.[47] Only much later were these stories simplified, cleaned-up, and given to children. Tolkien was very much influenced from an early age by collections of European folklore and fairy stories published in the eighteenth and nineteenth centuries. Charles Perrault's *Tales of Mother Goose* (1697), Jakob and Wilhelm Grimm's *Children's and Household Tales* (1812), Hans Christian Andersen's *Fairy Tales* (1837), Elias Lönnrot's *Kalevala* (1835), Lady Charlotte Guest's translation of the *Mabinogion* (1838), and the *Fairy Books* of Andrew Lang (1889–1910) all had an influence on Tolkien's writing.

Tolkien was unhappy both about the imprecision of our use of the term "fairy-story" and the relegating of such stories to the nursery. He explored the topic in a 1938 lecture at the University of St. Andrew's that was expanded and published in 1947 as the essay "On Fairy-Stories."[48] Here Tolkien dismisses the diminutive and delicate fairies of Shakespeare and Dryden and the high artifice of *Gulliver's Travels* and the Alice in Wonderland books, arguing that the true fairy story comes from a much older and communal tradition and concerns the realm of Faërie, a perilous realm filled with otherworldly beings great and small, magical and mundane. Fairy-stories offer Fantasy (the sub-creation of a secondary world of arresting strangeness), Recovery (regaining a clearer view of the primary world), Escape (an adventure to an archaic world where virtues shine more clearly), and Consolation (the essential happy ending). For this last attribution, Tolkien coins the term "eucatastrophe"—a sudden turning from catastrophe to joy, "Joy beyond the walls of the world, poignant as grief."[49] In an epilogue to the essay, Tolkien suggests that the Gospel works as a fairy-story, with the eucatastrophe of the Crucifixion leading to the happy ending of the Resurrection; indeed, all fairy-stories may offer a glimpse of the *evangelium*. This was the argument that Tolkien employed with C. S. Lewis on his path to conversion, convincing his friend and fellow myth-lover to view Christianity in a new way by seeing the Gospel as the "truest myth," that is, a story that is *both* historical *and* conveys great theological truths.

"It was in fairy-stories," writes Tolkien, "that I first divined the potency of words, and the wonder of the things, such as stone, and wood, and iron; tree and grass; house and fire; bread and wine." Words and wonder—these are the essence of Tolkien, and strange words of his making work on us an ancient magic and awaken our sense of wonder. Sam Gamgee hears stories of the Perilous Realm of the Elves and wants to venture there; he finds himself inside that world, a character in his own fairy story, and lives to record his adventures as a continuation of the tales of Bilbo and Frodo. Tolkien wrote encouragingly to his son Christopher, then training as a pilot in South Africa in 1944: "Well, there you are: a hobbit amongst the Urukhai. Keep up your hobbitry in heart, and think that all *stories* feel like that when you are *in* them. You are inside a very great story!"[50] This message is echoed in Aragorn's comment to Éomer in *The Two*

Towers, that man may walk inside a story, on a green earth that is itself a "mighty matter of legend."

The telling of stories and the singing of songs are as old as art and literature, probably older. What kinds of stories we tell matters too. "Books ought to have good endings," Bilbo tells Frodo before he leaves Rivendell with his companions. "How would this do: *and they all settled down and lived together happily ever after?*"[51] It is in our nature to want happy endings, and the stories that have provided such consolation are "the ones," as Sam would say, "that really mattered."

Service, Selflessness,

and Self-Sacrifice

On April 29, 2019, FBI agents arrested an American army veteran who was planning to detonate explosive devices throughout Los Angeles that would create mass casualties. The twenty-six-year-old man told an undercover agent that he was willing to die a martyr in these attacks. "Murder me. Kill me. I will die *shadid.*" *Shadid* is an Arabic word meaning "strong or powerful, brave." The willing martyrdom of such terrorists is a controversial interpretation of the Koranic concept of *jihad*, and a perversion of the martyrdom suffered by the nonviolent throughout history. It is not a sign of strength or bravery to murder innocent people, nor is it cowardly; it is what Aristotle would call foolhardiness or recklessness, throwing away one's life in service of hatred and the political agendas of others.

J. R. R. Tolkien saw the devastation of the world's first modern war, saw the heroism of the humble and the sacrifice of many young men from the perspective of the trenches of the Western Front. As he composed poetry then, and wrote novels later, Tolkien had no inclination to romanticize war or martyrdom. Barely surviving himself from trench fever, Lieutenant Tolkien had the greatest respect for the English privates and corporals—the "tommys," especially those from rural England—who served under him.[1] Two of his sons—Michael and Christopher—would go on to serve their country in the British military forces in the Second World War, while his daughter, Priscilla, became a social worker after witnessing wartime destruction in Bristol and Birmingham and the urban poverty that followed it.[2] Professor Tolkien served as an air warden during the war and trained to be a code-breaker for a short period. Still, "One War is enough for any man," he wrote to son Michael in 1941, and to Christopher in 1944 he penned these words:

> The utter stupid waste of war, not only material but moral and spiritual. . . . I sometimes feel appalled at the thought of the sum total of human misery all over the world at the present moment: the millions parted, . . . [the] torture, pain, death, bereavement, injustice. If anguish were visible, almost the whole of this benighted planet would be enveloped in a dense dark vapour, shrouded from the amazed vision of the heavens![3]

Although as a devout Catholic he believed in Just War Theory, never let it be said that Tolkien glorified war. Rather, his fiction receives its power from its depiction not of warriors who brag and taunt and humiliate their enemies, but rather of the humble who do service and sacrifice for others. In depicting Hobbit service and altruism, Tolkien drew from a long history of philosophical and theological traditions as well as from his own wartime experiences.

Service to Others

The oldest documents of civilizations in the East and the West indicate the existence of servitude and slavery. Egypt, Mesopotamia, the Levant, Arabia, Persia, the Celtic and Germanic worlds—every land that had war and hard labor utilized slaves to a greater or lesser degree. In the Greek world there were domestic slaves in the cities and slaves who worked in the very dangerous mining industries. Slaves were depicted in art and drama (especially comedy), and in some cases had access to religious cults. The tragic condition of women captured in war and being sold off as slave concubines is covered with great sympathy by Euripides in his play *The Trojan Women* (415 BC).

Like Greece and other ancient Mediterranean lands, Rome had always had slaves.[4] But it only became a slave economy after the vast lands conquered by its armies beginning in the 3rd century BC resulted in a large influx of prisoners of war who were sold as chattel slaves to work the large estates of the patricians. These luxurious villas, with their accompanying agricultural fields, were called *latifundia*, and many were owned by a relatively small number of senators and retired generals. Domestic servants in the cities were also usually foreign slaves, as were the gladiators who fought to the death for the enjoyment of Romans and provincials alike. There were two slave wars fought in Sicily in the 2nd century BC followed by the famous Spartacus uprising in 73 BC, sparked by the escape of seventy slaves from a gladiator training school in Capua that led to hundreds of thousands of fugitive slaves joining a rebel army that inflicted several defeats on Roman forces.[5] Fugitive slaves were a constant in Roman society, as is reflected in penal laws and the hiring of slave hunters to retrieve fugitives. In ancient Rome the head of the family (*pater familias*), normally the oldest adult male, had absolute power to dispense life or death to both family members and slaves. No abolition movement existed in the ancient world, and even Spartacus crucified his war prisoners or made them fight one another as gladiators in his funerary rites.[6]

From earliest times the ancient Hebrews had slaves, both fixed-term indenture (for members of the tribe) and lifetime slavery (for aliens), and many served as slaves themselves in Egypt, Assyria, Babylon, and elsewhere. Mosaic law covers a wide array of issues concerning slaves, including selling oneself or one's child into slavery to avoid debt (Lev 25:39), the court condemning someone to slavery for theft (Exod 22:2), occasional manumission, and slave circumcision and participation in Passover (Exod 12:44). Slaves were to have a day of rest on the Sabbath and it was forbidden to return a fugitive slave to his or her master (Deut 23:16). These practices continued while Judea was under foreign rule or influence, and thousands of Jews were sold into slavery following the revolt against Rome in AD 70.

This is the historical backdrop from which we must view comments made by Jesus, Paul, and Augustine on slaves and their masters. Jesus heals slaves on at least two occasions (Luke 7:1–10 and Luke 22:52) and refers to slaves often in his parables. Some slaves were drawn into the earliest community of Christians in Jerusalem (Acts 12:12–17), and the slave trade is condemned twice in the New Testament (I Tim 1:10 and Rev 18:13).

Paul picks up Jesus's metaphor of being "a slave to sin" and calls himself "a slave of Jesus Christ" (Rom 1:1). He wrote twice to Christians enjoining masters to treat their slaves justly and to give up the use of threats against them (Col 4:1 and Eph 6:9) and asking slaves and freemen alike to "serve with good will" (Eph 6:8). "Slaves, obey your earthly masters with respect and fear and sincerity of heart, just as you would show to Christ" (Eph 6:5).[7] These words will be seen by many modern readers as providing justification for slavery, as indeed they were used as such in previous centuries. But Paul's main point here is the universalizing of the Christian Gospel: "There is neither Jew nor Greek, there is neither slave nor free, there is no male and female, for you are all one in Christ Jesus" (Gal 3:28). In his short letter to Philemon, Paul enjoins a friend to take back his former slave, Onesimus, "no longer as a slave, but as more than a slave, a beloved brother" (Philem 16).

Had Jesus preached a message of abolition or emancipation, would anyone at the time have taken him seriously? Even Aristotle infamously provided justification for the practice of slavery in the ancient world, arguing that there are some who are "slaves by nature" (with limited use of reason, but able to perform physical labor) and those who become slaves by law or war.[8] Jesus and Paul do not appear to agree with Aristotle that slaves (and barbarians) are limited in their ability to reason, for the slave can grasp the virtue of humility needed in order to have a proper relationship with God. ". . . [H]umbling oneself, Christlike 'in the form of a slave' (Phil 2:7)," writes ethicist Timothy P. Jackson, "requires a self-emptying orientation toward the other, whose reality, need, and otherness count for everything."[9] Nietzsche despised weakness and excoriated Christianity for its "slave morality."[10] Theologian Roberta Bondi (who first introduced me to the voices of the Desert Fathers as a graduate student) responds to this same passage in Paul's letter to the Philippians with a question for our culture and age: "How does the need for assertiveness in a world that despises the weak fit with the Christ who '. . . emptied himself, taking the form of a servant'?"[11]

Augustine shows that little had changed in Roman society four centuries later.[12] In *The City of God* and elsewhere, Augustine argues that both war and slavery are products of Original Sin (*originale peccatum*), and that they will be a part of earthly existence until God changes the *ordo* (order):

> He did not intend that His rational creature, who was made in His image, should have dominion over anything but the irrational creature—not man over man, but man over the beasts. . . . The prime cause, then, of slavery is sin, which brings man under the dominion of his fellow. . . . But by nature, as God first created us, no one is the slave either of man or of sin. This servitude is, however, penal, and is appointed . . . until all unrighteousness pass away, and all principality and every human power be brought to nothing, and God be all in all.[13]

Christian clergy could and did own slaves, but they also regularly freed slaves when they entered more disciplined and ascetic lives. Augustine made public manumission part of his church services, and he did complain about the North African slave trade (c. 427), as did in Ireland Saint Patrick, who had himself been a victim of a slave raid on his father's British villa.[14] Patrick escaped from his enslavement in Ireland only to return to the island as a bishop and evangelist. By the time of Augustine and Patrick, the empire's agricultural lands had both slaves and *coloni* (tenant farmers) doing most of the manual labor.[15] As the imperial slave trade withered away with the rest of long-distant trade in the early Middle Ages, tenant farming and manors (*manses*) began to replace villas and slave-based agriculture.[16] Tenants could be free (*ingenuus*) or unfree (*servus*), with free tenants owing the lord of the manor rent in cash or goods and serfs owing, in addition to rent, a fixed number of days of labor. This manorial system was more profitable for landowners because, unlike with slaves, they had no obligation to house or feed serfs. While serfs gave up many of their freedoms, they were protected by the military might of the nobles and bishops who owned these estates. Free villagers also looked to local barons for protection and justice in the Middle Ages.

Medieval Europe thus inherited a widespread system of servitude without widespread chattel slavery. Burchard, bishop of Worms (ca. 1023), heard "the frequent lamentations of my unfortunate subjects" and had laws written to protect "the members of the family," which included serfs of different ranks. Even the political term "vassal"—used for aristocrats from knights to kings—derived from the Celtic word *gwas*, meaning "boy or servant." Royal courts had nobles performing servile tasks for the sake of title (steward, chamberlain, seneschal, etc.) and nearness to power. Thomas Aquinas discusses *dulia* (respectful service) as a part of justice, and feudal ceremonies mandated the types of service the vassal owed to his lord.[17] Still, medieval peasants, the vast majority of the European population, belonged to the Third Estate—"those who work"—and could accurately be described by Bishop Adalbero of Leon (ca. 977) as "an unfortunate class that possesses nothing without suffering."

Selflessness and Altruism

In the Greek philosophic tradition there is no particular emphasis on selflessness but there is much discussion of love of one's friend (*philia*). In book nine, chapter eight of the *Nicomachean Ethics*, Aristotle wonders "whether a man should love himself [*philautia*] most or if it is better to love others. People criticize those who love themselves most, and call them self-lovers, using this as an epithet of disgrace, and a bad man seems to do everything for his own sake. . . ." Some say that "one ought to love best one's best friend," and since "he is his own best friend therefore he ought to love himself best." Aristotle's response is to argue for a prudent self-love:

> . . . the good man should be a lover of self [*philautos*], for he will both himself profit by doing noble acts, and will benefit his fellows, but the wicked man should not; for he will hurt both himself and his neighbors, following as he does evil passions. . . . It is true of the good man too that he does many acts for the sake of his friends and his country, and if necessary, dies for them; for he will throw away both wealth and honors and in general the goods that are objects of competition, gaining for himself nobility. He would prefer to . . . live nobly for one year than indifferently for many. . . . Those who give up their lives perhaps achieve this, and they choose great nobility for themselves. [18]

Choosing to give up one's goods and even one's life is, in the Judeo-Christian tradition, a reflection of divine love. God commanded Moses and the Israelites to have no other gods before—or besides—Him and to offer their love in reflection of His own: "You shall love (*v'ahavta*) the Lord your God with all your heart, and with all your soul, and with all your might," for "I have loved [*chesed*] you [Israel] with an everlasting love."[19] While this is the highest form of love, the Israelites are also directed to "love thy neighbor as thy self."[20] In Judaism, "right action" toward others is demonstrated through *mitzvahs*, literally "commandments" but often interpreted as "good deeds." "Whoever is kind to the poor lends to the Lord, and will be repaid in full," states Proverbs (19:17).

Jesus of Nazareth continues the Hebrew teachings on love of God and love of neighbor, but he and most of his followers universalize "neighbor" to mean not just fellow Jews, but all people and especially strangers and the poor.[21] Jesus is asked by the Pharisee, "Rabbi, which commandment in the law is greatest?" He replies:

> You shall love [ἀγαπήσεις, *agapēseis*] the Lord your God with all your heart, and with all your soul, and with all your mind. This is the greatest and first commandment. And a second is like it: you shall love [*agapēseis*] your neighbor as yourself. On these two commandments hang all the laws and the prophets. (Matt 22:37–40)

In the Sermon on the Mount, Jesus goes even further, requiring a life of charity and loving one's enemies:

> Give to everyone who begs from you, and do not refuse anyone who wants to borrow from you. You have heard that it was said, "You shall love [*agapēseis*] your neighbor and hate your enemy." But I say to you,

love [*agapate*] your enemies and pray for those who persecute you, so that you may be children of your Father who is in heaven. . . . For if you love [*agapēsēte*] only those who love [*agapōntas*] you, what reward do you have? Do not even the tax collectors do the same? (Matt 5:42–46)

So powerful is this new manifestation of *agapē*—or *caritas*, in the Latin Vulgate—that the apostle John is able to say, "God is love [*agape*], and the one who abides in love abides in God, and God abides in him" (1 John 4:16). Similarly, Paul states, "So now faith, hope, and love abide, these three; but the greatest of these is love" (Corinthians 13:13). "Nothing in the classical cardinal virtues fully prepares one for the Gospel vision of *agape*," writes Jackson.[22] Aquinas, who accepts the four Cardinal Virtues but elevates the three Theological Virtues—faith, hope, and charity [*caritas*]—asserts, "No virtue is possible without charity."[23]

The Judeo-Christian concept of charity is echoed in Islamic *sadaq*, where the obligatory giving of alms (*zakat*) is one of the Five Pillars of the Faith.[24] The Quran states that it is good to give openly to the poor, and better to do so privately, and orphans are especially identified as in need of assistance.[25] The *Hadith* also describe charitable acts done by the Prophet and his family, and *karim*, meaning "generous one," is one of the ninety-nine names of God in Islam.[26] Eastern religions and philosophies show less agreement on the subject of charity than do the three great monotheistic faiths, but selflessness is still fundamental. In Hinduism *dāna* is the generosity that is part of one's duty (*dharma*).[27] Siddhartha the Buddha gave up all his princely riches to dedicate his life to understanding and alleviating the suffering of others; Buddhism thus teaches that individuals must sacrifice themselves in order to obtain salvation for others. While Confucius rarely singles out *shi* (giving) as a special subject for consideration, *ren* or *jen*, (human benevolence) and *yi* (righteousness) are linked to altruism by Confucian ethical teachers like Mencius. *Jen* may be the closest in meaning to *agape*; both are "not simply virtues" but "the root from which virtues grow."[28] The three key ethical guidelines of Taoism—compassion, moderation, and humility—lead to a willingness and ability to perform good deeds like acts of charity. *Agape* "is the kind of love," writes the philanthropist Sir John Templeton, "in which the religions of the world may find a basis for unity."[29]

Sacrifice

"Sacrifice has not proved the most glamorous of notions in the modern age," writes culture critic Terry Eagleton. "It smacks of self-abasement and punitive self-denial. It is what long-suffering wives do for their imperious husbands, maidservants for their pampered mistresses, nurses and steelworkers for the good of the economy and storm troopers for the Fatherland."[30] But *agape* love need not be destructive to one's self, nor aid destructive forces in society. In a truly loving relationship, observes Eagleton, "love enhances the self in the very act of decentering it."[31] This is why self-sacrifice can be viewed as a virtue in the Aristotelian sense, even if Aristotle did not himself include it in his list of moral virtues.

The practice of making sacrifices—of objects, animals, and humans—to a god or gods is at least as old as our earliest written records. Before writing appears, sacrifice is hard to interpret from archaeological evidence, but in all likelihood the practice existed in the Stone Age. Anthropologists suggest that the first sacrifices were human and often cannibalistic, and human sacrifice is recorded in nearly every part of the world. Homer and the Greek tragedians testify to the Greek practice of making human sacrifices to the Olympian deities. At some point animals were substituted for humans, possibly first in Mesopotamia in the third millennium BC. Ancient Egyptians, Israelites, Greeks, and Romans all embraced the practice of animal sacrifice. Jewish laws about sacrifice developed in antithesis to the practice of human sacrifice (often infants) by the worshippers of Baal, while Rome set out to exterminate the Druids in part because of their sacrificial rites and divination involving humans.[32] In Iron Age Britain, votive objects like swords and jewelry were deposited in shafts, graves, and bodies of water as offerings to the divine. Indeed, the reasons for sacrifice even within a single culture could vary from bribery or bargaining to gratitude or atonement.

The sacrificial tradition among the Israelites is first glimpsed in Genesis when God accepts the animal offering made by Abel and rejects the agricultural offering made by Cain. Both offerings are called *minchah* in Hebrew, though much later the word *korban* is used to designate animal offerings.[33] "The one who brings a sacrifice gives to God what God has given to him," writes Moshe Halbertal. "The sacrificial act is therefore a symbolic recycling of the gift to its origin."[34] The practice is put to the ultimate test when God commands Abraham to sacrifice his son Isaac as a burnt offering upon the mountain (Genesis 22). Abraham's duty and love for God is pitted against his love for his only son, not to mention the more general duty to love one's neighbor; ultimately God stops the sacrifice by substituting a ram for Isaac. This test of Abraham's faith has proved problematic for both Jews and Christians, especially post-Enlightenment. Jackson suggests a solution: that God's command to Abraham "is real but nonliteral, redemptive but rhetorical," and that it "actually empowers Abraham to abstain from bloodletting by bringing his conscience to a crisis . . . that requires a new understanding of divine love."[35] "To do righteousness and justice is more acceptable to the Lord than sacrifice," declares Proverbs 21. In Hosea, God says to Ephraim and Judah, "I desire steadfast love [*chesed*] and not sacrifice" (6:6). Abraham and his descendants must ultimately sacrifice the ancient practice of animal sacrifice itself in order to be fully God's children, creatures of conscience who love and seek both justice and mercy.[36]

But this is not fully realized until the period of the Roman occupation of Judea. While doves, bulls, rams, and other animals are sacrificed in the Hebraic legal tradition, the sacrificial lamb (הָלֶט, *tela*) holds special significance. When Isaac asks Abraham, "Father, where is the lamb for the burnt offering?" Abraham replies, "My son, God himself will provide the lamb for the burnt offering" (Genesis 22:7–9). The Paschal lamb was ordered by God to be slaughtered and eaten on the eve of the first Passover, before the Exodus from Egypt, and the tradition is to be preserved on the first day of every Passover celebration (Ex 12:3–11). Since many Egyptians worshipped deities with sheep or ram attributes (even mummifying rams), this act was probably seen as a political provocation that put the Hebrews at further risk with the pharaoh.

Jesus challenged religious authorities on sacrificial practices, even as he continued traditions like the Passover meal. He clearly had a problem with the money-changers in the Temple, but it is a matter of debate whether it was the financial transactions themselves or their association with animal sacrifice that led him to overturn their tables. Jesus allows himself to be arrested by the Temple guards, tried by the Sanhedrin, and executed by Pontius Pilate and the Roman soldiers. That he *became* the Lamb of God (Greek *Amnos Theou*; Latin *Agnus Dei*) is a central tenet of Christianity. "Behold, the

Lamb of God [Ἀμνὸς Θεοῦ], who takes away the sin of the world!" cried John the Baptist when he saw Jesus (John 1:29; c.f. John 1:36). Jesus was the "lamb without blemish or spot" (I Peter 1:19) and the Worthy Lamb of the Apocalypse to whom all "praise and honor and glory and power" are to be given "forever and ever!" (Rev 5:6–13). Eagleton points out rightly that Jesus and the Crucifixion do not meet the criteria for a proper sacrifice according to Jewish sacerdotal laws (he is a condemned man, there is no priest present, it does not occur in the Temple, etc.), and yet, "It is a sacrificial act because it concerns the passage of a humble, victimized thing from weakness to power."[37]

Before his ultimate self-sacrifice, Jesus tells his disciples, "This is my commandment, that you love [*agapate*] one another, just as I have loved [*ēgapēsa*] you" (John 15:12), and again, "As the Father has loved [*ēgapēsen*] me, so I have loved [*ēgapēsa*] you; abide in my love [*agapē*]" (John 15:9). "Greater love hath no man than this," continues Jesus, "that he lay down his life for his friends" (John 15:13). The Quran states similarly: "If you give your life in a cause, that is the greatest gift you can give."[38] Yet because the ritual remembrance of Jesus's self-sacrifice involved eating the body and blood of Christ, early Christians were the targets of pagan antipathy in the Roman Empire, whose officials tried and executed them for cannibalism and failure to make proper sacrifices to the Roman gods. Earlier, Rome had done the same thing to the worshippers of Bacchus for their alleged violent orgies, and Christians themselves in the Middle Ages would accuse Jews of killing and eating children. From the rounding up and slaying of Christians as spectacle in the coliseum by Nero in AD 64 to the purge of Christians from the Senate and the Roman army, for three hundred years the persecutions led to the creation of martyrs whose Christlike sacrifice made them the models of sanctity in the Church. When these persecutions ended with the conversion of the emperor Constantine I in

312, monastics (*monachi et virgines*) took over this role by sacrificing their physical desires to the contemplative life. The Desert Fathers (and Mothers) were the first to embrace extremes of self-sacrifice, and in doing so became sages whose word often carried great power.[39] Such extreme renunciation of worldly things is echoed in scripture related to Buddhist monks.[40]

In his magisterial poem cycle *Idylls of the King*, Alfred, Lord Tennyson gives us two depictions of humans imitating divine love and self-sacrifice: Sir Galahad and King Arthur. Galahad is the youthful knight whose purity and devotion lead to success in achieving the Quest for the Holy Grail, but his achievement means giving up all titles and privileges of being a Knight of the Round Table and even sacrificing his mortal life, galloping across a fiery bridge as he ascends to heaven with the Grail. Arthur, who mourns the departure of all his knights on the Quest, stays behind to fight for earthly justice, only to have his nephew, his wife, and his best friend betray him. On the eve of his last battle before being mortally wounded and departing for Avalon, Arthur reflects on his own *imitatio Christi*:

> I found Him in the shining of the stars,
> I marked Him in the flowering of His fields,
> But in His ways with men I find Him not.
> I waged His wars, and now I pass and die.
> O me! for why is all around us here
> As if some lesser god had made the world,
> But had not force to shape it as he would,
> Till the High God behold it from beyond,

And enter it, and make it beautiful?
Or else as if the world were wholly fair,
But that these eyes of men are dense and dim,
And have not power to see it as it is:
Perchance, because we see not to the close;—
For I, being simple, thought to work His will,
And have but stricken with the sword in vain;
And all whereon I leaned in wife and friend
Is traitor to my peace, and all my realm
Reels back into the beast, and is no more.
My God, thou hast forgotten me in my death;
Nay—God my Christ—I pass but shall not die. [41]

Sydney Carton in Charles Dickens's *Tale of Two Cities* (1858) provides yet another Victorian example of the ultimate self-sacrifice, both for the woman he loves and for the redemption of a life lived not often in pursuit of virtue. Fyodor Dostoevsky's Father Zosima in *The Brothers Karamazov* (1880) lives a life of constant love and self-abnegation. Even the philosophy of Stoicism popular in ancient Rome and throughout the Hellenistic world has elements of self-sacrifice for the greater good. The Desert Fathers and medieval theologians were thus not the only ones interested in exploring the links between *agape/caritas* and self-sacrifice. Modern philosophers and theologians like Immanuel Kant, Søren Kierkegaard, Reinhold Niebuhr, Paul Tillich, and Karl Barth all wrote about love and self-sacrifice. Niebuhr, for instance, claims that the "perfect disinterestedness of divine love can have a counterpart in history only in a life which ends tragically. . . . A love which seeketh not its own is not able to maintain itself in historical society."[42] Tolkien chose to illustrate that tragedy, as we shall see, with the sacrifices of the Hobbit Frodo Baggins.

The Good Servant: Samwise and Sméagol

When the Dwarves arrive at Bilbo's house each introduces himself followed by "at your service," and Bilbo replies, "at yours." It is a customary greeting, but nevertheless it is meant as a pledge: Only Thorin is haughty and does not offer his service.[43] Thorin does, along with the rest of the Dwarves, offer his service to Beorn, who gruffly refuses: "I don't need your service, thank you, . . . but I expect you need mine."[44] Beorn is right, and provides service to the Dwarves in the form of hospitality and ponies for their journey. Bilbo too continues to serve the Dwarves in ways beyond the scope of his employment contract, including rescuing them from the spiders of Mirkwood and from the dungeon of the Elvenking. He serves Bard twice, even though he has never met the bowman: once in discovering the weakness in the armor of Smaug and again by bringing him the Arkenstone. In this act of theft Bilbo is even still serving Thorin and the Dwarves, for it is in their best interest not to go to war under the spell of the dragon's gold.

Bilbo and Frodo are members of the squirarchy of the Shire and are thus used to being served rather than serving. Samwise and his father have served the Baggins family as gardeners for many years when we first meet the two Gamgees in *The Lord of the Rings*. Sam is always deferential to his employers—all "Yes, sir" and "Mr. Frodo, sir"—and gladly accepts his "punishment" for eavesdropping on Gandalf's conversation with Frodo.[45] Sam's constant deference and humility make many modern readers uncomfortable with its connotations of class difference, and in Peter Jackson's films this differential between Frodo and Sam is softened a bit. Regardless, Tolkien, I believe, meant to emphasize Sam's servant status in order to contrast his humble origins with his ultimate status as warrior-poet, hero, and mayor of the Shire.

Sam's constant service to Frodo manifests itself in many ways: carrying more than his share of baggage, helping tend his wounds, preparing meals, rationing water and *lembas* on the journey to Mordor. As these two Hobbits (along with Gollum) climb the stairs of Cirith Ungol, Sam's service takes on truly heroic proportions. His fight with Shelob over the body of Frodo begins with an instinctual ferocity that Tolkien compares to a small creature armed with nothing but little teeth fighting an enormous beast that threatens its mate.[46] This battle is followed almost immediately by Sam's daring rescue of Frodo from the orcs in the Tower: "His love for Frodo rose above all other thoughts," writes Tolkien, and forgetting his peril Sam cries aloud: "I'm coming, Mr. Frodo!"[47] When Frodo is so spent that he cannot even crawl any farther up the slope of Mount Doom, Sam demonstrates perhaps the most memorable example of his loving service when, starving and in pain himself, he vows to carry Frodo on the last steps toward the Crack of Doom:

> "Come, Mr. Frodo!" he cried. "I can't carry [the Ring] for you, but I can carry you and it as well. So up you get! Come on, Mr. Frodo dear! Sam will give you a ride. . . ."
>
> . . . Sam staggered to his feet; and then, to his amazement he felt the burden light. . . .

On he toiled, up and up, . . . and at last crawling like a small snail with a heavy burden on its back. When his will could drive him no further, he stopped and laid his master gently down. [48]

While Tolkien adds a bit of humor to this scene, Jackson films it in utter solemnity, and Sean Astin delivers what may be the greatest acting moment of his career. It is Frodo's *Via Dolorosa* ("Path of Sorrow"), and Sam is a willing Simon of Cyrene (Mark 15:21) helping his master carry the cross.

Merry and Pippin also grow in moral seriousness as they part on separate journeys, both of which require acts of service. Pippin, moved by guilt for the loss of Boromir, and also by a noble desire to honor his valiant sacrifice, offers his sword and his fealty to Denethor, Boromir's father and steward of Gondor: "Little service, no doubt, will so great a lord of Men think to find in a Hobbit, a halfling of the northern Shire; yet such as it is, I will offer it, in payment of my debt."[49] Merry makes a similar offer of service to King Théoden, to be his sword-thegn, but his motivation is different: "Filled suddenly with love for this old man, he knelt on one knee, and took his hand and kissed it. 'May I lay the sword of Meriadoc of the Shire on your lap, Théoden King?' he cried. 'Receive my service, if you will!'"[50] Merry's greatest act of service to Théoden is to ride into battle with Éowyn and help her kill the Witchking before the fell beast can devour Théoden's body. Pippin served Denethor by helping save the life of his son Faramir. Ironically, both Hobbits acted heroically but in defiance of their lords' commands in doing so.

Tolkien is also cognizant of the love that the master must demonstrate toward the servant and the slave (Lev 25:43 and Eph 6:9). This is demonstrated not only by Frodo toward Sam, who he comes to love deeply, but even in his interactions with Gollum.

Frodo restores to Gollum his real name, Sméagol, and tries hard to treat his guide with gentleness and dignity. When Frodo and Faramir discover Gollum eating fish from the forbidden pool of Henneth Annûn, Frodo at first considers allowing Faramir's bowmen to shoot Gollum to end his suffering and treachery. But he realizes that Gollum has a claim on him: "The servant has a claim on the master for service, even service in fear."[51] While Gollum resolves to betray both Hobbits to Sheelob after this incident, and attacks them at the Crack of Doom, Sam cannot bring himself to kill Gollum, for "now dimly he guessed the agony of Gollum's shriveled mind and body, enslaved to that ring."[52] Sam carries Frodo once again, after Gollum has bitten off his master's finger, and lying on the mountainside as it erupts with fire, Frodo asks Sam to forgive Gollum, admitting that if it weren't for Gollum he could not have destroyed the Ring.[53]

Love and Sacrifice in Middle-earth

When Bilbo is introduced to us in the opening pages of *The Hobbit*, it is clear that he is not someone who would gladly sacrifice the comforts of hearth and home. On the contrary, the hospitality which he is required to show to the Dwarves is quite the nuisance to him. We do not see Bilbo making willing sacrifices for others until his rescue of the Dwarves (twice) in Mirkwood. Since his escape plan from the Elvenking's palace is to stuff the Dwarves into barrels and drop them into a rushing river, the Dwarves are at first not at all grateful and Bilbo grows cross: "Well, are you alive or are you dead?"[54] Bilbo's most important sacrifice is renouncing his share of the dragon treasure when, at great risk, he brings the Arkenstone to Bard and the Elvenking so they can negotiate with Thorin and avoid war. "You are more worthy to wear the armour of elf-princes than many that have looked more comely in it," exclaims the Elvenking, offering Bilbo a place of high honor in his retinue.[55] Again, Bilbo sacrifices this to return to the Dwarves who have been his friends, though he hardly receives a friendly greeting from Thorin.

The central quest of *The Lord of the Rings* is a reversal of the traditional votive sacrifice to a deity: Instead of sacrificing a valued object to a god, Frodo's aim is to destroy the powerful object made by an evil spirit in the very fires that created it. The smaller sacrifices Merry, Pippin, and Sam make to accompany Frodo to Rivendell (beyond giving up meals!) are magnified when they volunteer to join the Company on its dangerous journey to Mordor. The aged Bilbo even offers in inimitable fashion to be the Ring-bearer once again—"It is a frightful nuisance. When ought I to start?"—but Gandalf gently lets him off the hook as the Nine Companions are chosen by Elrond. Each of them makes significant sacrifices along the way—Aragorn leaving behind Arwen, Gandalf and Boromir falling in battle, Merry wounded gravely—but it is Sam and Frodo upon which all hope rests, and their victory is paid for by sacrifice and loss. Theirs is also a demonstration of love.

Sam's service to Frodo leads to a deep and profound friendship, or *philia*. Tolkien's narrative in *The Lord of the Rings* often switches to Sam's perspective, as on the journey with Frodo and Gollum to Mordor when Sam first notices the way that the One Ring is affecting Frodo physically:

> Sam . . . shook his head, as if finding words useless, and murmured: "I love him. He's like that, and sometimes it shines through, somehow. But I love him, whether or no."[56]

Like David and Jonathan, the soul of Frodo seems bound to the soul of Sam, and Sam "loved him as his own soul" (1 Samuel 18:1). Sam's love for Frodo grows from affection to friendship to a service that is devotional and sacrificial. As David Rozema observes, this is in part a reflection of Frodo's moral growth:

> . . . in the end, Sam's loving affection for Frodo is manifested in ways that indicate a transformation from mere affection to charity itself; he sacrifices his own ration of food and water for Frodo; he carries Frodo up Mt. Doom on his back; and in the end, he pities and forgives Gollum too. The charity of Frodo both transcends and allows for the perfection of the affection Sam has for Frodo.[57]

Sam is demonstrating in these last steps of his quest *agape*, or *caritas*. "Love is patient, love is kind," wrote Paul to the Corinthians. "It bears all things, believes all things, hopes all things, endures all things" (I Cor 13:4–7). This describes Sam's attitude toward Frodo from their departure from the Shire to his helping Frodo escape the fires of Mount Doom.

"Love—*caritas*—is an extraordinary force," writes Pope Benedict, "which leads people to opt for courageous and generous engagement in the field of justice and peace."[58] This virtue—seeking both justice and peace—Sam demonstrates, as Boyd and Garcia point out, in the last and perhaps greatest self-sacrifice made by Sam in *The Lord of the Rings*.[59] After helping to defeat Sharkey and putting an end to his dark, industrial activities in the chapter titled "The Scouring of the Shire," Sam decides (with Frodo's encouragement) to use the gift of Galadriel—the earth from her own orchard in Lothlórien—not solely on his own garden, but rather to distribute it throughout the Shire, grain by grain, to ensure the growth of new trees to replace those that Sharkey's men had destroyed. "I'm sure the lady would not like me to keep it all for my own garden," says Sam, "now so many folk have suffered."[60]

Frodo's suffering is long and without end, at least in Middle-earth. The carefree young Hobbit who sings and jokes as he leaves the Shire is forever changed by being stabbed with a Morgul-knife on Weathertop. Although he survives being speared by an orc-chieftain in Moria, the venomous sting of Sheelob, and several attacks by Gollum—the last of which cost him a finger—it is the wound he receives from the Witchking that never heals. His pain, the loss of his finger, and the knowledge that he could not ultimately resist the Ring prevents Frodo from ever enjoying happiness and contentment in the Shire. "I am wounded," he explains to the worried Sam, "it will never really heal."[61] He tells Sam that he must not be torn between his love for his family and his love for adventure: "You were meant to be solid and whole, and you will be."[62] As happy as we are for Sam's domestic bliss, the reader can't help but be sad for the sacrifices and growing loneliness of Frodo Baggins.

The Batman in the Great War

Sam's dogged determinism as he carries Frodo up the slope of Mount Doom is demonstration of a very important—though hard to describe—virtue for Tolkien. He believed it was a particularly English characteristic, equating it with the medieval Anglo-Saxon concept of a strong will or spirit (*mod*), as in the lines from *The Battle of Maldon* (10th century) quoted earlier.[63] This virtue is not so different from that described by the Confucian philosopher Hsun-tzu: "Achievement consists of never giving up. . . . If there is no dark or dogged will, there will be no brilliant achievement." We also see it in the advice given by the Buddha to monks:

> When stricken by disease or hunger's pangs,
> Cold and excessive heat should he endure;
> When stricken sore by them, that homeless man
> Must stir up energy and strive with strength.[64]

Tolkien confesses, as discussed earlier, that he drew inspiration in creating Samwise from the English privates and the "batman," the common soldier assigned as a servant to commissioned officers in the British army. The "batmen I knew in the 1914 war," he writes in a letter to a fan in 1956, "[I] recognized as so far superior to myself."[65] These soldiers, often working-class men, looked after the officer's kit and cooked meals and cleaned for him. Tolkien may have had several batmen, as he served in multiple units during the Great War.[66] Their service and sacrifice seems to have stayed with Tolkien long after the war ended. As Tolkien biographer John Garth writes, "the fear, the resourcefulness, the demoralisation, the courage, the sorrow, the innocent laughter in the face of dreadful odds: all these things [Tolkien] had known [in the war], and he infused his fiction with them . . . [to] bring the hobbits vividly to life."[67]

Can Altruism be Explained by Biology?

Modern culture and politics have not been encouraging of altruism. The unleashing of the new god "Liberty" by the Enlightenment has led to many philosophies stressing that one's primary responsibility is to one's own life and political rights. This yields "a brand of ethics well suited to middle-class suburbia," remarks Eagleton.[68] Virtue ethics, of course, is not the usual way we now judge selfish or selfless behavior. The Harvard scientist E. O. Wilson wrote, in his landmark work *Sociobiology: The New Synthesis* (1975):

> Consider man . . . as though we were zoologists from another planet completing a catalog of the social species on Earth. In this macroscopic view the humanities and social sciences shrink to specialized branches of biology; history, biography and fiction are the research protocols of human ethology; and anthropology and sociology constitute the socio-biology of a single primate species.[69]

Contemporary psychology and neuroscience head down this same path, if on a micro rather than macro level. The theory of psychological egoism, for example, "makes a scientific claim that all humans (unless they are pathologically abnormal) will act to their own advantage," writes philosopher Michael Boylan.[70] This is taken as an absolute and universal law, involving no ethical choice. But we know from experience, counters Boylan, that there are many times when we do not act for our own benefit, that we do act altruistically. Evolutionary biologists would say that this instinct to be altruistic, though not always strong, has survived through natural selection because it was perceived by prospective mates to be an attractive quality. The jury is still out on whether psychological research can ever prove that altruism is simply part of human evolution.[71]

Can all human behavior and human culture, as Wilson suggests, be reduced to that of a more complex animal? C. S. Lewis satirizes such scientific aspiration in his novel *That Hideous Strength* (1945), in which sociology and psychology are employed to manipulate the masses so that they do not ask difficult questions about the nefarious "scientific" experimentation happening on both animals and humans in the N.I.C.E. (National Institute of Co-ordinated Experiments). Ransom, the hero of Lewis's space trilogy who literally fights on the side of the animals (and the angels), is a philologist modeled on none other than his friend Tolkien.

Sociobiology also does not get us beyond biological desires—or governmental restraints—controlling our interactions with others of our species, not to mention our relations with the natural world. Education, formal or otherwise, must play a role, as Plato and Aristotle and Aquinas all knew. Failing to educate the young in ways that informs their desires and trains their habits means that "their desires are evolving without any significant consideration of the needs of others," writes Thomas J. Lasley. This "desire-independent" approach leads children "to seek self-satisfaction without significant regard for larger moral consequences. The embodied self, not the immortal soul, constitutes the essence of the individual for those who view desire satisfaction as an end in and of itself."[72] Hence our obsession with the beautiful, youthful-looking and athletic body and our neglect of the beautiful soul.

Hobbits are defined by Tolkien not as beautiful but rather as having "good-natured faces."[73] Nor are they much interested in technology, beyond the tools of farmers and carpenters, nor in political power. These natural inclinations serve both Bilbo and Frodo well as they carry the One Ring and suffer under its malice. But beyond the natural virtues of a Hobbit, Bilbo and Frodo were capable under extraordinary duress of exhibiting one virtue that is at the very heart of Tolkien's whole mythology: mercy.

MERCY

In declaring 2016 "The Holy Year of Mercy," Pope Francis wrote in *Misericordiae Vultus*: "We need constantly to contemplate the mystery of mercy. It is a wellspring of joy, serenity, and peace. Our salvation depends on it." In many parts of the world, however, 2016 did not feel like a year of mercy. A brutal war in Syria left towns like Aleppo devastated and sent tens of thousands of refugees seeking asylum, many of them women and children. Al-Qaeda–linked gunmen attacked a hotel in West Africa, and terrorists linked to ISIS set off bombs at the Brussels Airport, killing dozens. In America a lone gunman shot and killed forty-nine people at a gay nightclub in Orlando, while "Big Pharma" fueled an opioid crisis responsible for an average of seventy-eight deaths a day. While the wrongful shootings by police continued to target young people of color, one angry sniper shot twelve police officers who were protecting a peaceful protest in Dallas. Anger and hatred, xenophobia and racism were on full display in national elections in the UK and America, backed by state-sponsored Russian hackers. One of the largest banks in America was fined for engaging in fraudulent behavior toward millions of its customers. Dozens of women who had been the targets of sexual harassment and assault on college campuses, in Hollywood, and on the US women's gymnastics team, among many others, spoke out about this abuse and helped launch the #MeToo movement. While the big and the powerful, the violent and the greedy exalted in their power and abuse in 2016, few were talking about mercy or forgiveness.

But there are small acts of mercy happening all around us, and heroic acts of forgiveness by people the world might consider to be small and unimportant. We must look harder to find the merciful, try harder to demonstrate pity, and in doing so hold up a mirror to the ugliness of violence, hatred, and abuse.

Mercy and pity, and their correlatives clemency and forgiveness, are virtues hardly touched upon by either classical or modern authorities on moral philosophy. "In both ancient heroic societies and in so-called modern meritocracies," asserts Ralph C. Wood, "pity is not a virtue but a vice. . . . Yet *Lord of the Rings* is a book imbued with such unmerited mercy and forgiveness."[1] Mercy is the chief virtue that unites *The Hobbit* and *The Lord of the Rings* and ties Bilbo and Frodo together to contest the power of the Ring. Their inner battles against fear, hatred, and vengeance are more important than those of all the armies of Middle-earth. "It is mercy," Peter Kreeft reminds us, "not justice or courage or even heroism, that alone can defeat evil."[2]

Mercy, Pity, and Forgiveness

Kyrie eleison
Christe eleison
Kyrie eleison

"Lord have mercy (upon us), Christ have mercy, Lord have mercy"

The *Kyrie* is one of the most ancient prayers in both the Eastern Orthodox and Catholic churches. It has precedents in both the Old (Psalm 4:2, 6:3, 9:14, 25:11, 121:3; Isaiah 33:2; Tobit 8:10) and New (Matthew 9:27, 20:30, 15:22; Mark 10:47; Luke 16:24, 17:13) Testaments, though its first recorded appearance in the liturgy of the Mass isn't until the 6th century.[3] God commands the ancient Israelites to exchange vengeance for love: "You shall not take vengeance or bear a grudge against any of your people, but you shall love [*v'ahavta*] your neighbor as yourself" (Lev 19:18).

The harshness of punishment in Deuteronomy, however, sometimes echoes that of the oldest of all legal documents, *Hammurabi's Code* (ca. 1780 BC): "Thus you shall not show pity [נחיה, *tachos*]: life for life, eye for eye, tooth for tooth, hand for hand, foot for foot" (19:21). Mercy is not a human obligation in most of the ancient world, but rather a plea from humans to the divine. There are several Hebrew words in the Bible that have been translated as "mercy," including *ahavah*, *rachamim*, and *chesed*. Psalm 85 brings together mercy and justice: "mercy [*chesed*] and truth have met together, righteousness and peace have kissed." Mercy is a divine quality in the Torah, and it took some time before the people recognized their obligation to act like God in demonstrating both justice and mercy.

Heroic Age Greece exalted a warrior ethos that had little room for mercy. When, in Book 6 of *The Iliad*, Andromache begs her husband Hector not to leave her for battle— "My lord, your passion will destroy you, and you take no pity / on our little child, nor me, ill-fated, your widow / soon to be"—Hector reminds her that his place is at the front of the battle lines, winning glory for his father and for Troy. Yet Homer does feel pity on this family, fated for tragedy, especially in the scene where King Priam comes before Achilles (the man who has just killed his eldest son and mutilated his body by dragging it behind his chariot around the walls of Troy) to retrieve Hector's body for proper burial:

> The majestic king of Troy slipped past the rest
> and kneeling down beside Achilles, clasped his knees
> and kissed his hands, those terrible, man-killing hands
> that had slaughtered Priam's many sons in battle.
> . . . Priam prayed his heart out to Achilles:
> "Remember your own father, great godlike Achilles—
> as old as *I* am . . . at least he hears that you are still alive
> and his old heart rejoices. . . .
> Revere the gods, Achilles! Pity me in my own right,
> remember your own father! I deserve more pity. . .
> I have endured what no one on earth has ever done before—
> I put to my lips the hands of the man who killed my son."[4]

Homer here links pity with respect for one's father and reverence for the gods. Other Greek writers, from the historians to the tragedians, define pity or compassion (*oiktos* and *eleos*) as an emotion, albeit an admirable one.[5] Plato, however, is suspicious that the poets are able to influence the *demos* by using their rhetorical abilities to manipulate their emotions—a technique called *pathos* (πάθος)—including pity.[6] In his *Poetics*, Aristotle defends the tragedians, declaring that the function of tragic drama is to arouse pity and fear through *catharsis*.[7] This can only happen if the tragic hero is a person who possesses great glory or fortune but also a fatal flaw or inadequacy of character (*hamartia*). Pity is defined in Aristotle's *Rhetoric* as "a feeling of pain at an apparent evil, destructive or painful, which befalls one who does not deserve it, and which we might expect to befall ourselves or some friend of ours, and moreover to befall us soon."[8] Pity is for Aristotle an emotion, or set of emotions, not a virtue.

The ancient Romans made a virtue of clemency (*clementia*), usually interpreted as restraint in punishing one's enemies. Cicero praised Julius Caesar for his clemency toward the senators who had opposed him in his war with Pompey. In 27 BC the Roman Senate presented Octavian Caesar with the title "Augustus" along with a golden shield inscribed with four virtues—manliness (*virtu*), clemency (*clementia*), justice (*iustitia*), and devotion (*pietas*)—used to describe the first emperor, while he himself states in his public will that he "spared all citizens who sought pardon."[9] The emperor Claudius made a public show of his *clementia* in pardoning the rebel British king Caratacus in a triumphal procession in the capital.[10] *Clementia* is a virtue of the ruling class in Rome, a demonstration of both their moderation and their superiority. The emperors Tiberius, Vitellius, Hadrian, Antoninus Pius, and Marcus Aurelius all boasted of this virtue by having CLEMENTIA stamped on their coinage.[11] Seneca wrote *De Clementia* to advise the young emperor Nero on "restraining the mind from vengeance when it has the power to take it," and to avoid cruelty (*crudelitas*): Nero repaid his teacher by forcing him to commit suicide.[12]

Mercy in the Latin Christian liturgy is often used in the closing phrase of prayer, *miserere domine*, "Lord have mercy." It is related to *misericordia*, "giving the heart [*cor*] to the wretched [*miseri*]." We are able to show mercy when we see the misery or wretchedness of the other and have compassion for their condition. This is no easy thing to do when the other is loathsome or has committed crimes against us or other people. Such is the way many Jews viewed the Roman army and administrators. Surely the Messiah will come, thought the Zealots and many others, as a conquering general and son of David who will seek justice and vengeance in restoring Jewish rule in Judea.

Neither John the Baptist nor Jesus of Nazareth appeared in such a guise. John embraced simplicity and preached repentance, while Jesus was a poor son of a craftsman who preached the Gospel of love and forgiveness. "Blessed are the merciful, for they shall obtain mercy," promised Jesus in the Sermon on the Mount (Matt 5:7). Even on the cross, where the Romans mocked him as "King of the Jews," Jesus was able to forgive the Roman soldiers and show mercy to the Good Thief. Terry Eagleton argues that the Crucifixion is "a carnivalesque parody of the practice" of sacrifice, for God himself "is the flayed, bloodied victim, and one, moreover, who identifies with his executioners by forgiving them. . . . The event is at once an act of murder and an act of pardon, for this and all other crimes."[13]

The Judeo-Christian view that mercy is a quality of the divine can be found in many world religions. The Quran from its first verses describes Allah as "the Merciful, the Compassionate." There are also many examples of the mercy of Allah in the *Hadith*. "Forgiveness is more manly than punishment," writes Gandhi. "The weak can never forgive. Forgiveness is the attribute of the strong."[14] One Hindu prayer in the *Rig Veda* ends each stanza with a plea similar to the *Kyrie*: "Have mercy, spare me, mighty Lord."[15] In Hinduism the god Vishnu is often seen as the embodiment of mercy; in Buddhism, Siddhartha Gautama perfected the pursuit of wisdom and compassion.

Mercy may be a quality of the divine, but so is justice. Many societies have struggled to balance both. "That I may mitigate their doom / On me deriv'd," offers the Son to the Father in Milton's *Paradise Lost*, "yet I shall temper so / Justice with mercy as may illustrate most / Them fully satisfied, and thee appease."[16] As the persecution of Christians came to an end in the 4th century, the church had to come to terms with embracing a Gospel of mercy while obeying often brutal secular authorities in charge of administering justice. Is it right, for example, that "judgment be without mercy to one who has shown no mercy," asks the apostle James? "Mercy triumphs over judgment" is his answer (James 2:13). Such sentiments were alien to the Vikings, however, nor were many Christian monarchs of the early Middle Ages interested in mercy: both practiced a culture of vengeance, mitigated occasionally by substituting the *wergild* (man-price) for bloodshed. The Peace of Christ and the Truce of Christ were attempts by the church to put restrictions on rampant aristocratic violence in the 11th century, including prohibitions against attacking women, children, and clerics. Little mercy was shown to heretics and nonbelievers by Christian emperors and kings, however, despite the voices of the theologians. "God acts mercifully, not indeed by going against His justice, but by doing something more than justice," writes Aquinas. "Mercy is the fulfillment of justice, not its abolition."[17]

Yet there was another force at work in medieval aristocratic culture that mandated mercy: chivalry. We see this in French romances and other chivalric literature, and occasionally in the behavior of actual knights in the historical record (chivalry was an ideal few could live up to).[18] There was a growing expectation of knights from the 12th century on to serve women, to protect all noncombatants, and to observe certain rules during combat with their peers: never attack an unarmed or unhorsed knight, never gang up to attack a single opponent, and always grant mercy to an opponent who begs mercy. "To be merciful is to treat a person less harshly than, given certain rules, one has a right to treat that person," states Jeffrie Murphy. "The rules of chivalry give me the right to kill you under certain circumstances of combat. If you beg for mercy, you are begging that I do something less severe than killing you."[19] Knights who joined orders were expected to do more than just show mercy to their enemies. In the 12th century, the Order of St. John of Jerusalem, also known as the Knights Hospitaller, established and staffed hospitals in the Holy Land, devoting themselves to healing the sick and wounded as well as providing food, drink, clothing, and shelter for the poor. Christine de Pizan suggested ca. 1400 that young noblemen should emulate the "good knight Jesus Christ" through an education stressing *misericorde et compassione.*[20] During the Hundred Years' War, however, the surrendering of nobility in battle was often simply a vehicle for collecting ransom. Lowly men-at-arms were not protected by the rule of mercy, and occasionally the rule was simply suspended based on national anger and prejudice.

Despite the harsh and chaotic reality of the battlefield, medieval and Renaissance writers continued to extol the virtue of mercy. The first words of Dante's *Divine Comedy* are *miserere di me*, "have mercy on me."[21] In *The Prince*, Machiavelli saw a merciful reputation as benefitting the public image of the monarch: "to slay fellow-citizens, to deceive friends, to be without faith, without mercy, without religion: such methods may gain empire, but not glory."[22] Mercy and pity appear throughout Spenser's *The Faerie Queene*. In Book I, "The Legend of Holiness," mercy is associated with charity and healing and serves as a divine nurse for the Red Cross Knight; in Book II, the Knight of Temperance praises the mercy of Gloriana (i.e., Queen Elizabeth I); and in Book V, "The Legend of Justice," Mercilia is the Queen of Mercy, but it is human mercy in pursuit of justice.[23] Shakespeare, in *The Merchant of Venice*, grasps the divine quality of mercy and advocates its employment by the mighty in Portia's courtroom plea to Shylock:

> The quality of mercy is not strained;
> It droppeth as the gentle rain from heaven
> Upon the place beneath. It is twice blest;
> It blesseth him that gives and him that takes:
> 'Tis mightiest in the mightiest; it becomes
> The thronèd monarch better than his crown:
> His sceptre shows the force of temporal power,
> The attribute to awe and majesty,
> Wherein doth sit the dread and fear of kings;
> But mercy is above this sceptred sway;
> It is enthronèd in the hearts of kings,
> It is an attribute to God himself;
> And earthly power doth then show likest God's
> When mercy seasons justice.[24]

Mercy and the Saving of Middle-earth

Tolkien probably did not set out to write *The Hobbit* to be a story about mercy. He certainly did not see that one single act of pity by a little creature would save his whole world. The Hobbits of the Shire expect kindnesses from Bilbo Baggins because he is their neighbor, in the literal sense. Over the course of his adventure, Bilbo grows morally to be able to have compassion for his "neighbors" in the universal sense, especially those who are pitiable and dispossessed.

When Bilbo encounters Gollum, both are wary of the other. The narrator states that Gollum had played riddle games long ago before he lost his friends and was driven away, creeping into the dark places under the mountains.[25] Though Bilbo won the riddle game and Gollum was bound by its ancient rules to show him the way out of the cave, Bilbo could not trust him to keep any promise and ran from the hungry and furious creature when Gollum suspected Bilbo had his ring.[26] With the ring making him invisible but Gollum blocking his path of escape, Bilbo prepared to fight:

> He was desperate. He must get away, out of this horrible darkness, while he had any strength left. He must fight. He must stab the foul thing, put its eyes out, kill it. It meant to kill him. No, not a fair fight. He was invisible now. Gollum had no sword. Gollum had not actually threatened to kill him, or tried to yet. And he was miserable, alone, lost. A sudden understanding, a pity mixed with horror, welled up in Bilbo's heart: a glimpse of endless unmarked days without light or hope or betterment, hard stone, cold fish, sneaking and whispering. All these thoughts passed in a flash of a second. He trembled.

And then quite suddenly in another flash, as if lifted by a new strength and resolve, he leaped. . . . Straight over Gollum's head he jumped. . . .[27]

There is a lot going on in this remarkable passage. Tolkien brings us deep into the psyches of both Bilbo and Gollum, and his constant use of pronouns leads the reader to confusion over which miserable creature the narrator is talking about. We must assume that the philology professor *wants* us to confuse the two because he wants us to experience Bilbo's compassion. It comes from "pity mixed with horror"—close to Aristotle's necessary ingredients for tragedy and catharsis—and is assisted by a mysterious new strength and resolve. "No great leap for a man," writes Tolkien, "but a leap in the dark."

This episode is the Hobbit's first display of physical courage in the novel, which is accompanied—if not enabled—by pity and understanding. "The pity that stays Bilbo's hand," writes Louis Markos, "is a pure expression of *caritas* that is born out of Bilbo's ability to move out of himself (out of his fear, hatred, and disgust) and feel a sympathetic (even empathetic) connection with the loathsome and deceptive Gollum."[28] No one is there to witness Bilbo's courage let alone perceive his compassion for Gollum. The moment exists for the sake of Bilbo and for us. Bard also asks for pity, from Thorin, when he asks for a share of the dragon hoard to help rebuild Lake-town: "The wealthy may have pity beyond right on the needy that befriended them when they were in want."[29] But Thorin, like Gollum and Smaug, has brooded too long on treasure to gift pity so easily.

Gandalf does not learn the full story of the ring and the riddle game from Bilbo. He must piece it together over many years, just as Tolkien took several years to figure out what roles Gollum and the ring would play in *The Hobbit*'s saga-sequel, *The Lord of the Rings*. Gandalf returns to Bag End seventeen years after Bilbo's disappearance at his birthday party and tells Frodo what he has learned about the nature of the Ring, how one of the River-folk named Sméagol came to possess the ring after murdering his friend Déagol, and how Sméagol took to thieving, was cursed and expelled from his home, and was called Gollum.

> "Gollum!" cried Frodo. "Gollum? Do you mean that this is the very Gollum-creature that Bilbo met? How loathsome!"
>
> "I think it is a sad story," said the wizard, "and it might have happened to others, even to some hobbits that I have known."[30]

Gandalf then admits that he talked with Gollum himself and figured out the truth about the riddle game and Bilbo's taking possession of the Ring:

> "What a pity that Bilbo did not stab that vile creature, when he had a chance!"
>
> "Pity? It was Pity that stayed his hand. Pity, and Mercy: not to strike without need. And [Bilbo] has been well rewarded, Frodo. Be sure that he took so little hurt from the evil, and escaped in the end, because he began his ownership of the Ring so. With Pity."
>
> "I am sorry," said Frodo, "but . . . I do not feel any pity for Gollum. . . . He deserves death."
>
> "Deserves it! I daresay he does. Many that live deserve death. And some that die deserve life. Can you give it to them? Then do not be too eager to dole out death in judgment. For even the very wise cannot see

all ends. I have not much hope that Gollum can be cured before he dies, but there is a chance of it. . . . My heart tells me that he has some part to play, for good or ill, before the end; and when that comes, the pity of Bilbo may rule the fate of many—yours not least." [31]

Frodo does not immediately grasp the full meaning of Gandalf's words at Bag End, but after his own suffering as the Ring-bearer he finally comes face-to-face with Gollum and has a change of heart. When Sam suggests tying up Gollum and leaving him in Emyn Muil, Frodo responds that it would be kinder to kill him outright, but he cannot do that. "Poor wretch! He has done us no harm." [32] Frodo agrees to let Gollum serve as their guide to Mordor and assumes the role of Gollum's "Master." Frodo's many acts of mercy toward the undeserving Gollum come about because of empathy: Frodo knows the corruptive power of the Ring. He thus tries to restore the good left in Gollum by calling him by his pre-Ring name, Sméagol, and acts with kindness toward him, perhaps even comes to love him. But Gollum knows that Sam is suspicious and interprets Frodo's actions at the Forbidden Pool as a betrayal:

> ". . . Nassty, wicked Men. Sméagol's neck still hurts him, yes it does. Let's go."
>
> "Yes, let us go," said Frodo. "But if you can only speak ill of those who showed you mercy, keep silent!"
>
> "Nice Master," said Gollum, "Sméagol was only joking. Always forgives, he does, yes, yes, even Master's little trickses. O yes, nice Master, nice Sméagol!" [33]

Sméagol does not forgive Frodo, of course, and his babbling makes sense if we see that he is confusing himself with Frodo here—in his mind, both play tricks, neither are "nice"—a distortion of the compassion both Bilbo and Frodo have displayed toward him.

Gollum attacks Sam while Frodo is fighting Sheelob, and later he attacks Frodo at the foot of Mount Doom. The Ring seems to give Frodo the power to throw off Gollum, who then faces a sword-wielding Sam. But another surprising act of mercy is done. Sam looks at the whimpering creature, "this thing lying in the dust," and hesitates; while he only wore the Ring briefly, he can appreciate the horrible toll it has taken on Sméagol, and he lets him go. "Sam has done more than choose to act (or not act) in a certain way," argues Markos, "he has chosen as well to be a different kind of person."[34]

Gollum returns for one last attack on Sam and Frodo. This time he bites off Frodo's finger to get at his Precious after Frodo claims it as his own, and, consumed with his obsession, he stumbles into the fires of Doom with the Ring. Frodo's failure to destroy the Ring, argues Kreeft, shows that pity is *necessary* to defeat evil.[35] We can even see Frodo's loss of a finger in his struggle with Gollum as an act of "severe mercy." The concept comes from C. S. Lewis, who wrote a letter in 1952 to a friend who lost the love of his life and was contemplating suicide. "You have been treated with a severe mercy," wrote Lewis. "You have been brought to see [by the loss of your wife] . . . that you are jealous of God."[36] These hard words, written from "my belief in you and love for you," helped Lewis's friend get to a greater appreciation of the woman he loved and of the God they had both loved together. The severe mercy shown to Frodo inside the Crack of Doom by that unseen but powerful force in *The Lord of the Rings* was, as Tolkien admits, a gift of grace to Frodo and to his world:

At this point the "salvation" of the world and Frodo's own "salvation" is achieved by his previous pity and forgiveness of injury. At any point any prudent person would have told Frodo that Gollum would certainly betray him and could rob him in the end. To "pity" him, to forebear to kill him, was a piece of folly or a mystical belief in the ultimate value-in-itself of pity and generosity even if disastrous in the world of time. He did rob him and injure him in the end—but by a "grace," that last betrayal was at a precise juncture when the final evil deed was the most beneficial thing anyone could have done for Frodo! By a situation created by his "forgiveness" he was saved himself and relieved of his burden. [37]

With the Ring and Gollum both gone, Frodo is saved from becoming Gollum. And as Sam picks up the bleeding Frodo and carries him away from the flames, Frodo recalls Gandalf's words about Gollum and thinks about the necessity for mercy. Let us forgive him, he tells Sam, knowing that Gollum did play an important role in bringing their quest to an end, bringing about the *eucatastrophe*. Mercy gives a person who does not deserve love, love, proclaims Sister Joan Chittester, because God knows of what we *all* are made:

> . . . clay, the dust of the earth, the frail, fragile, shapeless thing from which we come and to which we will all return someday. We are all capable of the same things. Our only hope is that when we are all sitting somewhere bereft, exposed, outcast, humiliated and rejected by the rest of society, someone, somewhere will "reach out a hand and lift us up." [38]

Gandalf too knows of what we are all made and what we are all capable of doing. He passes this wisdom on to Frodo, enabling him to reach out a hand and lift Gollum up—if briefly—out of his misery. Gandalf also demonstrates mercy in his treatment of Saruman after the Battle of Helm's Deep, and he and Galadriel offer it again when they come upon Saruman and Wormtongue on the road.[39] The Hobbits too look on Saruman with pity at this last meeting, and Merry even gives him his pouch full of pipe-weed.

Frodo is able to do much more when he discovers, upon returning to the Shire, that the "Sharkey," who has been causing so much destruction there, is none other than Saruman, doing one last deed of spite against the Hobbits, as Gandalf predicted:

> "You made me laugh, you hobbit-lordlings, riding along with all those great people, so secure and so pleased with your little selves. . . ."
>
> "I pity you. . . . Go at once and never return!" [said Frodo].
>
> The hobbits of the villages . . . murmured angrily:
>
> "Don't let him go! Kill him! He's a villain and a murderer. Kill him!"
>
> . . . But Frodo said: "I will not have him slain. It is useless to meet revenge with revenge: it will heal nothing. Go, Saruman, by the speediest way!"[40]

Even when Wormtongue tries to kill Frodo with his knife, Frodo remains merciful: "Do not kill him even now. . . . He is fallen, and his cure is beyond us; but I would still spare him, in the hope that he may find it." This causes Saruman to look at Frodo with eyes of mingled wonder and respect and hatred. "You have grown, Halfling!" he remarks. "You are wise, and cruel. You have robbed my revenge of sweetness, and now I must go hence in bitterness, in debt to your mercy."

All of Middle-earth is in debt to the mercy of Frodo, and that of Bilbo and Sam. The world was saved because three Hobbits took pity on a miserable, wretched, murderous creature full of malice and deceit. The little people *are* lordly, they have grown morally. There is *much* wisdom and *much* courage within them, but love and mercy sit above all their many Hobbit virtues.

Justice, Renewal, and Recovery

Despite Frodo's overwhelming acts of mercy toward Saruman and Wormtongue, both die hideous deaths in the Shire: Saruman's throat cut by Wormtongue, the latter shot by arrows as he tries to flee the murder. Still, Frodo looked at the body of Saruman "with pity and horror," and when Merry asks if this is the final end of the war, Frodo sighs, "I hope so. . . . The very last stroke. But to think that it should fall here, at the very door of Bag End!"[41] Tolkien stresses the Aristotelian tragedy in this chapter, "The Scouring of the Shire," and the devastation that war and industry can wreak on the homefront. Tolkien and his generation had experienced such devastation twice in less than thirty years. The antidote he suggests here at the close of *The Lord of the Rings* is justice tempered with great acts of mercy.

In a 1963 letter to a reader who asked about Frodo's failure to surrender the Ring at Mount Doom, Tolkien writes: ". . . that strange element in the World that we call Pity or Mercy, which is also an absolute requirement in moral judgment (since it is present in the Divine nature). In its highest exercise it belongs to God. For as finite judges of imperfect knowledge . . . we must estimate the limits of another's strength and weigh this against the force of particular circumstances."[42] It was *not* a moral failure on Frodo's part, Tolkien explains, for the Ring at this moment would have exerted maximum power over its bearer, impossible for anyone to resist. Frodo did what he could before providence took over. "His humility (with which he began) and his sufferings were justly rewarded by the highest honour; and his exercise of patience and mercy towards Gollum gained him Mercy: his failure was redressed."

Adam Smith and other legal theorists have suggested that retributive justice stems from our natural passion of resentment, and that the criminal justice system institutionalizes anger, resentment, and hatred toward wrongdoers.[43] Criminal law channels these passions and allows victims to achieve revenge while maintaining public order. Resentment is corrosive and generates false values, argues Nietzsche; the *übermensch* should be above the resentments of lesser folk, is strong, and therefore has no need for forgiveness or to forgive.

Retribution, even when just, is a dangerous thing, as Galadriel tells Sam when he suggests that she take the Ring and "make some folk pay for their dirty work."[44] That is how it would begin, she replies, but it would not stop there. *The Lord of the Rings*, writes Peter Candler, "celebrates all of those virtues Nietzsche found so hideous: pity, mercy, charity."[45] Tolkien reminds us of the strength to be found in the little people, whose humility in part generates their values. Hobbit virtues, however, are not only good for Hobbits. As we will see in the next chapter, Tolkien also wants us to be inspired by the virtues of Elves, Dwarves, Wizards, and Men, and be warned by their vices.

Virtue and Vice in Middle-earth

The critic Henry Giroux calls for us to "imagine a mode of civic courage and militant hope" in the current political moment, this "grim reality" that he calls "a failed sociality" and "a serious erosion of the discourses of community, justice, equality, public values, and the common good."[1] Are modern conceptions of social justice and equality compatible with traditional virtue ethics? I believe they are, as long as we do not lose sight of the common good. We can disagree about public policy, about international relations, even about civil rights, but our disagreements should be aired in an environment of commonly held virtues like civility and respect for truth, courage, love, and mercy.

There is a lengthy section in *The Fellowship of the Ring* in which there is no action, just a lot of talking by people who hold divergent views on many issues. At the Council of Elrond there are gathered peoples from every part of Middle-earth—Elves, Dwarves,

Men, and Hobbits—and many of them are suspicious of each other because of perceived insults and injustices past and present. They argue a lot, but they understand that there is a common threat to their freedom and way of life. Even the wisest counselors present, however, cannot convince this motley group to take common action toward this threat. It is only when the smallest, most humble in their midst speaks up with great courage and self-sacrifice do they stop their bickering and agree on a course of action. One "small voice" in the midst of the mighty says, "I will do it. I will take the Ring, though I do not know the way."[2]

Race, Class, and Gender in Middle-earth

Tolkien uses the term "Races" to describe the various peoples of Middle-earth, one of which is "Men." This terminology is, understandably, troubling to many contemporary readers of his fiction. It is not my intention to apologize for Tolkien's use of these words, but rather to explain the context and what he most likely meant—or did not mean—to imply with his usage. Race was a word commonly used in his day, even by academics, to divide humanity into overly neat biological or national categories. Tolkien is clearly doing the former, akin to the way a modern science fiction writer might use "species" to describe different beings on an alien planet. Within the Races of Middle-earth there are separate nations or kinship groups. What Tolkien does *not* do is make sweeping judgments about the superiority or inferiority of these Races, although he, like many of the Hobbits, is often admiring of the Elves as the "First Born," or eldest of the Children of Ilúvatar.

As a product of a Victorian childhood and coming of age in the Edwardian era, Tolkien and his Oxford friends reflect common British attitudes toward race, class, gender, and empire. The use of "Man" to describe humankind would not have troubled many of his readers in the 1950s, even if today we realize that linguistic choices like this one can marginalize some people and reinforce class and gender privilege. Tolkien was a cultural (if not political) conservative and was suspicious of many modern ideologies, but that does not mean he can't challenge his contemporaries' views about women, class, and empire. Careful reading of the stories of Galadriel and Éowyn, Frodo and Sam, and the Númenóreans do, I would argue, still challenge our views on these topics.

Galadriel tells Frodo that if the Elves remain in Middle-earth and do not depart into the West, they will "dwindle to a rustic folk of dell and cave, slowly to forget and to be forgotten."[3] This is how the Elves and fairies of European folk tradition are often viewed, and we should situate Tolkien's "Races" here. Hobbits and Elves are dwindling and hard to see, but not altogether gone in the Age of Man.

Treebeard and Tom Bombadil

In the *Nicomachean Ethics*, Aristotle describes a person who is the possessor of a great number of virtues such that he has "greatness of soul" (*megalopsychia*). This "great-souled man" (*megalopsychos*) has the appropriate amount of pride, for *megalopsychia* is the mean between the vices of "vanity" and "smallness of soul." The great-souled man "must be good" and must have "nobility and goodness of character [*kalokagathias*]."[4] "Honor and dishonor are the objects with which the great-souled man is especially concerned," but the achievement of common honors he holds as a little thing.[5] In *The Lord of the Rings* there are two characters who come close to the description of Aristotle's "great-souled man," and neither belongs to the Race of Men: Treebeard and Tom Bombadil. Both are ancient inhabitants of Middle-earth, powerful and wise, and held in great esteem by Galadriel, Elrond, and Gandalf.

The *megalopsychos*, writes Robin Lovin, "moves slowly and deliberately, never hurries himself at the behest of others, always maintains control of himself and the situation."[6] Aristotle says that he prefers "to be sluggish and to hold back except where great honor or a great work is at stake, and to be a man of few deeds, but of great and notable ones."[7] These qualities fit Treebeard to a tee. "Do not be hasty, that is my motto," proclaims the Ent when we first meet him.[8] Pippin's first impressions are that Treebeard was slow and steady thinking, with eyes that considered others with the same slow care they gave to considering the state of its own soul for endless years. He is rooted in the earth, and on fine mornings he stands looking at the sun and the grass, the horses and the clouds, "and the unfolding of the world."[9]

Aristotle states that the great-souled man "will also bear himself with moderation [*metriôs*] towards wealth and power and all good or evil fortune [*eutukian kai atukian*]," and "not even towards honor does he bear himself as if it were a very great thing."[10] Like the *megalopsychos*, Tom Bombadil cares for very few things that worry others. He is master of himself, and therefore can order his part of the Old Forest, wood, water, and hill. He has no fear, which gives him power over Old Man Willow and the Barrow-wights. But he does not grasp at higher power, nor seems much concerned with the wider world. He is content with Goldberry, his little house, and his songs.

The *megalopsychos* "knows how to hold his social inferiors at an appropriate distance," observes Lovin, but this strikes "us as arrogant, not virtuous."[11] The great-souled man is, for Aristotle, undeniably aristocratic. Treebeard and Bombadil, on the other hand, are singular entities; they do not derive their status from their relationship with others. They assist with the good quietly, behind the scenes, but both are primarily involved with the world of nature. They live in the present, with little worry about the future: "That is the business of Wizards," says Treebeard.[12] While the *megalopsychos* is singular and heroic, Aristotle suggests that *eudaimonia* ("good souled, thriving") and *makarios* ("blessed") are states of being available to all who habituate virtues into one's character.

Wizards: Gandalf and Saruman

Wizards are appropriately mysterious beings in Middle-earth. We learn almost nothing about their origins and purpose in *The Hobbit* and *The Lord of the Rings*; the bits of information about the Order to which Gandalf and Saruman belong come mainly from *The Silmarillion* and Tolkien's letters. They are possibly Maiar, lesser spirits present at the creation of Middle-earth itself, but of a special class designated as messengers of the Valar sent, in human shape, to assist the Children of Ilúvatar. The ones we hear about are Saruman the White, Gandalf the Grey, Radagast the Brown, and two Blue Wizards of whom Gandalf has lost track. Even Treebeard admits that he does not know the history of Wizards, only that they appeared in Middle-earth after the Númenórean ships first arrived.

The two virtues most associated with Gandalf are hope and wisdom. Gandalf goes by many names: Mithrandir among the Elves and in Gondor, Tharkûn to the Dwarves, Olórin in his "youth in the West that is forgotten," Incánus in the South, Stormcrow and Greyhame ("Grey Cloak") in Rohan, the Grey Pilgrim, and the White Rider.[13] He is a constant traveler, like Strider, though he spends a good deal of time at Minas Tirith and in the Shire. In Gondor he is a scholar and teacher, in Hobbiton the maker of grand fireworks displays. In Rohan he is accused of constantly bringing bad news and trouble—hence Stormcrow—but it is hope that he brings when Théoden and the Rohirrim need it most. Rozema argues that Gandalf is the constant dispenser of hope in *The Lord of the Rings*, indeed is the very embodiment of hope, especially after his transfiguration to become Gandalf the White.[14] He saves the Dwarves from the trolls and the goblins in *The Hobbit* through small magic and stratagems, while in *The Lord of the Rings* he defeats a balrog as "servant of the Secret Fire, wielder of the flame of Anor."[15] Even in the guise of Hope Militant—especially at Helm's Deep and in the defense of Minas Tirith—Gandalf is the white beacon of hope, the sight of which lifts others to action.

Gandalf is also one of the Wise, effectively taking Saruman's place as head of the White Council. Faramir describes him as one of great wisdom and power, "a great mover of deeds that are done in our time."[16] Gandalf himself says to Denethor: "the rule of no realm is mine," but "all things that are in peril . . . are my care. . . . For I also am a steward."[17] The Steward of Gondor, however, accuses him of having subtlety rather than wisdom.[18] If Gandalf's hope for Frodo's success in Mordor is "a fool's hope," as he and Denethor both suggest, Gandalf is like Shakespeare's fools, a speaker of wise words. As Gandalf carries wisdom from Valinor so too does he bring joy to Middle-earth, from his fireworks that entertain the Hobbit children to the merriment of the reunion of the fellowship and the celebration of Aragorn's coronation: a "fountain of mirth enough to set a kingdom to laughing" in the words of Pippin.[19] "For Joy is the other child of Hope," writes Rozema, "the sister of Wisdom."[20]

Saruman becomes increasingly the opposite of Gandalf, for he carries neither hope nor wisdom. Treebeard speaks of a time when Saruman was quiet and caused no trouble as he walked through Fangorn Forest, gathering information with a polite coldness. But he gave up being concerned about Men and Elves: "He is plotting to become a Power," says Treebeard. "He has a mind of metal and wheels; and he does not care for growing things, except as far as they serve him for the moment."[21] His pride grows as he gains more *epistēmē* and *technē*—he even thinks he can outsmart Sauron—but he loses wisdom and piety in the process. No longer Saruman the White, he is like a chameleon of character, changing colors constantly, his political and rhetorical skills becoming powerful spells over the "lesser folk," the "violent and ignorant"; appealing to Gandalf as "members of a high and ancient order," Gandalf's dismissive laugh breaks the spell just as he breaks Saruman's staff.[22] After his fall Saruman is described as snakelike and takes on the nickname "Sharkey," his power limited to petty acts of destruction and vengeance. Tolkien gives us a portrait of a pathetic figure who dies miserably and without hope.

Elves: Galadriel and Elrond Half-Elven

A different kind of sadness accompanies Tolkien's depiction of the Elves of Middle-earth. When we first meet them in *The Hobbit*, the Elves are merry and occasionally foolish. Elrond, however, is from the first instance "noble and fair in face as an elf-lord, as strong as a warrior, as wise as a wizard, as venerable as a king of dwarves, and as kind as summer."[23] When we get to *The Lord of the Rings*, gone are the silly Elves of *The Hobbit* who gently mock Bilbo and the Dwarves, replaced by a race of noble and powerful beings. Tolkien, in fact, seems to have created the very embodiment of the ancient Greek *kalos*: His Elves are both morally and physically beautiful. As Lord of the Last Homely House in the West, Elrond offers great hospitality (*themis*) in Rivendell to all the free races of Middle-earth. As head of the Council of Elrond he displays unrivalled prudence (*phronēsis*), or practical wisdom, to which even Gandalf defers. He is a member of the White Council, one of "The Wise" (*sōphrōn*), and shares with Galadriel the ability to communicate without movement or speech but only thought.

We learn in the Appendices to *The Lord of the Rings* that Gil-galad, Galadriel, and Círdan the Shipwright were given the Three Rings of the Elf-Lords. Elrond explains that the Three were not made by Sauron and were not made as weapons of war. "That is not their power. Those who made them did not desire strength or domination or hoarded wealth, but understanding, making, and healing. . . ."[24] Elrond inherits Vilya, the ring of Gil-galad, when the High King of the Noldor falls in battle against Sauron, and this ring may have enhanced Elrond's healing abilities. For example, he acts as surgeon in removing the splinter of the Morgul-knife from Frodo, saving the Hobbit from a fate worse than death.

The bearer of the ring Nenya is Galadriel, whose power sustains and protects Lórien. Galadriel and her husband Celeborn are both described as tall and beautiful and grave, their eyes profound with deep wells of memory. They offer hospitality and healing to the weary travelers, enabling Lothlórien to serve, like Rivendell, as a place of refuge. Galadriel exhibits both wisdom and sympathy at her first meeting with the Company in *The Lord of the Rings*. She corrects her husband when he expresses regrets about allowing Gandalf and the rest of the Company to enter Moria. None knew Gandalf's mind, she observes, and says that Gimli should not be blamed for wanting to see the ancient home of his people, for the Elves would have felt the same desire even though "it had become an abode of dragons."[25] In Lothlórien she can look into the hearts and minds of each member of the Company, speaking to each without voicing her thoughts aloud. She abstains from giving advice, but can tell "what was and is, and in part also what shall be."[26] "You are wise and fearless and fair," Frodo tells Galadriel before offering her the Ring of Power.[27] Her refusal is a demonstration of both wisdom and true humility.

Galadriel and Celeborn are both possessed with the medieval virtue of *largesse*. They bestow gifts "beyond the power of kings." Celeborn gives the Company boats for their river journey, while Galadriel's gifts include cloaks woven by her and her maidens, putting "the thought of all we love" into their making; a crystal phial in which is caught the light of Eärendil's star given to Frodo; and, for Gimli, the one thing his heart most desires: a lock of Galadriel's golden hair.[28] In these scenes with Galadriel and Gimli we see Tolkien tearing down the curtain of suspicion and hatred that divides races. "Indeed, in nothing is the power of the Dark Lord more clearly shown than in the estrangement that divides all those who still oppose him," remarks Haldir of Lórien as Legolas and Gimli recall the ancient enmity between Elves and Dwarves.[29] Yet Galadriel shows the way to heal enmity when she counsels her husband not to judge Gimli:

She looked upon Gimli, who sat glowering and sad, and she smiled. And the Dwarf, hearing the names given in his own ancient tongue, looked up and met her eyes; and it seemed to him that he looked suddenly into the heart of an enemy and saw there love and understanding.[30]

Respect, empathy, and a smile—powers of an Elf-queen, but virtues within the grasp of any mortal.

Dwarves

Much is said in Tolkien's fiction about the stubbornness and greed of the Dwarves. Yet there is virtue too in this race of sturdy miners and warriors. "Let none say again that Dwarves are grasping and ungracious," remarks Galadriel at Gimli's gesture of courtly love. "It is said that the skill of the Dwarves is in their hands rather than in their tongues, yet that is not true of Gimli."[31] Even the Dwarves of *The Hobbit* are courteous and loyal, and before his death Thorin's nobility is reasserted in the last battle and in his farewell to Bilbo.

Dwarves exceed all the other races of Middle-earth in their technical abilities, their craftmanship, and their mining skills. They were created by Aulë, the Vala who is lord of the substances of the earth and what lies below. From their earliest appearances in *The Silmarillion*, the Dwarves are builders of great underground cities and fortresses and craftsmen of remarkable ability, rivalling even the Eldar in the making of jewels and weapons. The mining and building of the Dwarves are best described by Glóin as he converses with Frodo in Rivendell:

> We make good armour and keen swords, but we cannot again make mail or blade to match those that were made before the dragon came. Only in mining and building have we surpassed the old days. You should see the waterways of Dale, Frodo, and the fountains, and the pools! You should see the stone-paved roads of many colours! And the halls and cavernous streets under the earth with arches carved like trees; and the terraces and towers upon the Mountain sides![32]

The great *technē* of the Dwarves would never have been possible without another virtue: their love of beautiful things. Thorin and his companions love music and their songs reveal part of the Dwarvish aesthetic, but more is revealed in *The Lord of the Rings* when we see the vast halls of Moria and hear, in Appendix A, about the glorious history of Khazad-dûm and the ferocity and hardiness of Durin's Folk. "They were made from their beginning of a kind to resist most steadfastly any domination," we learn in the appendix, and though "they could be slain or broken, they could not be reduced to shadows enslaved to another will. . . ."[33]

From Gimli we see that Dwarves are capable of great love and friendship. ". . . [T]he Lady Galadriel is above all the jewels that lie beneath the earth!"[34] Gimli not only appreciates here the beauty of Galadriel but also her kindness. Her response to his *courtoisie* is to forecast that Gimli's hands "shall flow with gold, and yet over you gold shall have no dominion."[35] The great danger for those who mine gold and jewels and craft them into objects of even greater beauty is that their hearts' desire will be on these things, that they will suffer from "dragon's sickness." It is this vice that ensnares Thrór and Thráin when they possess the last of the Seven Rings and this that overwhelms Thorin once he sees the dragon hoard in *The Hobbit*. But Dwarves are not the only Race in Middle-earth that is afflicted by greed, lust, and vengeance.

Men: Bard, Théoden, Faramir, and Aragorn

The otherness of Tolkien's secondary world, as first introduced to us in *The Hobbit*, means that the focus is not on the Race of Men. Indeed, in both books we begin in the world of Hobbits and Elves and Dwarves, and it takes a while before Men appear. The first Men of note in *The Hobbit* are the Master of Lake-town and Bard the Bowman. The Master is an utterly modern and misguided character, more like an embezzling accountant than a leader of Men. He did not think much of old songs, writes Tolkien, rather "giving his mind to trade and tolls, to cargoes and gold."[36] He is *politique*, obeying the general clamor of his people and pretending to be friendly to the Dwarves while grumbling to himself that the warm reception had turned into a long holiday "in which business was at a standstill."[37]

Bard is nearly the polar opposite of the Master. Tolkien depicts him as a grim and proud captain of the archers, whom he rouses to battle when the Master is busy trying to escape in his gilded boat. "I am Bard, of the line of Girion," the last Lord of Dale, he introduces himself. "I am the slayer of the dragon!"[38] When the survivors of Lake-town instantly proclaim Bard as their king, the Master protests that he was "elected . . . from among the old and wise," and that his town has "not endured the rule of mere fighting men." "We will have King Bard!" protest the people. "We have had enough of the old men and the money-counters!" Pecuniary prowess is clearly no match for courage. Tolkien does not fully develop the character of Bard, however. One of the successes of the Peter Jackson *Hobbit* films is that we get a more detailed and nuanced depiction of Bard: he is grim and bold, but he acts in the service of his family and his community.

In *The Lord of the Rings* our attention is focused for much of the story on two states governed by Men: Rohan and Gondor. Aragorn first describes the virtues of the Rohirrim: "They are proud and willful, but they are true-hearted, generous in thought and deed; bold but not cruel; wise but unlearned, writing no books but singing many songs. . . ."[39] Many critics have seen in the Rohirrim an homage by Tolkien to the Germanic peoples of the early Middle Ages, especially the Anglo-Saxons and the Goths. Their king is Théoden—the name is Anglo-Saxon and means "prince of people"—who, once freed from the spell of Saruman, displays the military virtues we would expect from a leader of the "horse people," close kin to the Bardings of Dale. Théoden has lost his son, slain by the Uruk of Saruman, and now faces tough decisions in war against his former ally. He must balance his desire for battle and vengeance with his need to protect his people. He is also a king who shows mercy, as in his treatment of Wormtongue, a loving foster-father to Éomer and Éowyn, and a kind lord to his smallest sword-thain, Merry.

Théoden serves as a contrast to Denethor, Steward of Gondor, and therefore ruler of the greater state of which Rohan is a vassal. When Pippin first sees Denethor he is impressed by his physical stature, thinking that he looked more like a Wizard than Gandalf, "more kingly, beautiful, and powerful."[40] But we soon see that Denethor's pride is hubris, his seeming wisdom really just *epistēmē* based on incomplete information derived from the Seeing Stone. His grief for Boromir, moreover, leads him to make bad military decisions, to hurt (physically and emotionally) his younger son, and to despair to the point of suicide. Pippin has chosen to serve a lord who does not deserve his service.

When Pippin first sees Faramir, in contrast, his heart is strangely moved by the young captain, so resembling his brother, lordly and kindly, yet with an air of high nobility closer to that of Aragorn, lesser perhaps but not as remote, "one of the Kings of Men born into a later time," though touched with the wisdom and sadness of the Elves, "a captain that men would follow, that he would follow, even under the shadow" of evil.[41] Faramir is perhaps the character most resembling the ancient Númenóreans, the one most dedicated to preserving their cities and culture. It is in these terms that Tolkien has Faramir express to Frodo his commitment to fighting against Sauron as a just war:

> "I would see . . . Minas Tirith in peace: Minas Anor again as of old, full of light, high and fair, beautiful as a queen among other queens: not a mistress of many slaves, nay, not even a kind mistress of willing slaves. War must be, while we defend our lives against a destroyer who would devour all; but I do not love the bright sword for its sharpness, nor the arrow for its swiftness, nor the warrior for his glory. I love only that which they defend: the city of the Men of Númenor; and I would have her loved for her memory, her ancientry, her beauty, and her present wisdom. . . ."[42]

Faramir describes the people of Gondor as still possessing many of the virtues of their Númenórean ancestors. "We are truth-speakers, we men of Gondor. We boast seldom, and then perform, or die in the attempt."[43] Oaths are important to Faramir, as they are to many of the peoples of the West. Faramir swears to Frodo that he would not take the One Ring even if he found it lying in the road. "Even if I were such a man as to desire this thing," he explains, "still I should take those words as a vow, and be held by them."[44]

Tolkien describes Faramir in a 1963 letter to a reader as "courageous and decisive, but also modest, fair-minded and scrupulously just, and very merciful."[45] Faramir also displays great *pietas* to his father and his ancestral home. Yet Denethor derides him and tries to make Faramir share guilt in the death of his brother. "Ever your desire is to appear lordly and generous as a king of old, gracious, gentle. . . ." When Faramir asks his father if he wishes that his and Boromir's places had been exchanged, Denethor replies, "Yes, I wish that indeed. For Boromir was loyal to me and not a wizard's pupil."[46] We often forget that Faramir was a student of Gandalf, or Mithrandir, as he was called in Gondor. They had a personal relationship that occurs offstage, so to speak, prior to the action in *The Lord of the Rings*. In the ancient and early medieval world, Peter Brown reminds us, no student ever went to an impersonal *school*: "He would always have gone to a *person*. . . . The most poignantly expressed relation in the ancient and medieval worlds was that between teacher and pupil."[47] Teachers—be they in the Academy or the monastic schools—often served as moral exemplars, not just distributors of knowledge.

Faramir's actions are guided by the virtue of prudence, which helps him to know who he is and to respect those around them for who they truly are. This is displayed when we first meet him in *The Lord of the Rings*, in his attitude toward the Hobbits Frodo and Sam. But prudence and humility can also be seen in "The Houses of Healing" chapter as he comes to win the heart of Éowyn by showing that he both understands her pain and appreciates her valor:

> "You desired to have the love of Lord Aragorn. Because he was high and puissant, and you wished to have renown and glory and to be lifted far above the mean things that crawl on the earth. And as a great captain may to a young soldier he seemed to you admirable. For so he is, a lord among men, the greatest that now is. But when he gave you only understanding and pity, then you desired to have nothing, unless a brave death in battle. . . ."[48]

Tolkien stated that the romance of Faramir and Éowyn was not "courtly love," but something "more primitive . . . and nobler."[49] Nevertheless, both Aragorn and Faramir owe much to the ideal chivalric knight of the medieval romance. Knights of the Round Table—Lancelot, Gawain, Tristan, Perceval, Galahad—are often depicted as coming very near to the knightly ideals expressed in romances and other medieval literature. In Sir Thomas Malory's late medieval prose masterpiece, *Morte D'Arthur*, we see this most clearly in the eulogy delivered by Sir Ector at the grave of his brother, Sir Lancelot:

> "Ah, Lancelot!" he said. "You were the best of all Christian knights! Now, I daresay," said Sir Ector, "you, Sir Lancelot, who lies there—you were never matched in combat by any earthly knight. You were the most courteous man to ever bear a shield, and the truest friend to your

lover of any man who ever rode a horse. Among sinful men, you were the truest lover who ever loved a woman. You were the kindest man who ever struck with a sword, and best person who ever came among any press of knights. You were the meekest and most gentle of any who ever ate in the hall among ladies, and you were the sternest man to your mortal foe of any man who ever bore a spear."[50]

Faramir pitied Boromir because his brother was always distressed that their father was not recognized as king of Gondor, even though he exercised the power of a king. Faramir, on the other hand, has no desire to be king, and is satisfied with the title Steward of the City. "The hero for Tolkien," states Boyd, "is not the person who desires to lead or the person who longs for greatness."[51] The true king is not one who is eager to grasp power; he is hesitant, turning only to his birthright out of necessity, to save a people who are leaderless. Aragorn first does this when Gandalf falls and the Company is in need of a leader, and he acts no differently on his path to the throne of Gondor.

The virtues of Strider, from his first meeting of the Hobbits at the Prancing Pony, reveal what kind of king Aragorn, son of Arathorn, will make. Service to others, especially to the humblest of creatures; prudence, learnt from years of experience as a ranger and from his companionship with Gandalf; courage in the face of the most extreme dangers; friendship and fellowship, helping dissolve enmity between Elf and Dwarf; respecting the authority and wisdom of others, especially Elrond and Galadriel; learning the customs and cultures of other peoples; sympathy for the plight of Éowyn; helping others to regain their honor, even the oathbreakers of the Shadow Host; healing Merry, Éowyn, and Faramir; displaying mercy to Gollum; and pardoning the slaves and allies of Sauron, even giving them lands. Daniel Rozema argues that Tolkien makes Aragorn especially the symbol of faith in *The Lord of the Rings*: faith in friends, faith in Gandalf's wisdom, and faith in Arwen, such that her hope becomes his hope.[52]

Most remarkable of all, given his military prowess and noble lineage, is Aragorn's humility. There is a scene in the Peter Jackson film *The Return of the King* that is not in the book—but I think Tolkien would have nonetheless approved—in which Aragorn displays his humility publicly, and at a moment when all those assembled are there to bear witness to *his* greatness and political authority. At his coronation, after Gandalf has placed the crown of Gondor on his head and Arwen (who presents him with his silver standard) is by his side as royal consort, Aragorn passes through a crowd of dignitaries and comes to the Hobbits Frodo, Sam, Merry, and Pippin, all four of them bowing before the High King of the West. "My friends," exclaims Aragorn in consternation, "you bow to no one." He then drops onto one knee and bows his head in respect to the role that the Hobbits have played in saving Middle-earth, and all his subjects do likewise while the halflings stand gazing in wonder.

It is a powerful scene, especially for those who have invested emotionally in the whole trilogy, and a wonder of cinematography as the camera pulls back to show the large number of people bowing at Minas Tirith, which then dissolves into an illustrated version on Bilbo's map.[53] Aragorn has performed so many physical and moral feats on his personal quest to kingship, and now in this scene he is the very embodiment of magnificence, the crowning virtue of chivalry. Magnificence is also a quality of the Divine, seen but rarely in the City of Man. Aragorn has quite literally "brought down the powerful from their thrones and exalted the lowly" (Luke 1:52). As we gaze in awe at his display of humility and respect to the Hobbits, it brings into stark contrast what we have so often accepted from our contemporary leaders. Democracy or no, we all know what a *true* king looks like, argues Peter Kreeft, and "something in us longs to give him our loyalty and fidelity and service and obedience. He is lost but longed for and will someday return, like Arthur. In *The Lord of the Rings*, Arthur's name is 'Aragorn.'"[54]

Women: Éowyn

It is a fair criticism of Tolkien to say that he gives us few examples of women playing major roles in either *The Hobbit* or *The Lord of the Rings*. This is absolutely true of the former, but in the latter the few exceptions are important.[55] We have already looked at Galadriel, but in some ways a more complex portrayal of womanhood is to be found in Éowyn, shieldmaiden of Rohan. Many have seen in Éowyn a Joan of Arc figure, challenging gender norms in both her appearance and her prowess on the battlefield. While Joan certainly had charisma and courage, she was not the warrior that Éowyn proved to be in the guise of Dernhelm. One of the great emotional moments, in book and film, is when the Witchking has her at his mercy, pronouncing, "No man can kill me!" and Éowyn's response, removing her helmet before delivering the fatal blow: "I am no man!"[56]

Tolkien said of Éowyn that he did not intend to create an Amazon warrior, "but like many brave women [Éowyn] was capable of great military gallantry at a crisis."[57] In this he is closer to Plato, who argued that women were capable of *arete*, than to Aristotle, who allowed women, at best, to be efficient in running a household.[58] Any writer can create a woman warrior, but Tolkien gives Éowyn a voice that, in her frustration with the limitations of what is expected of women, will strike many readers as surprisingly modern. It is especially poignant that she argues the point ("her eyes . . . on fire") to the man she admires and loves, Aragorn:

> "Lord," she said, "if you must go, then let me ride in your following. For I am weary of skulking in the hills, and wish to face peril and battle."
>
> "Your duty is with your people," he answered.
>
> "Too often have I heard of duty," she cried. "But am I not of the House of Eorl, a shieldmaiden and not a dry-nurse? . . . may I not now spend my life as I will?"
>
> "Few may do that with honour," he answered. "But as for you, lady: did you not accept the charge to govern the people until the lord's return? . . ."
>
> "Shall I always . . . be left behind when the Riders depart, to mind the house while they win renown, and find food and beds when they return?"
>
> "A time may come soon," said he, "when none will return. Then there will be need of valour without renown, for none shall remember the deeds done in the last defense of your homes. Yet the deeds will not be less valiant because they are unpraised."
>
> And she answered: "All your words are but to say: you are a woman, and your place is in the house. But when the men have died in battle and honour, you have leave to be burned in the house, for

the men will need it no more. But I am of the House of Eorl and not a serving-woman. I can ride and wield blade, and I do not fear either pain or death."[59]

This is a hard conversation for the reader to respond to, because we admire both characters and they are both right. It *is* a gender double-standard that Aragorn expresses, and Éowyn *did* agree to her charge to stay behind and rule in Théoden's stead. She breaks her promise to her king and nearly dies in battle, but in doing so she preserves the king's honor and stops the enemy's most deadly weapon, perhaps saving Gondor *and* Rohan in the process. She is, to quote Faramir, "a lady high and valiant," possessor of great renown, but also "beautiful . . . beyond the words of the elven-tongue to tell."[60]

Éowyn is fiercely independent, but she is also fiercely loyal and capable of great love and friendship. She loves and reveres Théoden as a father and defends his broken body from being eaten by the fell beast of the Witchking. She also relates to the marginalization that Merry feels and helps him fulfill his warrior service by carrying him to battle. After accepting the love of Faramir and leaving the House of Healing, Éowyn vows to herself become a healer. She is a woman who takes charge of her decisions and her life.

The Seven Deadly Sins: Violence and Vice in Middle-earth

Over the span of seven days in late July/early August 2019 there were four mass shootings in the United States. Thirty-six men, women, and children were murdered, and dozens more injured, at a festival in northern California; at Walmart stores in

Southaven, Mississippi, and El Paso, Texas; and at a popular restaurant district in Dayton, Ohio. Three of the incidents were labeled hate crimes and domestic terrorism, and at least one of the shooters was motivated by hatred of recent emigration from Latin America. Similar shootings have taken place in Orlando, Las Vegas, Pittsburgh, and New Zealand since 2016, targeting immigrants, Jews, and members of the LGBTQ community. While America struggles to pass federal legislation against gun violence while balancing Second Amendment rights, and while the world continues well after the fall of the Twin Towers on 9/11 to witness suicide bombings targeting civilians and various ethnic and religious groups, scholars and political pundits debate the causes of bigotry, hatred, and terrorism. "The world changes," remarks Théoden, king of Rohan, "all that once was strong proves unsure. How shall any tower withstand . . . such reckless hate?"[61]

Tolkien could not have foreseen our age of global terrorism and domestic gun violence, but he did witness much reckless hate in his lifetime. He saw up close and personal the unparalleled carnage of the First World War, which was started by an act or terror; the Second World War threatened his sons and his home, and by 1945 it proved responsible for an even greater number of deaths, caused by the combination of hatred, nationalism, and technology. While not a pacifist, Tolkien did fill his fiction with cautionary tales relevant to modern warfare and many examples of vices ancient and contemporary. "For nothing is evil in the beginning," states the wise elf-lord Elrond. "Even Sauron was not so." Nevertheless, as Aragorn reminds us, "there are many evil and unfriendly things in the world," and not all are "in league with Sauron, but with purposes of their own."[62]

The history of vice and sin is too vast to cover here. Let it suffice to say that Tolkien inherited classical ideas about vice, especially those of Aristotle, as well as the Catholic concept of the Seven Deadly Sins, first articulated by the Desert Father Evagrius Ponticus, in the late 4th century.[63] Evagrius and his disciple John Cassian channeled Hellenistic philosophy through the lens of ascetic theology to identify the demons with which all humans struggle: greed, pride, envy, sloth, gluttony, lechery, and anger. While there are demonic beings in Middle-earth, Tolkien does not treat these sins allegorically in *The Hobbit* and *The Lord of the Rings*, and seems most interested in exploring greed, pride, and anger.[64]

Greed, as we have seen, is one of the main themes of *The Hobbit*. It is a vice associated with the aristocratic Dwarves (especially Thorin), with the Master of Lake-town, with the goblins, and most vividly with the dragon Smaug. Tolkien describes the depiction of *Beowulf*'s dragon not as *draco* but *draconitas* (being dragon-like), "a personification of malice, greed, destruction (the evil side of heroic life), and of the undiscriminating cruelty of fortune that distinguishes not good or bad (the evil aspect of all life)."[65] Smaug is all this and more because he is intelligent evil. Bilbo not only survives his encounter with Smaug but also learns a lesson about greed from the dragon. Smaug warns Bilbo that, even if he were able to steal the treasure, how would he get even a fourteenth-share down the mountain and safely through the long passage home. Gold is a heavy burden, both literally and metaphorically, as the Taoist sages taught.[66] After Thorin's death Bilbo comes to fully understand this and chooses to carry very little treasure back with him to the Shire, even offering to give Gandalf all of the trolls' gold that they had buried on his journey home. Bilbo learns years later about the fate of the greedy Master of Lake-town, who had fallen under the dragon-sickness, taken most of the gold given by Bard for the rebuilding of the town, and fled into the Waste where he died of starvation in misery and abandoned by his companions.[67]

In *The Lord of the Rings* the demonic Balrog is unleashed because the Dwarves delved too deep in their search for the precious *mithril*. But it is one act of greed—and violence—perpetrated by a small creature that begins the War of the Ring. Sméagol, one of the Hobbit-like creatures who lived along the river, kills his friend to possess a golden ring. His transformation into Gollum begins with some of Tolkien's most poignant prose: "He wandered in loneliness, weeping a little for the hardness of the world. . . ."[68] Through Gollum, his most original creation, Tolkien is able to explore topics like addiction and loss of self, all by-products of greed and violence. "He hated [the Ring] and loved it, as he hated and loved himself. He could not get rid of it. He had no will left in the matter."[69]

Some theologians have argued that greed is the original sin, since Adam and Eve broke God's prohibition by stealing the one object they were forbidden to have. Others have pointed to disobedience and concupiscence. But thinkers from Augustine to Milton identify pride as the root of all sin. Sinful pride is a total preoccupation with self, a feeling that one is capable of divine autonomy. It is Lucifer's sin and leads to rebellion against God. Tolkien was very interested in exploring this view of pride, but he was also drawn to various pagan perspectives on pride, including seeing it as a virtue when held in moderation. The eagles, for example, are described as "proud and strong and noble-hearted" in *The Hobbit*, and Tolkien describes many admirable characters who are warriors or of noble houses as proud: Bard, Thorin, Éowyn, and Túrin, to name just a few.

But, for Tolkien, pride is more often at the center of malice, bad decisions, and evil characters in Middle-earth: the rebellions of Morgoth and Sauron, the disobedience of the Dark Elves, the stubbornness of Fëanor, the cursed House of Húrin, the Fall of

Númenor, Bilbo's riddling with Smaug, the scheming of Saruman, the strategic miscalculations of Denethor. Tolkien must be thinking of two types of pride, which we might call "authentic pride" (a quality of Aristotle's "great-souled man") and "hubristic pride" (from the Greek *hubris*). Aristotle thought so highly of authentic pride (*megalopsychia*) that he described it as "a sort of crown of the virtues; for it makes them greater, and it is not found without them."[70] Aquinas believed that Aristotle was not contradicting Christian ethics here, suggesting that this authentic or proper pride is related to the virtue of temperance.[71] As Garcia points out, it was proper pride that Bilbo felt after battling the spiders and rescuing the grateful Dwarves.[72] However, Bilbo succumbed to hubristic pride in his encounter with the dragon Smaug. Because he could move about the dragon's lair unseen with the help of the Ring, Bilbo answered Smaug's questions with taunting riddles, giving away too much information to the crafty dragon. Bilbo made too much of his own cleverness and thought too little of Smaug's intelligence, and as a result Smaug realized that Bilbo had come from Lake-town and rained down fiery vengeance on its inhabitants. Like Odysseus in his encounter with the cyclops Polyphemus, Bilbo's hubris resulted in the death of innocent people and great destruction.

Bilbo learned from this lapse in judgment, however, and risked his own safety and share of the treasure in bringing the Arkenstone to Bard and the Elves. Either their size or their moral natures seem to prevent Hobbits from giving in to vanity and hubris. It is more often the great lords who succumb to these vices brought to Arda by the rebel Morgoth, and in *The Lord of the Rings* this is the fate of Denethor and Saruman. In both cases their hubristic pride comes as they are deceived by the partial knowledge gained from using the Seeing Stones. Saruman's "knowledge is deep," remarks Gandalf, "but his pride has grown with it. . . ."[73] Professor Tolkien was on his guard for intellectual pride.

Saruman also spirals into an abyss of anger and hatred after his defeat, and his mistreatment of Wormtongue brings the latter slave-like into his misery. The goblins, orcs, and Uruk-hai as a whole show an inclination to reckless hate and violence throughout the books, and one of the criticisms of Tolkien is that there are whole Races of evil beings in Middle-earth, creatures seemingly born evil, incapable of moral choice. Tolkien gives two explanations for this: 1) orcs, goblins, and other monsters were made or "counterfeited" by the First Enemy, and 2) orcs are a Race of "rational incarnate" beings (possibly Elves) who have been horribly corrupted by Morgoth and Sauron, since evil cannot create.[74] Men obviously can make right or wrong moral decisions, and both the Black Riders and the Armies of the Dead bring a macabre character to the violence in *The Lord of the Rings* as a result of their lust for power and treachery, respectively. From *Beowulf* and other Anglo-Saxon literature Tolkien found the *orcneas*, translated variously as "demons" and "animated corpses," while one medieval inspiration for the Black Riders and Armies of the Dead may be the Arthurian romance *Perlesvaus* (early 13th century), which features black knights with flaming swords and lances who hack their victims (and occasionally each other) into pieces and "screamed like demons" when they fought Arthur, Lancelot, and Gawain.[75]

Violence is played out in large scale and in small in Tolkien's fiction. Torture was introduced to Middle-earth by the Diabolus Morgoth, the original Dark Lord, and became a favorite tactic of his lieutenant and successor Sauron. We see the torture of Elves and Men throughout *The Silmarillion*, and in *The Lord of the Rings* it is used most vividly by servants of Sauron against Gollum. His mistreatment is part of why Gandalf, Aragorn, and Frodo take pity on Gollum. Individual acts of murder are perpetrated by

Sméagol and Wormtongue, and a result is that they appear as the two most miserable and wretched characters in the book.

There is a long and memorable passage in *The Fellowship of the Ring* in which Frodo, wearing the Ring and sitting on the Seat of Seeing at Amon Hen, looks out in every direction and sees the signs of war.[76] For Tolkien war itself was not an evil (he adhered to Just War theory) but rather an arena in which individuals are constantly tested to make moral choices. There can be heroism in war and cowardice, just as in peace. But Tolkien was especially critical of mechanized warfare. Aragorn tells Théoden, for example, that the orcs have brought "a devilry from Orthanc," "a blasting fire" that they have used against the defenses of Helm's Deep.[77] Saruman breeds goblins and orcs to create a genetically superior fighting machine, the Uruk-hai, and the orcs and their allies bring to Pelennor Field huge siege towers and great engines. Tolkien had seen the machines, the flames, and the explosions of the first mechanized war: "One War is enough for any man," he wrote to his son Michael, then in training for yet another war.[78]

Gandalf tells Frodo at the beginning of *The Lord of the Rings* that he had been deeply concerned about all the "charming, absurd, helpless hobbits," that the Dark Power should overcome the Shire and enslave its "kind, jolly, stupid" inhabitants.[79] Tolkien wrote much of *The Lord of the Rings* at the same time that he was writing to his sons, in training or in combat during the Second World War, trying to lift their spirits. "All we do know," he wrote to his son Christopher in 1944, ". . . is that evil labours with vast power and perpetual success—in vain: preparing always only the soil for unexpected good to sprout."[80] This is the lesson that Morgoth and Sauron never learn: There is always hope.

Multiculturalism and Diversity in Middle-earth

One difference between the "real" (Primary) world and the one he was creating in his fiction, writes Tolkien in another letter to Christopher, is that in real life there are orcs on both sides.[81] Racial superiority and tribalism held no appeal for Tolkien. Although he could be patriotic, and certainly proud of English culture, he was also critical of Empire and Commonwealth. At the end of the War of the Ring he gives us a racially diverse Middle-earth, temporarily at peace, with a high king in Gondor, several vassal kingdoms, and one tiny little "half republic, half aristocracy"—the Shire.[82] Tolkien was suspicious of words like politics, state, and government (especially when capitalized), and believed that Frodo's mission was universal and humane, not primarily political. Frodo was carrying the Ring for all the Races of Middle-earth.

Yet we look for political answers and trust democracy to provide solutions to our differences. We are told to celebrate diversity (and rightly so) but are surprised when there is no common vision of the Good. "[H]ow can respect for diversity be encouraged," asks economist Rick Szostak, "but also honesty, responsibility, and a host of other desirable attitudes, values, and behaviors . . . [when] individuals are urged to respect the views of others [and] are told that knowledge is not absolute, that neither scientific nor philosophical statements can be proved?"[83] We have embraced a host of seeming contradictions.

Thomas Lasley makes an argument for the importance of teaching virtue ethics, especially selflessness, as a counter to selfish tribalism:

> Such a selfless disposition is essential because of the inherent pluralism
> of American culture. Without a certain cultural extra-centeredness,

the myriad racial, ethnic, and ideological differences will begin to tear American society apart. America will become increasingly a people of competing tribal interests who struggle for sufficient power in order to disdain or reject others who do not hold the "right" views.[84]

Hobbits are not immune to these kinds of sociopolitical difficulties. As much as he loves the Shire, Tolkien calls to our attention the small-mindedness and xenophobia common there. Bilbo must overcome his provincial prejudices to begin his quest and see that he is only a small person in a big world. Frodo and Sam must likewise leave behind the Gaffer and others in Hobbiton who think their way of life superior to others and have no interest in the politics and wars of the Big Folk. "Elves and dragons! Cabbages and potatoes are better for me and you."[85]

The answer to this dilemma may lie with Aragorn, who spends much of his life with Elves and Dwarves and who becomes a just and respectful ruler over many disparate peoples. When he first meets Éomer and tries to convince him to join the fight against Saruman, Éomer asks how a man should judge who to trust in such times of political and moral complexity. Aragorn responds: "As he ever has judged. Good and ill have not changed since yesteryear; nor are they one thing among Elves and Dwarves and another among Men."[86] Virtues, in other words, are not values, they do not change with the calendar or with geography. Different cultures can be respected—even protected—but moral relativism is to be avoided. It is the way of Saruman, not of Gandalf; and it is the isolationism that Bilbo and Frodo must both reject in order to serve the common good of all Middle-earth.

BEING SMALL

IN A BIG WORLD

*G*lobalization. It is a word that we hear constantly in our public discourse, whether we are talking about politics, economies, violence, communication, or climate change. It is a big world and we often feel small in it—or alienated from it. "The risk for our time," writes Pope Benedict, "is that the *de facto* interdependence of people and nations is not matched by ethical interactions of consciences and minds that would give rise to truly human development."[1] Instead of ethics we turn to technological development—in energy, medicine, artificial intelligence—to save us. Tolkien, reflecting in 1945 on the mass destruction wrought by machines during the Second World War, was skeptical: "As the servants of the Machine are becoming a privileged class, the machines are going to become enormously more powerful. What's their next move?"[2]

At the very end of *The Hobbit*, Bilbo and Gandalf have a short but important conversation (while smoking their pipes, of course) about prophecies and luck and a Hobbit's place in the wide world:

> "You don't really suppose, do you, that all your adventures and escapes were managed by mere luck, just for your sole benefit? You are a very fine person, Mr. Baggins, and I am very fond of you; but you are only quite a little fellow in a wide world after all!"
>
> "Thank goodness," said Bilbo laughing, and handed him the tobacco-jar.[3]

This conversation returns us to the prime virtue—humility—which Aquinas suggested "tempers the appetite from aiming at great things contrary to right reason."[4] Gandalf helps remind Bilbo, using right reason, that despite his great adventures against trolls and giant spiders and a dragon, he is not the sole reason that things worked out for the good. "Right reason dictates how we should value ourselves," writes Craig Boyd, "in light of the fact that we are neither the most important person in the cosmos nor the most worthless."[5] Right reason directs us toward true humility, steering away from overweening pride (*hubris*), on the one extreme, and self-loathing on the other. "If you are humble," observes Robert Adams, "you do not think that what happens to you *matters* more, objectively, than what happens to other people. . . ."[6] At the end of his great adventure, Bilbo is exactly this kind of humble person, and his humility (and later that of Frodo) perhaps saved him from becoming utterly corrupted by the One Ring.

The conversation is also cosmological, Gandalf reminding Bilbo that there are a lot of forces at work in the universe, though Tolkien is by turns hesitant and vague in naming them. Luck, fate, prophecy, love—these are just some of the metaphysical forces in Middle-earth that are powerful but unpredictable. Virtue and vice are defined, in part, by how each character responds to these forces as well as to physical danger and political power. In this final chapter, I want to discuss various other Hobbit virtues not covered earlier, and finally to ask the question: Is there a unity and a purpose to virtue?

Country Walks and Mathoms

Can taking long walks in the countryside be a virtue?[7] Is it good for us to hold onto old things? We begin with what might seem trivial and idiosyncratic Hobbit habits, but perhaps Tolkien would not have considered them so. Nature, growing things, and rural life were very dear to the professor, in part because they reminded him of his happiest moments as a youth, living in rural Sarehole (outside of Birmingham) with his mother, Edith, and brother, Hilary, just before his mother died. John Ronald's adventures with Hilary in the woods and fields of Sarehole (and with the miller and his son) were the genesis of some of his Hobbit tales.[8] Years later, as we have seen, Professor Tolkien enjoyed long walks in the Oxfordshire countryside with his Inkling friends, though his constant pauses to inspect trees and plants sometimes annoyed the Lewis brothers. Long after his rugby playing years were over, these long walks became Tolkien's chief form of exercise, all the more enjoyable if the journey ended at a country pub.

In *The Hobbit* we are told that the respectable Bilbo Baggins "had settled down immovably" in his hobbit hole by the time Gandalf offered him the chance of adventure. The Dwarves stirred up his Tookish blood and he took a very long walk indeed across Middle-earth; there and back again. Strolling contentedly through the summer grass on his way back to the Shire, Bilbo even composes a walking song, "The Road Go Ever On." It would be the first of many after his adventure with the dragon, for Bilbo now had lost his respectability among his neighbors through a constant desire to travel and visit the Elves and the Dwarves. Still, his travels made him appreciate even more the comforts of home—one of the great benefits of travel.

Bilbo shared his love of country walks with his young cousin, Frodo Baggins, as we learn at the beginning of *The Lord of the Rings*. After his party, Bilbo leaves the Shire because he wanted to see "the wild country again before I die," as he tells Gandalf, "and the Mountains," while Frodo loves the "woods and fields and little rivers" of the Shire.[9] What Frodo really loved was tramping in the countryside with Bilbo, and after the latter's disappearance he continues his walks with companions from Buckland. In *The Lord of the Rings*, many of the most endearing characters—Bilbo, Frodo, Sam, Merry and Pippin, Gandalf, Strider, Faramir—spend a good deal of time walking and exploring Middle-earth. Even Tom Bombadil and Treebeard are constantly moving through their little realms. Sam, growing up listening to the stories of Bilbo's adventures, develops a great desire to travel to see the Elves. Legolas and Gimli dedicate their days after the coronation of Aragorn to traveling together, and in the end Legolas followed the great desire of his heart and sailed over the Sea.

When Bilbo returns from his first adventure he hangs his sword above the mantle and donates his coat of *mithril* mail to a museum called the Mathom-house. Anything that Hobbits had no immediate use for, but were unwilling to throw away, they called *mathoms*.[10] Hobbit houses were often cluttered with mathoms, for they were constantly giving them to each other as birthday presents. Tolkien knew well that the Old English word *māpum* could mean both "treasure" and "gift," and that the word had become extinct sometime after Middle English went out of use. So he revived it—unwilling to throw away perfectly good words!—just as he revived ancient legends and discarded history in his Middle-earth writings. Part of history is writing memoirs, as Bilbo did soon after his return from the Lonely Mountain, and we are told in the Prologue to *The Lord of the Rings* that these were recorded in the Red Book of Westmarch, along with Frodo's account of the War of the Ring and additional notes from Samwise.[11] The Red Book was first copied by Pippin in Gondor at the request of King Elessar (Aragorn), where, along with the addition of *The Tale of Aragorn and Arwen*, it became known as the Red Book of the Periannath. Material about the history of Rohan was added to this by Merry, who became well-known as the author of *The Herblore of the Shire* (with a history of pipe-weed!) and an expert on calendars and place names.

This rather academic sounding literary conceit should draw our attention to the importance of history to Tolkien, a professional historian of words and languages. The inclusion of the Shire in the Reunited Kingdom, we are also told in the Prologue, awakened a widespread interest among the Hobbits in their own history and traditions, with many members of the great families taking to the study of ancient histories and legends.[12] This led to the founding of libraries and the writing of official records in many towns in the Shire. The Hobbits pass from a stage where only oral histories were kept to becoming a book-writing and book-loving culture. Latter day Hobbits who become fans of Tolkien's works are often of the same culture.

Oaths and Promises

Historians who study ancient and medieval lands where written records are scarce know the importance of oaths in these societies. Legal disputes, for example, often centered on formal oaths given before witnesses, while treaties were often in the form of personal oaths given by kings and warlords set down in writing before witnesses. At the end of *The Hobbit* there is a saga-like dispute between three peoples—Thorin's Dwarves, the Elves of Mirkwood, and the Men of Lake-town—that devolves into open warfare because there is no written record of promises to divide the dragon hoard other than among Bilbo and the Dwarves.

Frodo begins his quest with an oath to carry the Ring out of the Shire, and when he offers to continue that journey all the way to Mordor at the Council of Elrond, others agree to accompany him after Elrond has weighed in. The Lord of Rivendell explicitly does not make the rest of the Company take oaths, for he wants them to go as "free companions," and no further than their will can bear. Of the many who do make oaths and give promises in *The Lord of the Rings*, it is Sam and Faramir who stand out. Sam sticks to his original promise to Gandalf and never leaves Frodo's side through all the trials and travails on the road to Mordor.[13] Even when he thinks Frodo is dead Sam argues with himself about whether he should take the Ring and continue on or stay by his master's side. "Don't go where I can't follow! Wake up, Mr. Frodo . . . me dear," is his heartbreaking lament.[14] By the end of their journey it has become part of Sam's character to not give up and not break his promise to help Frodo. Likewise, we learn that truth and loyalty are part of Faramir's character. "I would not snare even an Orc with a falsehood," he declares to Frodo, and, when guessing that Boromir was tempted by a weapon of the Enemy, he states, "I would not take this thing if it lay by the highway."[15] When he discovers that Frodo is carrying the Ring and has a chance, like Boromir, to seize it, Faramir remarks that even if he were such a man who desired glory brought by such a weapon, "still I should take those words as vow, and be held by them."[16]

We live in a world where we expect the politically powerful to make promises and to break them in short order, where oaths and vows taken in courts and in churches are broken every day. Part of what makes *The Lord of the Rings* so remarkable and so refreshing is that we get to know characters like Sam and Faramir who would rather die than break a promise, for death is a lesser thing to them than dishonor.

Honor and Nobility

Honor is not a very fashionable virtue in our time, while nobility is more of an embarrassing anachronism. We expect men and women in the military and in the police force to "serve with honor," but otherwise it makes little impact in our routine discourse. This in an age when every other schoolchild is an "honors student" and when academic "honors" in American higher education have grown exponentially, as have honors programs and honors colleges, based originally on the Oxford model of an honours degree. Possessing honors and having honor are now two very different things.

Historically, honor was the terrain of the privileged few, the nobility, the military aristocracy. Honor (*timê*), or glory (*kûdos*), was one of the highest virtues of the Greek Homeric Age, just as it would be in medieval Europe. *Kavod* (דובכ) is the Hebrew word for "honor or respect" when associated with people, but often translated as "glory" when expressed as a quality of God. It's roots too are military, often referring to the shield or armament of the Lord. In Plato's *Republic*, those ruled by spirit (*thumos*), the military guardian class, are motivated by love of honor (*philotimia*), and in his *Symposium* the discourse begins this way before Socrates shifts it to a higher love of wisdom (*philosophia*). Aristotle describes honor as "the greatest of external goods" and "the prize of excellence and virtue," a recognition of genuine value in a person who is truly good, not just fame or notoriety.[17] In the Roman Republic, *honores* were "the prizes, the tokens of the esteem and recognition that one received from others and that gave one status," including titles, offices, laurels and, under the emperors, crowns, statues, and panegyrics.[18] Honor was the domain of noblemen, the *honestiores*; honor among Roman women and the poor are harder to grasp from the sources. Honor in Celtic and Germanic societies of the early Middle Ages was almost entirely male and military, bearing great similarity to that of the Greek Heroic Age. This was later enshrined in feudal hierarchies and in the chivalric code, with knights—whose very being depended on gaining and maintaining honor—expected to practice *noblesse oblige*, an obligation to protect women and the poor.

Tolkien knew well the history of the concepts of honor and nobility and constructed Middle-earth (or at least large parts of it) in the semblance of medieval Europe. From *The Hobbit* and *The Lord of the Rings*, however, we learn that the Halflings are as capable of honor and admiration as are any of the peoples of Middle-earth. Both Thorin and the Elvenking bestow honor upon Bilbo in *The Hobbit*, as do Elrond and Galadriel in *The Lord of the Rings*. Faramir, on meeting Sam, supposes that gardeners are held "in high honour" in the Shire. Aragorn, as King Elessar, honors his four Hobbit companions with titles and gifts. Affording Bilbo and Frodo places on the White Ship is perhaps the greatest of all honors bestowed upon Hobbits.

"I loved [the Hobbits] myself, since I love the vulgar and simple as dearly as the noble," confesses Tolkien, "and nothing moves my heart (beyond all the passions and heartbreaks of the world) so much as 'ennoblement' (from the Ugly Duckling to Frodo)."[19] The Bagginses are a well-to-do family in the Shire and Frodo is thus already a member of the gentry of Hobbiton when he embarks on his quest and becomes "ennobled" by its seriousness and self-sacrifice, more so than even Bilbo. Tolkien, while still working out the plot of *The Lord of the Rings*, describes this process of ennobling in a letter to his son Christopher:

> Frodo . . . has to be high-minded, and has (as it were) a vocation. The book will prob. end up with Sam. Frodo will naturally become too ennobled and rarified by the achievement of the great Quest, and will pass West with all the great figures.[20]

Hope

One of the consistent themes throughout *The Lord of the Rings* is the tension between hope and despair, a tension in the hearts and minds of even the most admirable characters. This was identified in preproduction by Peter Jackson, Fran Walsh, and Philippa Boyens, the screenwriters for the *The Lord of the Rings* film trilogy, and part of their magnifying the role of Arwen for the films was to have her be the constant voice of hope, even in the face of the doubts of her father and her lover. In Tolkien's novel the most dramatic example of this struggle is within the patriarchs Théoden and Denethor;

the former finds his hope and retains his honor, the latter falls deeply into despair when he sees a second son mortally wounded and gives in and commits suicide. Even the greatest figures of Middle-earth—Gandalf, Elrond, Galadriel, Aragorn—are not immune to doubt, though their hope shines through the cloud of darkness. And, each in their own moment, the four Hobbit companions voice hope to others.

"Hope, after all, is a virtue, perhaps the most political virtue in our times," write Stanley Hauerwas and Charles Pinches.[21] Hope is also political in the Third Age of Middle-earth, in that the solution to the One Ring requires community action, associations of good people coming together for the Common Good. The Shire, Rivendell and Lothlórien, Rohan and Gondor—these communities must cooperate, not just fight as allies, if there is to be any hope of defeating the enemy. But defeating the enemy is not defeating pain and death, as many of the characters must face when they return home. Hope is not only one of the three theological virtues in Christianity, it is perhaps the most Christian of virtues. The consolation—as Tolkien calls it in his essay, "On Fairy-Stories"—that Christianity offers is not a "happily ever after" life on earth, but the hope for a healing and a grace beyond "the circles of the world," as Aragorn tells Arwen before his own death.[22] "In sorrow we [Men] must go, but not in despair. Behold! we are not bound for ever to the circles of the world, and beyond them is more than memory."

Wisdom

Socrates, according to Plato, was the truest "lover of wisdom" (*philosophia*) and gave his life for this love. Wisdom is perhaps the most consistently esteemed virtue across most world philosophies and religions. In Hebrew the word *chokmah* (המכח) is used for both divine (Prov 3:19) and human (Dan 1:17) wisdom; the *Book of Wisdom* (1st century BC), a work of the Apocrypha attributed to Solomon, is dedicated to this virtue. In Hinduism, wisdom (*prajña*) ultimately leads to becoming one with the Supreme Being (*Brahman*) and enables one to achieve salvation (*moksha*). Wisdom (*sapientia*) is one of the chief virtues of Stoicism, as it is in Buddhism, and is part of the *Dao* in Chinese philosophy. As prudence (*prudentia*), or "practical wisdom," it was to have an important role in shaping Christianity, while *hikmah* (حكمة) is mentioned several times in the Quran as a characteristic of the righteous. While Athena/Minerva embodied wisdom in the Olympian pantheon, in Norse mythology the gods Mimir and Odin are both associated with wisdom.

Given its associations with the high and the learned, one might not expect to find wisdom among the Hobbits. Indeed it is most often associated in Middle-earth with the highest of the Elves and with the Wizards. Gandalf, Elrond, and Galadriel are counted among "the Wise" because they possess *both* knowledge and (through eons of experience) wisdom. But Thorin, on his deathbed, tells Bilbo the Hobbit that he has both some wisdom and some courage blended in just the right amounts. Galadriel likewise tells Frodo that he has enough courage and wisdom to endure the visions shown in her mirror. Wisdom is not the same as knowledge or intelligence in Hellenic philosophy. Socrates explains the difference to the sophist Protagoras in Plato's dialogue of that name: when Protagoras says that it would be "shameful" for him "to say that wisdom (*sophia*) and knowledge (*epistēmē*) are not the best (*kratiston*) thing in human affairs," Socrates responds that "knowledge (*epistēmē*) is a noble (*kalon*) thing, and able to rule the human being; and if one knows what is good and bad, one will not be conquered by anything so as to do anything other than what knowledge commands, but practical wisdom (*phronēsis*) is sufficient help for the human being."[23] Aristotle tends to use *sophia* to mean "theoretical wisdom" while *phronesis* implies "wisdom in action," and it is thus a moral intelligence. Hence Hobbits with little or no formal or scientific learning—like Bilbo, Frodo, and Sam—are still capable of acting wisely, while at least one of "the Wise" (i.e., most learned) of Middle-earth—Saruman—slips from wisdom to folly.

Piety

Saruman willingly gives up his white robes for robes of many colors, while Gandalf the Grey passes through death to become Gandalf the White. White is, of course, a sign of purity and holiness in many cultures, associated with priests, monastics, and saints. In the extended edition of Jackson's film *The Return of the King*, Saruman mocks Gandalf for his "newfound piety." In ancient Greece, piety (*eusebeia*) was seen as an obligation to various institutions, but particularly a religious obligation; one of the charges against Socrates was *asebeia*, "impiety," or offending the gods in some way.[24] In Rome citizens had a moral obligation of piety (*pietas*) toward the family and ancestral gods as well as a legal obligation to make sacrifices to the state gods, including (from Augustus to the adoption of Christianity) the cult of the emperors. In Confucianism, piety (*xiao*) is the duty and respect owed to both one's parents and to dead ancestors, the latter also practiced as far away as pagan Ireland. The early Christians, however, because they could not make public sacrifices to the Roman gods and did not worship the spirits of their ancestors, were breaking Roman law and subject to persecution. After surviving nearly three centuries of such persecution, the now legal Roman Christians practiced their *pietas* toward Christ and his mother, the apostles, and the martyred saints.

Is it possible to have piety in Tolkien's Middle-earth when there are, seemingly, no gods and no religions?[25] If it is, then Frodo is the Hobbit who most demonstrates piety. He shows great filial respect toward Bilbo and Gandalf, loves the Shire deeply, and has learned from the Elves to pay reverence to their stars. Sam learns this piety as well from his master. But despite Tolkien calling *The Lord of the Rings* a "Catholic novel," he is clear that the Third Age of Middle-earth is pre-Christianity. If anything, the virtuous figures in the novel are pious pagans, inspired by Tolkien's love of the pre-Christian, Northern mythologies. Tolkien writes that he saw in *Beowulf*, for example, a "*pietas* which treasures the memory of man's struggles in the dark past, man fallen and not yet saved, disgraced but not dethroned."[26] That same spirit pervades *The Lord of the Rings* and *The Silmarillion*. Philologist and Tolkien scholar Tom Shippey has commented that Tolkien's heroes "are so virtuous that one can hardly call them pagans at all."[27] Yet that is what they remain, "virtuous pagans," at least within "the circles of this world."

Little People

"Against the grain of both ancient and modern paganism," observes Wood, "Tolkien makes the little people of Middle-earth—the seemingly insignificant hobbits and their allies—into his truly exemplary figures."[28] When he first began planning his great Middle-earth mythology, his *legendarium*, as a student at Oxford and as a soldier in the trenches of the First World War, Tolkien envisioned a world of heroic Elves and Men, with battles on an epic scale. Hobbits were certainly not in his thoughts until the 1930s, when he began telling an unrelated tale to his own children about Bilbo Baggins. In a letter from 1956, however, Tolkien admits that *The Lord of the Rings* would never have seen publication had it not been for the public's clamor for "more hobbits" after the success of his first book in 1937: "The 'Little People' floated the whole unwieldy ship, bless them."[29]

The Hobbits go by many names in Middle-earth—they are the Little Folk or Little People, the Halflings and the Shire Folk, the *Periain* or *Periannath* in Gondor, the *Holbytla* ("Hole-dwellers") in Rohan. They have no clear antecedent in any mythology, nor would we expect such humble creatures to play among the gods and the fairies. But Tolkien's faith, and his experiences with the common soldiers who served alongside him in the war, told him not to overlook the virtues of the little people in a big world. "Truly I say to you," Jesus tells his disciples, "just as you have done to the least of these [ἐλαχίστων, *elachistōn*] who are of my family, so have you done to me" (Matt 25:40). Mother Theresa reports that Jesus spoke these words to her when inviting her to found the Missionaries of Charity: "You are I know the most incapable person, weak and sinful, but just because you are that I want to use you, for My Glory!"[30]

Hobbits can themselves be quite provincial, distrusting not only the other Races in Middle-earth but even other Hobbits who live across the Brandywine River. As Dennis Knepp points out, Bilbo Baggins overcomes this provincialism and becomes a true cosmopolitan, caring dearly about Dwarves, Elves, and "the Dunedain" (Aragorn).[31] The philosophy of cosmopolitanism originated among such ancient Greek philosophers as Socrates and Diogenes of Sinope (412–323 BC). It is said that when Diogenes was asked where he came from, he replied, "I am a citizen of the world [*kosmopolitês*]."[32] Alexander the Great is said to have been attracted to the idea of a commonwealth of all peoples, and Polybius argued that the Romans were following Alexander in creating their multiethnic empire. Roman Stoics like Cicero and Seneca adopted a cosmopolitan stance in many of their writings, though the center of their world was the *patria* of Rome to which all citizens owed obligations. Queen Victoria's British Empire exceeded even that of the Romans, but the human cost of importing tobacco, tea, and potatoes was high indeed in the colonies.

Being little in a big world can be one way of describing people who are marginalized socially and politically. While Tolkien certainly enjoyed aspects of white privilege and served in the military of an imperialist power, he wrote about a multicultural secondary world, discussed race relations in that world, and chose to write frequently from the perspective of the little people (Hobbits), of lands threatened by industrialization (the Shire, Fangorn Forest), and of women whose power is dismissed or misunderstood (Éowyn, Galadriel). It would be far off the mark to describe Tolkien as progressive, but it is equally erroneous to dismiss him as an imperialist, a racist, or a sexist (as some critics have done).

As Garcia points out, Thorin at first displays a "'haughty disregard' of hobbits, dismissing them as 'simpletons' and 'food-growers.'"[33] Saruman has this attitude to the very end, mocking them and calling them "urchins." But the wisest of the Wise—Galadriel, Elrond, and Gandalf—do not. "This quest may be attempted by the weak with as much hope as the strong," counsels Elrond. "Yet oft is the course of deeds that move the wheels of the world: small hands do them because they must, while the eyes of the great are elsewhere."[34] Both Bilbo and Frodo offer to take the Ring to the fires of

Mordor, and neither Elrond nor Gandalf are surprised by their valor. "This is the hour of the Shire-folk," declares Elrond, "when they arise from their quiet fields to shake the towers and counsels of the Great."[35]

The Unity of Virtue

An early, anonymous reviewer of *The Lord of the Rings* remarked that all "right-thinking hobbits, dwarves, elves and men" in the novel share only "the warrior's code of courage," while Tolkien "never explains what it is they consider the Good."[36] I hope that the present book has shown that Tolkien's Hobbits have more virtues than just courage, as important as that virtue is. The criticism does beg the question, however, about the good toward which these virtues all point. It is, and has been, a controversial topic among philosophers since the days of Socrates.

In Plato's *Protagoras*, Socrates makes the argument that all virtue is one, that a person cannot possess any of the particular virtues unless one has them all, and that one cannot be called virtuous without having all of the particular virtues.[37] Aristotle agrees to some extent, interpreting Plato's concept of a singular "Good" (*nous*) as the goal of all virtues, "the unmoved first mover," which some (certainly Aquinas) interpret as God.[38] "For [Aristotle], the virtues are not so much the means of happiness, as they are its form," write Hauerwas and Pinches. "It follows . . . that neither can be conceived independently of the other. . . ."[39]

The critique of the theory of the unity of the virtues comes from simple observation: Most people we see exhibiting a virtue do so to a certain degree, not perfecting the virtue, and certainly do not seem to possess *all* the virtues. Christianity offered something of a compromise. There exists a unity of the virtues in God (as in Plato and Aristotle), but after the Fall in the Garden of Eden, men and women are tempted constantly by evil and cannot obtain perfection, or perpetual virtue, in this life. Augustine expressed this concept of unity through his theory of perfected love:

> As to virtue leading us to a happy life, I hold virtue to be nothing else than perfect love of God. For the fourfold division of virtue [i.e. the Cardinal Virtues] I regard as taken from four forms of love. . . . I should have no hesitation in defining them: temperance is love giving itself entirely to that which is loved; fortitude is love readily bearing all things for the sake of the loved object; justice is love serving only the loved object, and therefore ruling rightly; prudence is love distinguishing with sagacity between what hinders it and what helps it. The object of this love is not anything but God, the chief good, the highest wisdom, the perfect harmony.[40]

Aquinas put it in a slightly different way: We are destined to be friends with God, something unthinkable from Aristotle's point of view.[41] Love and friendship, however, seem central to our Hobbits' path of virtuous behavior. Though no single Hobbit possesses all virtues, nor perfects any one of them, their seemingly meandering journeys through Middle-earth lead Frodo, Sam, Merry, and Pippin to the same place—Mordor—and in that evil place there is an unexpected turn to the good for all Middle-earth, a *eucatastrophe*. It is enough to make one laugh *and* cry.

Recovering the Language of Humanity in Society

Another way of interpreting "little people" is to think about children. Tolkien began his Hobbit-talk as stories told to his children, and both he and C. S. Lewis continued to be interested in an academic way about how we write for and educate our children. Both, I have argued, wrote literature that illustrated virtue ethics in a classical educational mode: i.e., they thought stories about virtuous behavior helped inculcate virtue in both children and adults. We have more recently sacrificed traditional virtue ethics, along with religious ethics, in our pluralistic society in favor of "value education."[42] The semantic move from virtues to values weakens ethics in an attempt to be more inclusive, argues the philosopher and education critic Allan Bloom:

> The moral education that is today supposed to be the great responsibility of the family cannot exist if it cannot present to the imagination of the young a vision of a moral cosmos and of . . . the drama of moral choice, a sense of the stakes involved in such choice, and the despair that results when the world is "disenchanted." Otherwise, education becomes the vain attempt to give children "values." . . . [But] values are such pallid things. What are they and how are they communicated? . . . [They] are will-o'-the-wisps, insubstantial, without grounding in experience or passion, which are the bases of moral reasoning. Such "values" will inevitably change as public opinion changes.[43]

Furthermore, when there are no shared goals or vision of the public good, Bloom asks, is the social contract any longer even possible? We are increasingly abandoning Aristotle's view of *paideia*—learning and habituating virtues for personal flourishing and the common good—in favor of technical-instrumental education leading to private wealth for some, argues philosopher Richard Eldridge: "to abandon the cultivation of virtues and instead to teach only in order to produce measurable outcomes is to capitulate to an individualist culture of instrumental control and private satisfactions."[44]

Thankfully, where our modern educational theories have failed, great stories have continued to appeal to the moral imagination of the young. Their "escape"—to Middle-earth and to Narnia, to Hogwarts School of Witchcraft and Wizardry and to the Olympian world of Percy Jackson—is the escape of the prisoner to enchanted worlds where their moral choices *really* matter. When the fate of all of Middle-earth is dependent on the moral choices of one little Hobbit, the reader—young and old—will pay attention to those choices, especially if the story is told well.

William Caxton, England's first printer, published Malory's *Morte D'Arthur* in 1485, in part as a handbook on moral virtue, as he explains in the preface:

> I have followed my copy and set the story down in print with the intent that noble men may read and learn the noble acts of chivalry—the noble and virtuous deeds performed by some knights in days of yore. The story tells how honor came to some knights, and how those that were vicious were often shamed and rebuked. I humbly beseech all noble lords and ladies, and the people of all other estates—whatever their status or degree—that when they read this book, they remember

the good and honest acts and follow their example. . . . Herein can be seen chivalry, courtesy, humanity, fellowship, endurance, love, friendship, cowardice, murder, hate, virtue, and sin. Follow the example of the good and leave the evil, and it shall bring you good reputation and renown.[45]

Tolkien hints that his own fiction performs a similar role, writing in a 1951 letter to the editor Milton Waldman: "Myth and fairy-story must, as all art, reflect and contain in solution elements of moral and religious truth (or error), but not explicit."[46] By not writing religious allegory or overtly preaching morality, Tolkien was able to construct compelling characters whose moral choices came naturally from the action of a good plot. He wrote quest tales—nothing new, in fact, as old as literature itself. But then, his aim was not novelty; it was to help us rediscover a lost language of humanity through the vehicle of the fantastic; or, as he puts it, to illustrate virtues and encourage moral reasoning through the ancient practice of exemplifying them in "unfamiliar embodiment."[47]

Tree and Leaf

Tolkien wrote a very personal allegorical short story called "Leaf by Niggle," about an artist trying to work hard, find purpose in his art, and at the same time be a good neighbor and a good person. Each leaf painted by Niggle was done in great detail. But could he capture the meaning of the entire wood?

After the climactic battle before the Black Gate in *The Lord of the Rings*, and after the coronation of Aragorn as King of Gondor, Gandalf takes Aragorn up into the hills so that he can survey his new kingdom. At this moment Gandalf also tells the king that he will be leaving Middle-earth because his time, the Third Age, is over, and it is the dawn of the Fourth Age, the Age of Man. The Wizard then points out a small tree, just a sapling, but a descendant of Telperion, the Eldest of Trees. Life within a seed may lie sleeping through many long years and none can foretell the time of its awakening, he tells Aragorn. "Remember this. For if ever a fruit ripens, it should be planted, lest the line die out of the world."[48]

Ancient virtues may lay for many years dormant. It does not mean that they are dead. We Hobbits need merely discover them, plant them in new soil, tend our little garden with care, and wait with sunlit hope for them to spring leaf and flower again in a new age.

APPENDIX A

ARISTOTLE'S MORAL VIRTUES

Vice of Excess	Aristotle's Moral Virtues	Vice of Defect
Recklessness	**Courage**	Cowardice
Licentiousness	**Moderation**	Insensibility
Prodigality	**Liberality**	Stinginess
Vulgarity/Crassness	**Magnificence**	Parsimony
Vanity	**Greatness of Soul**	Smallness of Soul
Grasping Ambition	**Ambition**	Lack of Ambition
Irascibility	**Gentleness**	Meekness
Boastfulness	**Truthfulness**	Irony
Buffoonery	**Wittiness**	Dourness
Obsequiousness	**Friendliness**	Surliness
Dourness	**Tact**	Tactlessness
Vengeance	**Justice**	Silent Malice

In ancient Greece, there are the Heroic Age virtues most vividly described by Homer (e.g., *thumos*, "spirit," and *technē*, "skill"), and the virtues of the Classical Age *polis* (in particular Athens) discussed and debated by the playwrights, the philosophers, and the historians. Plato discusses virtues throughout the Socratic dialogues and in *The Laws*, defining four—courage, temperance, justice, and wisdom—as the Cardinal Virtues. Aristotle adapted and expanded Plato's list to come up with the twelve moral virtues in his *Nichomachean Ethics* (ca. 350 BC), and argues that, in order to be virtuous, one has to practice or habituate virtue (*aretē*). Aristotle's virtues are often made to fit his doctrine of the mean, that is, each virtue can be found in the Golden Mean between two vices. There is debate about how to translate some of Aristotle's terms: for example, *megalo-psychia*, which I translate as "greatness of soul," is often translated as "high-mindedness" or "magnanimity." The four Cardinal Virtues of the ancient Greeks and Romans were adopted by medieval philosophers as temperance, fortitude, justice, and prudence.

APPENDIX B

THE CATECHETICAL VIRTUES

Theological Virtues	Cardinal Virtues	Gifts of the Holy Spirit	Fruits of the Holy Spirit
Faith	Prudence	Wisdom	Charity
Hope	Justice	Understanding	Joy
Charity	Fortitude	Counsel	Peace
	Temperance	Fortitude	Patience
		Knowledge	Kindness
		Piety	Goodness
		Fear of the Lord	Generosity
			Gentleness
			Faithfulness
			Modesty
			Self-Control
			Chastity

The Seven Deadly Sins	The Saintly Virtues
Greed	Generosity
Pride	Humility
Envy	Meekness
Sloth	Zeal
Gluttony	Abstinence
Lechery	Chastity
Anger	Patience

The Christian virtues are rooted in the Gospel and developed out of both the Classical and Hebraic traditions. From Saint Thomas Aquinas and church councils came the articulation of the three Theological Virtues, the four Cardinal Virtues, and the Gifts and Fruits of the Holy Spirit. The medieval church developed, over time, the definition of the Seven Deadly Sins and the corresponding Saintly Virtues. These groups of virtues were enshrined in the catechism of the Catholic Church.

APPENDIX C

VIRTUES OF THE EAST AND WEST, ANCIENT AND MEDIEVAL

Grk = Greek

Lat = Latin

OE = Old English, Anglo-Saxon

OFr = Old French

OIr = Old Irish

ON = Old Norse

OW = Old Welsh

San = Sanskrit

HEBREW

These Hebrew virtues are derived from the Torah, from Talmudic commentaries, and from Mussar practices.

Awareness (*zehirut*): "Awareness brings one to enthusiasm [*zerizut*]" (*Avodah Zarah* 20b).

Enthusiasm (*zerizut*): *Zerizut* is variously translated as "enthusiasm," "zeal," or "alacrity."

Generosity (*nedivut*): Generosity, kind-heartedness.

Graciousness (חֶסֶד, *ḥesed* or *chesed*): Early on the word *ḥesed* indicated "loyalty," "fidelity," and even "compassionate love," but in post-Biblical Judaism it came to connote "graciousness," "generosity," "hospitality," or "kindness."

Gratitude (*hakarat ha tov*): Be aware of the good and give thanks for it.

Honor (כבוד, *kavod*): Glory, honor, and respect.

Humility (עֲנָוָה, *anavah*): Humility, modesty, or lowliness of spirit.

Justice (צְדָקָה, *Tzedakah* or *Ṣ'daqah*): *Tzedakah* means literally "justice" or "righteousness," but is often used to describe an act of charity (i.e., a gift given justly).

Love (*ahaba*): The most commonly used word for "love" in the Torah. It is used in contexts of love of God, friendship, sexual love, affection, and desire of various sorts.

Order (*seder*): Each thing in its place.

Patience (*savlanut*): Bearing the burden of a difficult situation.

Person of Integrity (German/Yiddish *mensch*): Literally "a man" or "a human," the term came to describe a person of great strength, honor, and integrity, a person who can be relied on to do the right thing.

Person of Virtue (*tzaddik*): Cognate with the word "saint" in Christianity, the Jewish *tzaddik* denotes the most spiritually and morally righteous member of the community. The *tzaddik* strives to live their entire life in the highest ethical manner as an exemplar to their neighbors.

Strength (הגבורה, *gevurah*): Refers to inner strength.

Trait or **Virtue** (*middah*): Part of the daily Mussar practice is the *cheshbon ha'nefesh*, "accounting of the soul." According to this Jewish ethical movement (begun by

Orthodox Jews in 19th-century Lithuania), there are thirteen virtues or traits (*middot*) that are part of this inner reckoning: humility, gratitude, patience, honor, generosity, kindness, strength, tranquility, trust, enthusiasm, order, awareness, and truth.

Tranquility (*menuchat ha'nefesh*): Rising above the good and the bad.

Trust (*bitachon*): Especially trust of God.

Truth (תֶמֶא, *emet*)

Wisdom (המכח, *chokmah*)

GREEK (Classical Age)

The virtues of Classical Age Greece come almost exclusively from Athens and its famous philosophical teachers: Socrates, Plato, and Aristotle. The historians (Herodotus, Thucydides, and Xenophon) and dramatists (Aeschylus, Euripides, and Sophocles) contributed somewhat to this picture. Plato, in the *Republic* (4.444e) defines virtue as the "health and beauty and well-being of the soul."

Ambition (*philotimia*): Literally "love of honor." One who is ambitious is one who loves honor (*timē*) in the proper measure.

Blessed (*makaria, makarios*): "Blessed" or "supremely happy," a god-given state. Cf. *eudaimonia*, literally "the condition of having a good *daimon*," describing a philosophical happiness attained by man through his own efforts.

Character (*ēthos*): "Ethics" are things that pertain to one's character.

Contemplation (*theōria, theōrein*): For Plato and Aristotle, the act of looking upon something so as to understand it, an understanding that is sought as an end in itself.

Courage (*andreia*): Etymologically related to "man" (*an*), thus could be translated as "a *real* man" or "manliness." The mean whose extremes are the vices of "recklessness" and "cowardice."

Decent (*epieikēs*): Description of those who are "upright" or "equitable," i.e., those who stand for "equity" (*epieikeia*). An *epieikēs* person is one who is decent, fair, equitable, honest, etc.

Divine (*theios*): Adjective relating to "god" (*theos*), thus a "heroic and divine" virtue.

Education (*paideia*): For Aristotle, the actualization of rational powers requires *paideia* in its broadest sense—education, socialization, and apprenticeship. The imitation, training, and the habituation of virtue that are part of proper education is, for Aristotle, central to human flourishing.

Excellence (*aretē*): Originally, the excellence of a noble or brave warrior, in Homer *aretē* is nearly synonymous with courage. Later, with the development of the *polis*, the term *aretē* could connote "civic virtue" and moral qualities other than physical courage. In its broadest sense, excellence is that thing which enables its possessor to perform its own particular function well. In Aristotelian virtue ethics, it is the virtue that makes a man function well in relation to his fellow men.

Friendliness (*philia*): Aristotle uses the same term to describe "friendliness" and "friendship" itself. The mean whose extremes are the vices of "obsequiousness" and "surliness."

Gentleness (*praotēs*): The mean whose extremes are the vices of "irascibility" and "meekness."

Glory (*kûdos*): In the Heroic Age, glory "belongs to the individual who excels in battle or in contest as a mark of recognition by his household and his community."[1] Divine glory, or immortality, is *kleos*.

Good (*agathos*): In Homer, *agathos* usually has military connotations, hence "brave" or "of noble birth." Later, with the development of civic virtues, it came to have a broader meaning. With the definite article, "*the* good," i.e., the goal of all human striving and happiness. Also, *to ariston*, "the highest" or "chief good."

Good Sense (*gnōmē*): Good judgment, sound understanding, etc. Part of *syngnōmē*, "forgiveness, sympathy," and *eugnōmōn*, "kindly, well disposed."

Greatness of Soul (*megalopsychia*): A complete virtue, the sum of all virtues within a person. Also "magnanimity" or "high-mindedness," an appropriate amount of pride. Aristotle may have had Socrates in mind when he described "the Great-Souled Man." The mean whose extremes are the vices of "vanity" and "smallness of soul."

Happiness (*eupraxia*): Both "to act well" (i.e., a good action) and "to be happy," *eupraxia* is, for Aristotle, the principle ingredient in the good life.

Hospitality (*themis*): Hospitality is part of the customary law shared by civilized peoples, particularly that part which dictates the behavior toward strangers and guests. Homeric literature is filled with examples of those who keep and those who break the law of hospitality.

Justice (*dikaiosunē*): Aristotle uses *dikaiosunē* to connote both "justice" in a narrow or particular situation as well as the more general quality of "righteousness" or "honesty," a virtue that regulates all proper conduct within society. Also used to mean "the just" (*to dikaion*) and a "just deed" (*dikaiōma*).

Liberality (*eleutheriotēs*): Generosity or freedom from undue attachment to money. The mean whose extremes are the vices of "prodigality" and "stinginess."

Love: The Greeks had many terms for many types of love, including "friendship" (*philia*), "erotic" or "passionate love" (*eros*), and "affection" (*storgē* and *agápe*). In *The Symposium*, Plato's speakers give many different definitions of *eros*, from the "desire" of the body (*epithumia*) to the "longing" (*orexis*) of the soul.

Magnificence (*megaloprepeia*): Literally "befitting greatness." The mean whose extremes are the vices of "vulgarity" and "parsimony."

Moderation (*sōphrosunē*): The proper disposition toward the bodily desires and pleasures. "Nothing in excess," in the words of the Temple of Apollo at Delphi. The mean whose extremes are the vices of "licentiousness" and "insensibility."

Noble (*kalos*): That which is "fine," both physically and morally beautiful. The opposite is that which is "shameful" (*aischros*). Cf. "the beautiful" (*to kalon*), and "a gentleman" (*kalokagathia*), literally one who is both good and noble.

Piety (*eusebia*): Literally "good reverence." Respect for the gods and for the religious customs of the family, especially burial rites. In *The Iliad*, Priam admonishes Achilles for the desecration of his son's body: "Revere the gods, Achilles [and] remember your own father!" In Sophocles' *Antigone*, a sister's duty to give her brother a proper burial is at odds with the views of a tyrant who believes traitors and rebels do not deserve pious funerals.

Prudent (*pronimos*): That which possesses "prudence" (*phronēsis*) or practical wisdom.

Science (*epistēmē*): Pure science or scientific knowledge, valuable in and of itself as opposed to *technē*, applied science whose value resides in its product. Cf. *theōria*, the mental activity we engage in for its own sake or for the attainment of truth.

Self-restraint (*enkrateia*): Self-control, the capacity to withstand the pull of the bodily pleasures, as opposed to lack of self-restraint (*akrasia*). For Aristotle, an *enkratēs* is a morally strong man.

Self-sufficiency (*autarkeia*): For Aristotle, a happiness defined as a life in need of nothing else.

Shame (*aidōs*): A proper sense of shame is required when confronted with the possibility or evidence of wrongdoing.

Skill (*technē*): The skill, art, or craft that enables a person to produce something. *Technē* is an applied science, as opposed to *epistēmē*.

Spirit, Spiritedness (*thumos*): Θυμός is usually translated as "spirit" or "heart," the seat of both anger and natural courage. In Book IV of *The Republic*, Plato identifies *thumos* (also *thymos*) as one of the three parts of the soul, along with reason and appetite.[2] The spirited part of the soul responds to injustices, both personal and communal, and makes one demand rights, recognition, and honor. It encourages pride and expects esteem for oneself and others deemed worthy. The desire to be recognized as superior to others is *megalothymia*.

Tact (*epidexia*): The mean whose extremes are the vices of "crudity" and "dourness."

Truthfulness (*alētheia*): The mean whose extremes are the vices of "boastfulness" and "irony."

Wisdom (*sophia*): The highest intellectual or philosophical excellence of which the human mind is capable. For both Plato and Aristotle, *sophia* is that which the philosopher ("lover of wisdom") most seeks. "The Wise" (*sōphrōn*) is a self-controlled man who knows well both his limits and his abilities (as Plato often depicts Socrates). He has "soundness of mind" (*sōphrosynē*).

Wittiness (*eutrapelia*): The mean whose extremes are the vices of "buffoonery" and "boorishness."

HINDU

Hindu virtues and other religious and ethical practices in India were collected ca. 400 BC–ca. AD 400 in *The Bhagavad Gita*, part of the Indian war epic, *Mahabharata*. English terms are translation of the Sanskrit.

Action (*karma*): The inescapable force of moral actions toward making one's own destiny.

Compassion (*karuna*): "The sentiment of pathos."

Devotion (*bhakti*): A discipline involving the performance of disciplined action without personal attachment.

Discipline (*yoga*): The spiritual and physical discipline binding one to Krishna's divine purpose. In Hindu culture in India, a "man of discipline" is a *yogī*. In *The Bhagavad Gita*, "disciplined action" is *karmayoga*.

Generosity (*dāna* or *daana*): *Dāna* is the Sanskrit word that indicates the virtue of generosity, charity, or the giving of alms in Indian philosophies and religions.

Knowledge (*jñāna*): Spiritual knowledge of transcendental reality.

Mercy (*daya*): Feeling compassion and wanting to help another person.

Pity (*ghrna*): Revulsion over the suffering of others.

Relinquishment (*tyāga*): Action performed without concern for the fruit of that action.

Renunciation (*sannyāsa*): Giving up action based on desire.

Sacred Duty (*dharma*): *Dharma* represents order, while *adharma* represents chaos.

Wisdom (*prajña*): The highest form of wisdom, intelligence, and understanding in Hinduism.

ROMAN

Roman Republican virtues were identified and defined by a number of writers, including the historians Sallust (ca. 40 BC) and Livy, statesmen like Cato and Cicero, poets like Virgil, and the emperor Augustus. Many of these could pertain to both individuals and the state (in his statuary and in the *Res Gestae*, Augustus presented himself as an embodiment of the virtues of the Roman state) and were stamped on imperial coinage from Augustus on. Panegyrics present the *princeps* (emperor) as the incarnation of all virtues. Since the Roman Empire was a multicultural state, there were many different ideas about virtue circulating, including those of the Stoics and the Christians. Stoicism was one of the most popular of the Hellenistic philosophies in the Empire, especially among Roman aristocrats. While Zeno the Cypriote was the founder of Stoicism, Seneca, Epictetus, and the emperor Marcus Aurelius largely defined Roman Stoicism. The four chief virtues of Stoicism are courage, wisdom, self-control, and justice.

Calmness (*tranquilitas*): "Quietness" or "calmness," a sign of peace.
Clemency (*celementia*): A noble showing of mercy or restraint from punishing one's enemies.
Constancy (*constantia*): This virtue became popular in late Roman naming practices, giving us several generals and emperors named Constans, Constantine, Constantius, etc.
Courage (*virtus*): Literally "manliness," this was a public virtue of the ruling class exemplified by military distinction and holding office. Results in achieving *gloria*.
Discipline (*disciplina*): A military virtue.
Equity (*aequitas*): A mark of fair dealing, calmness of mind.

Fidelity and **Honesty** (*fides*): Keeping faith in relationships, especially between patrons and clients. For Cicero, *fides* represented "a willingness to keep faith and deal honorably with all men at all times."

Fortitude (*fortitudo*): Cicero prefers *fortitudo* to *virtus*.

Friendship (*amicitia*): Being true to one's friends, including clients and patrons, and thus to the state. The opposing vice is *factio*, loyalty to a group/faction rather the state.

Frugality (*frugalitas*): The prudent and judicious management of property. "Parsimony," but other qualities too that should be possessed by a man of moderation.

Generosity (*munificentia*): "Munificence," a benevolent generosity.

Glory (*gloria*): Fame, repute, or accomplishment, usually related to military victory. Confers *dignitas* (prestige) and *auctoritas* (moral authority) upon self and family.

Gratitude (*grātia*): According to Cicero, "Gratitude is not only the greatest of virtues, but the parent of all the others."

Gravity (*gravitas*): Seriousness of purpose.

Greatness of Soul (*magnanimitas*): "Magnanimity" or "high-mindedness."

Justice (*iustitia*): "Righteousness, equity," from *jus* (law).

Leisure (*otium*): A productive leisure or retirement from affairs of state.

Liberality (*liberalitas*): The quality of a free man (*liberalis*) as opposed to a slave (*servus*). Can mean "generosity," but other qualities too that should be possessed by a free man.

Magnanimity (*magnitudo animi*): Literally, "greatness of spirit." Cicero believes magnanimity includes *patientia* and bravery.

Magnificence (*magnificentia*): "Loftiness," "greatness," or "grandeur."

Moderation (*moderatio*): Self control, restraint.

Modesty (*pudicitia*): "Modesty" or "chastity."

Nobility (*nobilitas*): Dignity, nobility of character.

Patience (*patientia*): Also, "tolerance" or "forbearance."

Piety (*pietas*): Fulfillment of religious obligations toward one's parents, ancestors, and gods (e.g., making sacrifices). In the Roman Empire, these obligations were linked with patriotism.

Pity (*misericordia*): "The sorrow of the mind brought about by the sight of the distress of others." Seneca thought pity and pardon were "counterfeit virtues."

Prudence (*prudentia*): A common-sense wisdom. Equivalent of Greek *phronēsis*.

Simplicity (*simplicitas*): Straightforwardness.

Temperance (*temperantia*): A Stoic virtue, sometimes *continentia*.

Wisdom (*sapientia*): Equivalent to Greek *sophia*.

CHINESE

The following Chinese virtues are derived mainly from *The Analects* of Confucius (or *Kongzi*, "Master Kong") and from *The Tao Te Ching* of Lao-Tzu.

Courage (*yong*): Can describe either physical or moral courage.

Courtesy (*gong*): Both courtesy and politeness are implied.

Deference (*rang*): Describes the ceremonious behavior of the gentleman, as in deferring to one another.

Filial Piety (*xiao*): The duty and respect owed toward one's parents and dead ancestors. Reverence connected to Chinese ancestor-worship.

Gentleman (*junzi*): While the term literally means "ruler's son," *junzi* is used in both social and ethical senses. A "noble man" or "exemplary man" are other acceptable translations. The *junzi* was expected to practice six "arts": ritual, music, archery, charioteering, writing, and mathematics. A *junzi* is the opposite of a *xiao ren*, a "small man."

Good Faith (*xin*): A virtue associated often with loyalty (*zhong*) and relationships with friends. Sincerity and trustworthiness are included in this virtue.

Goodness (*shan*): As in "being good at" something; competent or efficient. Used in the technical sense rather than the moral sense.

Humaneness (*ren* or *jen*): The key virtue in *The Analects*, *ren* embraces all the social virtues and summarizes ideally how a human being should act toward other human beings. Kindness, goodness, benevolence, in action not just in thought. Confucius established the importance of this virtue, which bears some semblance to the Christian *agápe*.

Loyalty (*zhong*): Conscientiousness or doing one's best for something or someone.

Men of Quality (*xian*): Admirable men, men of quality or worth ("worthies").

Reciprocity (*shu*): "Do not impose on others what you yourself do not desire." Akin to the Golden Rule.

Reverence (*jing*): The respect owed to one's ancestors, often displayed through ritual (*li*).

Rightness (*yi*): The gentleman (*junzi*) is concerned with what is right, while the small man (*xiao ren*) is concerned with profit.

Sage (*sheng*): A sage or sage-person (*sheng ren*) is one who benefits the people through their practical wisdom.

Understanding (*zhi*): A broad term encompassing understanding, knowledge, awareness, and appreciation. Confucius stressed acquisition of *zhi* through studying (*xue*).

Virtue (*de*): A term with a broad ethical sense, but also a virtue that is specifically Heaven-sent. Early connotations of spiritual power and charisma. In Taoism, *de* is "the *tao* within."

The Way (*dao* or *tao*): As in the Way of One's Father, the Way of the Gentleman, etc. Loosely defined in *The Analects*, this is key virtue in Taoism, where it connotes living in harmony with all things (synonyms: the course, the method, the practice, etc.). *Dao* in Chinese philosophy is the rough equivalent of "being" or "truth" in Western philosophy.

BUDDHIST

The most significant virtues in Buddhism are the ten *Pāramitās* ("Perfections"): energy, equanimity, determination, generosity, good-will, honesty, patience, proper conduct, renunciation, and wisdom. English terms are translations of the Sanskrit.

Ease (*Sukha*): An absence of suffering.

Energy (*Viriya*): Diligence, enthusiasm.

Equanimity (*Upekkhā*): Serenity, not overreacting.

Dharma: The one ultimate reality; also, virtue or righteousness.

Determination (*Adhiṭṭhāna*): Will, resolution.

Generosity (*Dāna*): Giving freely, alms.

Goodwill (*Mettā*): Loving-kindness to all.

Honesty (*Sacca*): Truthfulness.

Karma: An action that is either good or bad and is met with the just reward or punishment.

Nirvana: The ultimate goal of all striving in Buddhism, total extinction of craving.

Patience (*Khanti*): Gentle forbearance.

Proper Conduct (*Sīla*): Virtue, morality.

Saints (*Aryas*): Those who have won the Path, the straight and direct road to *Nirvana*. *Arbat* is the highest kind of saint.

Renunciation (*Nekkhamma*): Giving up worldly desires.

Wisdom (*Paññā*): Understanding, knowledge, or insight.

CELTIC AND GERMANIC

These "barbarian" virtues are derived from early texts in the Celtic and Germanic languages, especially Anglo-Saxon poetry and biblical exegesis, Irish and Norse sagas, and Welsh myth and romances. While the texts date to the Middle Ages and were often preserved by Christian scribes, older indigenous pagan attitudes can often be glimpsed.

Boldness (Gothic *balþei*, OW *blew*, OE *beald, mōdig*, ON *ballr*): Daring, bold, impetuous, but also high-minded and magnanimous.

Courage (OIr *meisnech*, ON *frami*): Keeping one's head, being in control of one's emotions.

Determination (OE *willa*): Denotes strong will, purpose, or determination.

Fellowship (OE *fēolagscipe*): Also "union" or "association."

Generosity (OE *bēaggyfu*, ON *stórmenska*): Literally "ring-giving."

Glory (OE *þrym, wuldor*, ON *hróðr*): Glory and praise.

Grimness (OE *grimness*, ON *grimmr*): The Old English adjective *grimm* can mean either fierce or cruel. Tolkien uses it as a positive description of a warrior's visage or character.

Honesty (OIr *indracus*): Showing integrity.

Honor (OE *ār*, Ir *ainech*, ON *vegr*): The supreme virtue in warrior aristocracies of the early Middle Ages. Other virtues, like boldness, courage, and hospitality, led to achieving or maintaining honor. The Old English word *ār* can mean grace (i.e., "gift"), honor, or mercy. In the Celtic world, "face" (OIr *enech*, Welsh *wyneb*) is a cognate, as in "saving face."

Hospitality (OIr *oígidecht*, ON *risna*): Expected in all aristocratic circles. Guests brought gifts to lords and expected gifts in return. Eating together was a sign of friendship; refusing to do so a sign of hostility. Alcohol was always present and often consumed immoderately, which led to warriors boasting of their deeds. The "feast" (OIr *feis*) is central to aristocratic culture.

Humor: Humor is a personal quality treated as a virtue in much northern European vernacular literature of the Middle Ages. The Norse/Icelandic sagas seem to especially value a wry sense of humor, while Anglo-Saxon poetry celebrates riddles and humorous understatement.

Justice (OIr *cóir*, Welsh *cywir*): Literally "correct," "in accordance with the truth."

Loyalty (OIr *tairisiu*, ON *hollr*): Loyalty was expected to be shown to one's lord and to one's kin. Sometimes these dual loyalties came into conflict. Also "steadfastness."

Spirit (OE *mōd*, OIr *brádach*): The Anglo-Saxon word *mōd* means literally "mood," but can connote heart, pride, spirit, courage, etc. Too much pride is *ofermōd*, "overmastering or destructive pride" (i.e., arrogance), the equivalent of the Greek *hubris*. The Old Irish *brádach* means literally "large-chested," (i.e., a man of spirit).

Wonder (OE *wundor*): In Anglo-Saxon literature a "marvel" or "miracle," but also that quality within one's character (i.e., the ability to marvel at something awesome).

CHRISTIAN

The Christian virtues are rooted in the Gospel and developed out of both the Classical and Hebraic traditions, though Jesus parted ways with Greek and Hebrew thinkers in several instances. Christianity rejects the worldliness implicit in much of the pagan virtues, such as pride, the desire for honor and wealth, and obsession with physical beauty.[3] Christian virtue ethics developed in the exegesis on scripture provided by the Patristic authors, especially Saints Basil, Gregory of Nyssa, and Augustine. Augustine, in *The City of God*, described virtue as "a right ordering of the loves" (*ordo amoris*).

Charity (Lat *caritas*): Jesus's so-called New Commandment, to love others as the Father loved the Son, and as the Son has loved us (by sacrificing His life for us).[4] The Gospel writers used the Greek term *agápe* to describe this selfless love, while later Latin Bibles like the Vulgate employed the word *caritas*. Hence, in English translations we see both "love" and "charity" used.

Empathy (Grk *empátheia*) and **Compassion** (Lat *compassio*): Both words convey feeling the suffering of another. Through the Passion of Christ, God displays His willingness to feel human suffering. Empathy (German *Einfühlung*) is the more modern term, coined in 1908 by the German philosopher Rudolf Lotze as a translation of the Greek *empátheia*.

Faith (Lat *fides*): Faith is, according the Catholic catechism, "the theological virtue by which we believe in God and believe all that he has said and revealed to us. . . ."[5]

Fortitude (Lat *fortitudo*): Firmness and constancy in the pursuit of the good, the resolve to resist temptations and to overcome obstacles in the moral life. That which enables one to conquer fear, even fear of death, and to face trials and persecutions.

Hope (Lat *spes*): Hope is "the theological virtue by which we desire the kingdom of heaven and eternal life as our happiness, placing our trust in Christ's promises and relying not on our own strength, but on the help of the grace of the Holy Spirit."[6]

Justice (Lat *ius, iustus, iustitia*): "The constant and firm will to give their due to God and neighbor," according to the catechism.[7] Justice disposes one to respect the rights of others and to establish in human relationships the harmony that promotes equity with regard to persons and to the common good. *Justitia* conveys both "righteous judgment" and "equitable treatment."

Mercy and **Pity** (Grk *eleos*): The term *eleos* conveys the meaning of both mercy and pity in Greek Christian writings.

Prudence (Lat *prudentia*): Practical wisdom or reason, sober thought. Aquinas follows Aristotle in defining prudence as "right reason in action." Catholic writers sometimes refer to it as *auriga virtutum*, "the charioteer of the virtues," because it guides the other virtues. Prudence, for example, helps us apply moral principles to particular cases without error.

Temperance (Lat *temperantia*): The moral virtue that moderates the attraction of pleasures and provides balance, ensures the will's mastery over biological instincts, and keeps bodily desires within the limits of what is good and honorable. In the New Testament, synonymous with "moderation" and "sobriety."

MUSLIM

These Muslim virtues are derived from the Koran, or Quran (Qur'ān; Arabic القرآن), and the Ḥadīth (canonical oral tradition). The five "pillars," or fundamental obligations, of Islam are the profession of faith (*shahada*), prayer (*salat*), giving alms to the poor (*zakat*), annual fasting during the holy month of Ramadan (*sawm*), and the pilgrimage to Mecca (*hajj*). All terms given in Arabic.

Charity (*sadaqa*): The Quran uses the Arabic word *sadaqa* to connote charity or philanthropy in general, while the obligatory giving of alms is called *zakat*.
Justice (*salihat*): Literally "performing just deeds."
Manliness (*muruwwa*): A pre-Islamic, Arab martial virtue that encompassed courage, generosity, loyalty to kin, and mercy shown to one's enemies.
Saint (*wali*): Literally a "friend" or "protégé," someone "near to God."
Signs of the Prophets (*ayāt*): Facts that deviate from God's customary way of ordering the universe.
Tradition (*sunna*): The Arabic word *sunna* is often translated as "way" or "tradition."

Valor (Arabic *futuwwa*, Persian *javan-mardi*): The Islamic concept of a young man of valor, usually in martial contexts but also (as in Sufism) one striving for virtue.

CHIVALRIC

Chivalric virtues are derived mostly from the medieval romances—especially those of Chrétien de Troyes—and feudal ceremonies of Western Christendom. Chrétien defined the virtues specific to knights as prowess, loyalty, generosity, courtliness, and franchise. Medieval Islam developed parallel concepts of chivalry and courtliness.

Courage (OFr *corage*)

Courtesy (OFr *courtoisie*): Literally "courtliness," i.e., proper conduct or behavior at court. Courtesy went well beyond manners and included the arts of love.

Fidelity (Lat *fidelis*) and **Loyalty** (OFr *loyauté*)

Fortitude (OFr): From Latin *fortitudo*, "strength or courage."

Franchise: Historian Maurice Keen's definition: "the free and frank bearing that is visible testimony to the combination of good birth with virtue."[8] A generosity of spirit, present in "fellowship." Opposite vice is churlishness.

Gallantry: To be described as a *preux chevalier* ("gallant knight") was both an historical aspiration and a literary idealization.

Generosity (OFr *largesse*): The term *largesse* was given to the "magnificent, great-hearted generosity" that was the exclusive domain of the knightly class.[9]

Honor (OFr *onur*)

Justice (OFr *justise*): From Latin *iustitia*.

Magnificence (OFr): Splendor, nobility, or grandeur.

Mercy (OFr *merci*): Pity, followed by an act of kindness to an opponent.

Prowess (OFr *prouesse*): In the romances, love most often inspired a knight's prowess, and prowess in turn inspired courtly love.

Valor: The *preux chevalier* is also expected to be *vaillans* (valiant).

RENAISSANCE

The sources for the following Renaissance virtues include Desiderius Erasmus; Thomas More; Baldesare Castiglione, *The Book of the Courtier*; Niccolo Machiavelli, *The Prince*; Edmund Spenser, *The Faerie Queene*; William Shakespeare; and Ben Jonson, *Cynthia's Revels*. In his *Education of a Christian Prince*, Erasmus describes the qualities of the Christian prince as "wisdom, justice, moderation, foresight, and zeal for the common welfare" and argues that the prince must learn that the teachings of Christ apply to "no one more than to himself." The rediscovery of Plato's writings in the 16th century was also to have a profound impact on European art, literature, and theology.

Benevolence (OFr *benivolence*): Kindliness, or granting a favor (grace).

Boldness (Middle English): Fearlessness, valorous.

Charity (Lat *caritas*)

Civility: "The humanists' idea was that civility, which they called *humanitas*, was itself a virtue and needed to be cultivated," writes James Hankins. "They sought to school *humanitas* into the character of the ruling class by study of the classics, make it part of an educated person's self-concept, and support that self-concept through informal social pressure."[10]

Courage: "Stoutness of courage" is one translation of the Italian Humanist virtue *magnanimità*, while "valiant courage" renders *fortezza*.[11] For Machiavelli, courage is the highest expression of *virtú*.

Elegance (Lat *elegantia*): Tastefulness, refinement, graceful.

Eloquence: Fluency, an expressive style of speaking or writing.

Fortitude

Gentleness

Good Judgment

Grace (Italian *sprezzatura*): In *The Book of the Courtier*, Castiglione cites this as one of the defining virtues of the Renaissance courtier. *Sprezzatura* has no exact English equivalent, but means doing something difficult but making it look easy (i.e., doing it with a cultivated grace or style). Studied carelessness, effortless ease.

Justice

Love of Virtue

Moderation

Piety: Erasmus promoted the concept of learned piety (*docta pietas*), or what he termed the "philosophy of Christ."

Prudence

Temperance

Virtú: "Excellence."

Wit

APPENDIX D

C. S. Lewis and the Tao

In his book *The Abolition of Man* (1944), and later in *Mere Christianity* (1952), C. S. Lewis makes the argument for existence of a universal "Natural Law," which he calls the *Tao*, that is both inherent and taught, with a virtue ethics reflected in most world religious codes and many Western philosophies. He attaches as an appendix to *The Abolition of Man* a number of "Illustrations of the *Tao*," summarized below (I have added other examples in bold):

I   The Law of General Beneficence

"Thou shalt not murder" (Exodus 20:13)

"In Hell I saw . . . murderers" (Old Norse: *Voluspa*)

"Never do to others what you would not like them to do to you" (Confucius, *Analects* 15.23)

"Do to men what you wish men to do to you" (Matthew 7:12)

"Speak kindness . . . show good will (Babylonian: *Hymn to Samas* 5.445)

"Love thy neighbor as thyself" (Leviticus 19:18)

II The Law of Special Beneficence

"Natural affection is a thing right and according to Nature" (Epictetus 3.24)

"Part of us is claimed by our country, part by our parents, part by our friends" (Cicero, *De Officiis* 1.7)

"If any provide not for his own, and especially for those of his own house, he hath denied the faith" (1 Timothy 5:8)

"Be blameless to thy kindred. Take no vengeance even though they do thee wrong" (Old Norse: *Sigdrifumal*, 22)

III Duties to Parents, Elders, and Ancestors

"Honor thy father and thy mother" (Exodus 20:12)

"Your father is an image of the Lord of Creation, your mother is an image of the earth, For him who fails to honor them, every work of piety is in vain. This is the first duty" (Hindu: Janet 1.9)

"Care for parents" (Epictetus 3.7)

"When proper respect towards the dead is shown at the end and continued after they are far away, the moral force of a people has reached its highest point" (Confucius, *Annalects* 1.9)

IV   Duties to Children and Posterity

"Respect the young" (Confucius, *Analects* 9.22)

"Nature produces a special love of offspring" (Cicero, *De Officiis* 1.4)

V   The Law of Justice

"Thou shalt not commit adultery" (Exodus 20:14)

"Thou shalt not steal" (Exodus 20:15)

"To wrong, to rob, to cause to be robbed" (Babylonian list of sins)

"Whoso takes no bribe . . . well pleasing is this to Samas" (Babylonian)

VI   The Law of Good Faith and Veracity

"I have not spoken falsehood" (Ancient Egyptian, "Confession of the Righteous Soul)

"The gentleman must learn to be faithful to his superiors and to keep promises" (Confucius, *Analects* 1.8)

"Thou shalt not bear false witness against thy neighbor" (Exodus 20:16)

"The foundation of justice is good faith" (Cicero, *De Officiis* 1.7)

"I sought no trickery, nor bore false oaths" (*Beowulf*, l. 2738)

"In Hell . . . I saw the perjurers" (Old Norse: *Voluspa*, 39)

VII   The Law of Mercy

"Whoso makes intercession for the weak, well pleasing is this to Samas" (Babylonian)

"I have given bread to the hungry, water to the thirsty, clothes to the naked, a ferry boat to the boatless" (Ancient Egyptian)

"Nature confesses that she has given to the human race the tenderest of hearts, by giving us the power to weep. This is the best part of us" (Juvenal 15.131)

"Blessed are the poor in spirit, for theirs is the kingdom of heaven. Blessed are those who mourn, for they shall be comforted. Blessed are the meek, for they shall inherit the earth" (Matthew 5:3–5)

VIII   The Law of Magnanimity

"To take no notice of a violent attack is to strengthen the heart of the enemy. Vigor is valiant, but cowardice is vile" (Ancient Egyptian: Pharaoh Senusert III)

"Courage has got to be harder, heart the stouter, spirit the sterner, as our strength weakens" (Anglo-Saxon: *Battle of Maldon*, 312)

"Love learning and if attacked be ready to die for the Good Way" (Confucius, *Analects* 8.13)

"Is not the love of Wisdom a practice of death?" (Plato, *Phaedo* 81a)

"He who loves his life loses it" (John 12:25)

Glossary of Philosophical Terms

Aesthetics The branch of philosophy dealing with beauty and things considered beautiful, especially in the arts.

Altruism The ethical theory that people should act on principle or duty rather than for personal advantage.

Applied Ethics A branch of **Moral Philosophy** concerning the application of the general principles of **Normative Ethics** to particularly unique or difficult cases. Medical ethics, business ethics, etc., are types of applied ethics.

Aretaic Ethics The theory, first proposed by Aristotle, that the basis of ethical assessment is character or the disposition of the agent rather than their actions or duties.

Bioethics The application of ethics to the biological sciences, medicine, health care, and related public health policies. Sometime called Biomedical Ethics.

Biological Determinism The theory that our biology determines everything about us, including moral reasoning and emotions.

Consequentialism The ethical theory that judges whether or not an action is right by its consequences. Both **Hedonism** and **Utilitarianism** are consequentialist philosophies. Jeremy Bentham was an early proponent of Consequentialism.

Cynicism The Hellenic philosophy that stressed living a simple, self-sufficient life independent of material things and devoted solely to the pursuit of virtue. Diogenes of Sinope (a contemporary of Plato) and Epictetus were two ancient Cynics.

Deontological Ethics An ethical theory based on following a list of rules or doing one's duty regardless of the consequences. Such duties and obligations include beneficence and non-maleficence, caring for children and parents, honesty, fidelity to friends and spouses, gratitude, reciprocity and fair play, political justice, and duty to other species. Derived from the thinking of Immanuel Kant, who believed that morality was based on a universal and impartial law of rationality.

Emotivism The theory that moral judgments are not a matter of truth but simply an expression of our individual attitudes or emotions.

Epicureanism Used generally to mean the pursuit of pleasure, Epicurus (341–270 BC) strove to avoid pain in the body and trouble in the mind. The Roman poet Lucretius (ca. 99–55 BC) further developed Epicurus's materialist metaphysics in his *De Rerum Natura*, including his theory of atoms.

Epistemology The branch of philosophy that deals with categories of knowledge, how we know what we know.

Ethical Egoism The theory that everyone ought to act to satisfy what they perceive to be in their own best interest, and that it is our ethical duty to do so in order to bring about social harmony and happiness.

Ethics (1) The rules or guidelines for right and wrong conduct; (2) a field of study, often by philosophers and theologians, of moral principles and dilemmas. Ethics in the first sense is often (though not always) used interchangeably with **Morals**.

Ethology The modern study and depiction of character, often specifically animal behavior in its natural environment.

Existentialism The modern philosophy that developed from the anxiety of trying to find meaning in a meaningless world, and the struggle to find personal freedom and authenticity. Søren Kierkegaard, Friedrich Nietzsche, Jean-Paul Sartre, and Simone de Beauvoir are all considered Existentialist philosophers. The writer Albert Camus, who never considered himself a philosopher, defined existentialism as "how to behave when one does not believe in God or reason."

Hedonism The philosophy of pursuing personal pleasure and avoiding personal pain as the highest good.

Human Flourishing A **Naturalist** or **Sociobiological** account of what Aristotle called the good life. A wide range of modern theorists have attempted to identify "flourishing," from the philosopher Alasdair MacIntyre to the socio-psychologist Corey Keyes.

Intuitionist Ethics Or ethical intuitionism, a theory in **Moral Philosophy** that there are real moral principles that can be immediately apprehended through intuition alone and taken as self-evidently true. Henri Bergson, John Rawls, and C. S. Lewis all made use of this ethical theory.

Metaethics The branch of **Moral Philosophy** that asks epistemological questions about ethics itself and questions about the definitions of moral terms like right, wrong, good, bad, killing, lying, etc.

Moral Philosophy The branch of philosophy that contemplates what is right and wrong behavior and explores the nature of morality. Socrates is commonly held to be the founder of moral philosophy, though hardly the first to ask questions about morality.

Moral Relativism The position that what is perceived as right or wrong human action is defined entirely within communities and not subject to judgment from without. Outsiders must respect the rights of these communities as they are based on long-held historical, religious, or cultural beliefs. Moral absolutism and moral realism are antithetical to moral relativism.

Moral Virtue Persisting excellence in being for the good.

Morality A code of conduct that can either be descriptive of what is acceptable by a person or group or universal, i.e., what any rational being should do under the same circumstances.

Morals Or moral principles, the standards of behavior or beliefs that enable people to live cooperatively in groups. Morals often refers to what societies sanction as right and acceptable.

Naturalism Or naturalist ethics, reduces all ethical concepts to concepts of natural science (especially biology and psychology) or sociology. Naturalism derives primarily from the philosophy of G. E. Moore.

Normative Ethics A branch of **Moral Philosophy** concerning the fundamental and universal principles governing how to act, how to live one's life ethically, or what kind of person to be.

Objectivism The view that moral principles have objective reality, whether we recognize these truths or not. These truths are not relative to culture or societal pressures.

Positivism Auguste Comte (1798–1857) is largely responsible for the belief that science should displace theology and metaphysics and be the basis for seeking truth, human action, and governing society. Later called "logical positivism."

Pragmatism A belief that all philosophical concepts should be tested via scientific experimentation, that a claim is true only if it is useful (e.g., contributes to social progress), and that language itself is problematic when trying to get at truth. Founded in late-19th-century America by Charles Sanders Pierce and William James, famous pragmatists include John Dewey, Jane Addams, and Richard Rorty.

Psychological Egoism The theory that all humans, unless they are pathologically abnormal, will always act to their own advantage.

Sociobiology The combination of **Ethology**, evolutionary biology, and sociology to reach a metatheory of human behavior. E. O. Wilson and Richard Dawkins are two of its more famous proponents.

Stoicism The Hellenistic philosophy that argued nothing is worth having in life except the exercise of the virtues.

Teleological Moving toward an ultimate end. Aristotle's ethics, for example, are teleological in that they aim toward an ultimate end, that of human happiness (*eudaimonia*).

Universalizability The theory that if an action is morally right for one person in a given situation then it is right for all people in similar situations.

Utilitarianism The ethical theory that states that the right action is that which benefits the most people. Jeremy Bentham and John Stuart Mill advocated for utilitarianism.

Values Individual beliefs (inherited or taught) that motivate people to act one way or another, that serve as a guide for human behavior. Weighing personal values that conflict with one another or with those of other people leads to ethical decision-making. Values can have inherent worth, be seen as sacred, or be a means to an end.

Virtue Virtues (*aretai*), according to Aristotle, are "excellences" that must be habituated in order to be virtuous. Thus, an Aristotelian definition of the virtuous life is a life of excellence in accord with right reason.

Virtue Ethics A theory of **Moral Philosophy** based on the ethical teachings of Socrates, Plato, and, especially, Aristotle. Focuses on character-building through the practice or habituation of virtuous actions and dispositions. Also called agent-based ethics, character ethics, and areteological ethics.

ACKNOWLEDGMENTS

I would like to thank, for their support of my research, the Judy and Bobby Shackouls Honors College at Mississippi State University; the History Faculty at the University of Oxford; and the Washington International Studies Council. Dr. Michael Boylan, Professor of Philosophy at Marymount University, generously shared his insights on ethics and fiction with me; Dr. Seth Oppenheimer, Associate Dean and Professor of Mathematics (MSU), encouraged my efforts and helped me understand Jewish ethical traditions; and I benefited from conversations with the Philosophy faculty at West Virginia University as well. Thank you to Dean Greg Dunaway (WVU) and Debbie Dunaway for their constant friendship. The Bodleian Library (Oxford), the Georgetown University Library, the Wise Library (WVU), and the Mississippi State University Libraries were essential to my research.

To my Tolkien Reading Group at MSU—Sam, Brady, Delaney, and Liz—thank you for your feedback on the manuscript and for your love of all things Tolkien. Thank you to my colleagues Dr. Tommy Anderson and Dr. Eric Vivier for our Oxford conversations and explorations. To my agent Mark Gottlieb, my publisher Claiborne

Hancock, and my Pegasus editors Mary O'Mara, Meredith Clark, Maria Fernandez, and Victoria Wenzel, thank you for all your hard work and encouragement. Lastly, to my family—my father Donald Snyder, my wife Dr. Renée Baird Snyder, and my daughter Carys Glynne Snyder—thank you for your love and support.

Bibliography

PRIMARY SOURCES

Aristotle. *The Eudemian Ethics*. New York: Oxford University Press, 2011.

———. *Nichomachean Ethics*. Translated and Introduction by Robert C. Bartlett and Susan D. Collins. Chicago: University of Chicago Press, 2011.

———. *Aristotle: Nichomachean Ethics*. Translated and Introduction by Martin Oswald. Upper Saddle River, NJ: Prentice Hall, 1999.

Bentham, Jeremy. *An Introduction to the Principles of Morals and Legislation*. Edited by J.H. Burns. Oxford: Clarendon Press, 1996.

Beowulf. Trans. by Seamus Heaney. New York: Farrar, Straus and Giroux, 2000.

The Bhagavad-Gita. Translated by Barbara Stoler Miller. New York: Bantam, 2004.

Castiglione, Count Baldesare. *The Book of the Courtier*. New York: Penguin, 1976.

Catechism of the Catholic Church. "Part III: Life in Christ," section I, chapter I, article VII. http://www.vatican.va/archive/ccc_css/archive/catechism/p3s1c1a7.htm.

Confucius. *The Analects*. New York: Oxford University Press, 2008.

Conze, Edward (ed. and trans.). *Buddhist Scriptures*. New York: Penguin, 1959.

Hobbes, Thomas. *Leviathan*. New York: Collier Books, 1962.

Homer. *The Iliad*. Translated by Robert Fagle. New York: Penguin, 1998.

Hume, David. *A Treatise on Human Nature*. London: Dover, 2003.

Kant, Immanuel. *Groundwork of the Metaphysics of Morals*. Edited and translated by Mary Gregor. Cambridge: Cambridge University Press, 1998.

———. *Practical Philosophy*. Edited and translated by Mary Gregor. Cambridge: Cambridge University Press, 1996.

Kierkegaard, Søren. *Fear and Trembling*. New York: Penguin, 1986.

Laertius, Diogenes. *Lives of the Eminent Philosophers*. Oxford: Oxford University Press, 2018.

Lewis, C.S. *The Abolition of Man*. New York: HarperCollins, 2015.

———. *The Four Loves*. London: Harcourt, 1960.

———. *Mere Christianity*. London: Fontana, 1955.

Locke, John. *Second Treatise of Government*. New York: HarperCollins, 2015.

Malory, Sir Thomas. *Morte D'Arthur*. Translated by Dorsey Armstrong. Anderson, SC: Parlor Press, 2009.

Mill, John Stuart. *Utilitarianism*. Edited by George Sher. Indianapolis, IN: Hackett, 1979.

Moore, G.E. *Principia Ethica*. London: Dover, 2004.

Nietzsche, Friedrich. *Thus Spoke Zarathustra* (*Also Sprach Zarathustra*, 1883-85). Translated by R. J. Hollingdale. New York: Penguin, 1973.

———. *Beyond Good and Evil* (*Jenseits von Gut und Böse*, 1886). Translated by Walter Kaufman. New York: Vintage, 1966.

———. *The Anti-Christ* (*Der Antichrist*, 1888). Translated by R. J. Hollingdale. New York: Penguin, 1968.

———. *The Will to Power* (*Der Wille zur Macht*, 1901). Translated by Walter Kaufmann and R. J. Hollingdale. New York: Vintage, 1967.

———. *Ecce Homo* (1908). Translated by R. J. Hollingdale. New York: Penguin, 1992.

Plato. *The Essential Plato*. Translated by Benjamin Jowett. New York: Quality Paperback Book Club, 1999.

———. *Protagoras*. Translated by C.C.W. Taylor. Oxford: Oxford University Press, 2009.

———. *The Symposium*. Translated by Seth Bernardette. Chicago: University of Chicago Press, 2001.

———. *The Republic*, second edition. Translated by Allan Bloom. New York: Basic Books, 1991.

The Tanakh. "Sacred Writings Vol. I: Judaism." New York: Jewish Publication Society/Book-of-the-Month Clubs, 1992.

Tolkien, J. R. R. *The Hobbit*. Boston: Houghton Mifflin, 2001.

———. "On Fairy-Stories." In *Essays Presented to Charles Williams* (1947). Republished in. Verlyn Flieger and Douglas A. Anderson (eds). *Tolkien on Fairy-Stories*. London: HarperCollins, 2014.

———. *The Lord of the Rings*. Fiftieth Anniversary Edition. Boston: Houghton Mifflin, 1994.

———. *The Tolkien Reader*. New York: Ballantine Books, 1966.

———. *The Silmarillion*. Edited by Christopher Tolkien. Boston: Houghton Mifflin, 1977.

———. *The Letters of J.R.R. Tolkien*. Edited by Humphrey Carpenter. Boston: Houghton Mifflin, 2000.

———. *The Children of Húrin*. Edited by Christopher Tolkien. Boston: Houghton Mifflin, 2007.

———. *The Fall of Arthur*. Edited by Christopher Tolkien. Boston: Houghton Mifflin, 2013.

SECONDARY LITERATURE

Abels, Richard and Phyllis Culham. "Roman Republican Virtues." https://www.usna.edu/Users/history/abels/hh205/romevirt.htm.

Adams, Robert Merrihew. *A Theory of Virtue: Excellence in Being for the Good*. Oxford: Clarendon Press, 2006.

Annas, Julia. *The Morality of Happiness*. Oxford: Oxford University Press, 1993.

Anscombe, G.E.M. "Modern Moral Philosophy." *Philosophy* 33 (1958). Reprinted in Crisp and Slote, eds., *Virtue Ethics*, 26–44.

Athanassoulis, Nafsika. *Virtue Ethics*. London: Bloomsbury, 2013.

Barton, Carlon A. *Roman Honor: The Fire in the Bones*. Berkeley: University of California Press, 2001.

Bassham, Gregory, and Eric Bronson, eds. *'The Hobbit' and Philosophy*. Hoboken, NJ: John Wiley & Sons, 2012.

Beauchamp, Tom L. *Philosophical Ethics: An Introduction to Moral Philosophy*. New York: McGraw-Hill, 1982.

Beauregard, David N. *Virtue's Own Feature: Shakespeare and the Virtue Ethics Tradition*. Newark, NJ: University of Delaware Press; London: Associated University Presses, 1995.

Benedict XVI. *Charity in Truth (Caritas in Veritate)* (Encyclical Letter). San Francisco: Ignatius Press, 2009.

Bloom, Allan. *The Closing of the American Mind*. New York: Simon and Schuster, 1987.

Bondi, Roberta. *To Love as God Loves*. Philadelphia: Fortress Press, 1989.

Boyd, Craig A. "Nolo Heroizari: Tolkien and Aquinas on the Humble Journey of Master Samwise." *Christianity & Literature* 68, no. 4 (2019). https://doi.org/10.1177/0148333119827022.

Boylan, Michael. *Basic Ethics*. 2nd ed. Upper Saddle River, NJ: Prentice Hall, 2009.

———. *Fictive Narrative Philosophy: How Fiction Can Act as Philosophy*. New York: Routledge, 2019.

———. *The Good, the True and the Beautiful*. New York: Continuum, 2008.

———. *A Just Society*. Lanham, MD, and Oxford: Rowman & Littlefield, 2004.

Brady, Michael and Duncan Pritchard, eds. *Moral and Epistemic Virtues*. Oxford: Blackwell, 2003.

Buckley, F.H. *The Morality of Laughter*. Ann Arbor, MI: University of Michigan Press, 2003.

Bull, Malcolm. *On Mercy*. Princeton, NJ: Princeton University Press, 2019.

Carpenter, Humphrey. *The Inklings*. London: HarperCollins, 1997.

Casey, John. *Pagan Virtue: An Essay in Ethics*. Oxford: Clarendon Press, 1990.

Childress, James F., and John MacQuarrie, eds. *The Westminster Dictionary of Christian Ethics*. Philadelphia: Westminster Press, 1986.

Chittester, Sr Joan. *God's Tender Mercy: Reflections on Forgiveness*. New London: CT: Twenty-Third Publications, 2010.

Crisp, Roger and Michael Slote, eds. *Virtue Ethics*. Oxford: Oxford University Press, 1997.

Curzer, Howard J. *Aristotle and the Virtues*. New York: Oxford University Press, 2012.

Dancy, Jonathan. *Moral Reasons*. Oxford: Blackwell, 1993.

Darling-Smith, Barbara, ed. *Courage*. Notre Dame, IN: University of Notre Dame Press, 2002.

Darwall, Stephen, ed. *Consequentialism*. Oxford: Blackwell, 2003.

———. *Deontology*. Oxford: Blackwell, 2003.

Davidson, James. *Courtesans & Fishcakes: The Consuming Passions of Classical Athens*. New York: HarperCollins, 1997.

Eagleton, Terry. *Radical Sacrifice*. New Haven, CT: Yale University Press, 2018.

Fimi, Dimitra, and Thomas Honnegar, eds. *Sub-Creating Arda: World-Building in J.R.R. Tolkien's Work, its Precursors and its Legacies*. Zurich: Walking Tree, 2019.

Fink, Charles K. "The Cultivation of Virtue in Buddhist Ethics." *Journal of Buddhist Ethics* 20 (2013): 668–701.

Finley, Moses I. *Ancient Slavery and Modern Ideology*. Edited by Brent D. Shaw. Princeton, NJ: Markus Wiener, 1998.

Flescher, Andrew Michael. *Heroes, Saints, and Ordinary Morality*. Washington, DC: Georgetown University Press, 2003.

Flieger, Verlyn. *There Would Always be a Fairy Tale: More Essays on Tolkien*. Kent, OH: Kent State University Press, 2017.

Foot, Phillippa. *Natural Goodness*. Oxford: Oxford University Press, 2001.

Garth, John. *Tolkien and the Great War: The Threshold of Middle-earth*. Boston: Houghton Mifflin, 2003.

Gert, Bernard. *Common Morality: Deciding What to Do*. Oxford: Oxford University Press, 2004.

Gordon, John-Stewart, ed. *Morality and Justice: Reading Boylan's 'Just Society.'* Lanham, MD: Rowman & Littlefield, 2009.

Graham, Gordon. *Eight Theories of Ethics*. London: Routledge, 2004.

———. *Evil and Christian Ethics*. Cambridge: Cambridge University Press, 2001.

Guinlock, James. *Rediscovering the Moral Life*. Buffalo, NY: Prometheus Books, 1993.

Halbertal, Moshe. *On Sacrifice*. Princeton, NJ: Princeton University Press, 2012.

Hammond, Wayne G. and Christina Scull. *'The Lord of the Rings': A Reader's Companion*. Boston: Houghton Mifflin, 2005.

Hansen, William, ed. and trans. *The Book of Greek and Roman Folktales, Legends, and Myths*. Princeton, NJ and Oxford: Princeton University Press, 2017.

Harris, John. *How to be Good: The Possibility of Moral Enhancement*. Oxford: Oxford University Press, 2016.

Hauerwas, Stanley, and Charles Pinches. *Christians among the Virtues: Theological Conversations with Ancient and Modern Ethics*. Notre Dame, IN: University of Notre Dame Press, 1997.

Hawley, John Stratton, ed. *Saints and Virtues*. Berkeley, CA: University of California Press, 1987.

Hazlitt, Henry. *The Foundations of Morality*. Princeton, NJ: D. Van Nostrand Company, 1964.

Hill, Susan E. *Eating to Excess: The Meaning of Gluttony and the Fat Body in the Ancient World*. Oxford: Praeger, 2011.

Hinman, Lawrence M. *Ethics: A Pluralistic Approach to Moral Theory*. 4th ed. Boston: Wadsworth, 2008.

Irwin, Terence. *The Development of Ethics: A Historical and Critical Study. Volume I: From Socrates to the Reformation*. Oxford: Oxford University Press, 2007.

———. *The Development of Ethics: A Historical and Critical Study. Volume II: From Suarez to Rousseau*. Oxford: Oxford University Press, 2008.

Ivanhoe, Philip J. *Ethics in the Confucian Tradition: The Thought of Mengzi and Wang Yangming*. 2nd edition. Indianapolis, IN: Hackett, 2002.

Jackson, Timothy P. *Love Disconsoled: Meditations on Christian Charity*. Cambridge: Cambridge University Press, 1999.

———. *Political Agape: Christian Love and Liberal Democracy*. Grand Rapids, MI: William B. Eerdman's, 2015.

Kaeuper, Richard W. *Chivalry and Violence in Medieval Europe*. Oxford: Oxford University Press, 2006.

Kagan, Shelly. *Normative Ethics*. Boulder, CO: Westview Press, 1998.

Kane, Robert. *Ethics and the Quest for Freedom*. Cambridge: Cambridge University Press, 2010.

Keen, Maurice. *Chivalry*. New Haven, CT: Yale University Press, 1984.

Kort, Wesley A. *Reading C.S. Lewis: A Commentary*. Oxford: Oxford University Press, 2016.

Kruschwitz, Robert B. and Robert C. Roberts, eds. *The Virtues: Contemporary Essays on Moral Character*. Belmont, CA: Wadsworth, 1987.

Lasley, Thomas J. *Teaching Peace: Toward Cultural Selflessness*. London: Bergin & Garvey, 1994.

Lee, Stuart D., ed. *A Companion to J.R.R. Tolkien*. Oxford: Wiley Blackwell, 2014.

Leontsini, Eleni. "The Motive of Society: Aristotle on Civic Friendship, Justice, and Concord." *Res Publica* 19, no. 1 (2013): 21–35.

Lovin, Robin W. *Christian Ethics: An Essential Guide*. Nashville: Abingdon Press, 2000.

MacIntyre, Alasdair. *After Virtue*. 3rd ed. Notre Dame, IN: University of Notre Dame Press, 2015.

———. *Dependent Rational Animals: Why Human Beings Need the Virtues*. Chicago: Open Court, 2001.

Markos, Louis. *On the Shoulders of Hobbits: The Road to Virtue with Tolkien and Lewis*. Chicago: Moody Publishers, 2012.

Massey, Irving. *Find You the Virtue: Ethics, Image, and Desire in Literature*. Fairfax, VA: George Mason University Press, 1987.

McIntosh, Jonathan S. *The Flame Imperishable: Tolkien, St. Thomas, and the Metaphysics of Faërie*. Kettering, OH: Angelico Press, 2017.

Meri, Josef W., ed. *Medieval Islamic Civilization: An Encyclopedia*. 2 vols. New York: Routledge, 2006.

Morinis, Alan. *Accounting of the Soul: Cheshbon Ha'Nefesh*. Jewish Pathways, 2007.

Munteanu, Dana LaCourse. *Tragic Pathos: Pity and Fear in Greek Philosophy and Tragedy*. New York: Cambridge University Press, 2012.

Murphy, Jeffrie G., and Jean Hampton. *Forgiveness and Mercy*. New York: Cambridge University Press, 1988.

Outka, Gene. *Agape: An Ethical Analysis*. New Haven, CT: Yale University Press, 1972.

Pangle, Lorraine Smith. *Aristotle and the Philosophy of Friendship*. Cambridge: Cambridge University Press, 2003.

Pellowski, Anne. *The World of Storytelling*. Expanded and revised edition. New York: The H.W. Wilson Company, 1990.

Pojman, Louis P. *Ethical Theory: Classical and Contemporary Readings*. Belmont, CA: Wadsworth, 1989.

Post, Stephen G. *A Theory of Agape*. Lewisburg, PA: Bucknell University Press, 1990.

Putman, Daniel. "Psychological Courage." *Philosophy, Psychiatry, & Psychology* 4, no. 1 (March 1997): 1–11.

Rabieh, Linda R. *Plato and the Virtue of Courage*. Baltimore, MD: Johns Hopkins University Press, 2006.

Rateliff, John D. *A Brief History of 'The Hobbit.'* London: HarperCollins, 2015.

Ridley, Matt. *The Origins of Virtue: Human Instincts and the Evolution of Cooperation*. New York: Penguin, 1996.

Rozema, David. "*The Lord of the Rings*: Tolkien, Jackson, and 'The Core of the Original.'" *Christian Scholar's Review* 37, no. 4 (2008): 427–445.

Schmid, W. Thomas. "The Socratic Conception of Courage." *History of Philosophy Quarterly* 2, no. 2 (1985): 113–29.

Scull, Christina and Wayne G. Hammond. *The J.R.R. Tolkien Companion and Guide: Reader's Guide*. Boston: Houghton and Mifflin, 2006.

Shaw, Brent D., ed. and trans. *Spartacus and the Slave Wars: A Brief History with Documents*. Boston: Bedford/St Martin's, 2001.

Singer, Amy. *Charity in Islamic Societies*. Cambridge: Cambridge University Press, 2009.

Snyder, Christopher A. *The Making of Middle-earth*. New York: Sterling, 2013.

Sober, Elliott and David Sloan Wilson. *Unto Others: The Evolution and Psychology of Unselfish Behavior*. Cambridge, MA: Harvard University Press, 1998.

Statman, Daniel, ed. *Virtue Ethics*. Edinburgh: Edinburgh University Press, 1997.

Sternberg, Rachel Hall, ed. *Pity and Power in Ancient Athens*. New York: Cambridge University Press, 2005.

Swanton, Christine. *Virtue Ethics: A Pluralistic View*. Oxford: Oxford University Press, 2003.

Szostak, Rick. *Unifying Ethics*. Lanham, MD: University Press of America, 2005.

Templeton, Sir John. *Agape Love: A Tradition Found in Eight World Religions*. Philadelphia: Templeton Foundation Press, 1999.

Tigner, Steven S. "Cultivating Virtue?" *Journal of Education* 182, no. 2 (2000): 1–20.

Urmson, J.O. "Saints and Heroes." In *Essays in Moral Philosophy*. Seattle: University of Washington Press, 1958.

Wallace-Hadrill, Andrew. "The Emperor and His Virtues." *Historia: Zeitschrift Für Alte Geschichte* 30, no. 3 (1981): 298–323. www.jstor.org/stable/4435768.

Wilburn, Josh. "Courage and the Spirited Part of the Soul in Plato's *Republic*." *Philosopher's Imprint*, 15, no. 26 (October 2015): 1–21.

Wickham, Chris. *The Inheritance of Rome: Illuminating the Dark Ages 400-1000*. New York: Viking /Penguin, 2009.

Williams, Gardner. *Humanistic Ethics*. New York: Philosophical Library, 1951.

Wilson, E.O. *On Human Nature*. Cambridge, MA: Harvard University Press, 2004.

Wolfe, Regina Wentzel, and Christine E. Gudorf, eds. *Ethics and World Religions: Cross-Cultural Case Studies*. Maryknoll, NY: Orbis Books, 1999.

Wood, Ralph C. *The Gospel According to Tolkien*. Louisville, KY: Westminster John Knox Press, 2003.

———. "Review Essay: Following the Many Roads of Recent Tolkien Scholarship." *Christianity and Literature* 54, no. 4 (summer 2005): 587–608.

———. ed. *Tolkien Among the Moderns*. Notre Dame, IN: University of Notre Dame Press, 2015.

Yao, Xinzhong. *Confucianism and Christianity: A Comparative Study of Jen and Agape*. Brighton: Sussex Academic Press, 1996.

Yu, Jiyuan. "Virtue: Confucius and Aristotle." *Philosophy East and West* 48, no. 2 (April 1998), 323–47.

Zafiropoulos, Christos A. *Ethics in Aesop's Fables: The 'Augustana' Collection*. Leiden: Brill, 2001.

Zaleski, Philip, and Carol Zaleski. *The Fellowship: The Literary Lives of the Inklings*. New York: Farrar, Straus and Giroux, 2016.

INTERNET RESOURCES

Ethics Unwrapped, University of Texas at Austin (https://ethicsunwrapped.utexas.edu).

Honor Ethics: Devoted to the Study of Honor as an Ethical Value (https://honorethics.org/about/).

The Stanford Encyclopedia of Philosophy (https://plato.stanford.edu).

ENDNOTES

PREFACE

1 *The Lord of the Rings* (published originally, against Tolkien's wishes, as three separate novels—*The Fellowship of the Ring, The Two Towers,* and *The Return of the King*) currently stands as the number one best-selling single novel of all time with over 150 million copies sold worldwide. *The Hobbit* is at number four with over 100 million copies sold.

2 Not all scholars are comfortable with the practice of apologue, or using fictive narrative to teach ethics. See, however, Michael Boylan, *Fictive Narrative Philosophy: How Fiction can Act as Philosophy* (New York: Routledge, 2019), esp. ch. 6.

3 See Josef Pieper, "Tradition: The Concept and its Claim on Us," *Modern Age* 36, no. 3 (Spring 1994).

4 See especially Gregory Bassham and Eric Bronson (eds.), *'The Hobbit' and Philosophy* (Hoboken, NJ: John Wiley & Sons, 2012).

5 Christopher A. Snyder, *The Making of Middle-earth: A New Look Inside the World of J.R.R. Tolkien* (New York: Sterling, 2013).

6 Aristotle's Golden Mean is a near-equivalent to Confucius's *yi* and Buddhism's Middle Way.

7 Julia Annas, *The Morality of Happiness* (Oxford: Oxford University Press, 1993), 5.

1: TENDING YOUR GARDEN

1 J. R. R. Tolkien, *The Lord of the Rings* (Boston: Houghton Mifflin, 2004), 1. Hereafter *LOTR*.

2 *LOTR*, 681.

3 *LOTR*, 358.

4 C. S. Lewis, *The Four Loves* (London: HarperCollins, 1960), 116–17.

5 Note that the tyrants Morgoth, Sauron, and Saruman all destroy trees and other living things to increase their power, while Aragorn, Faramir, and Treebeard all restore trees and gardens in their rule. Bombadil is wed to a nature spirit, Goldberry, daughter of the River.

6 *LOTR*, 48. In a 1971 letter to Roger Lancelyn Green, Tolkien claims that hobbits are "a diminutive branch of the human race" (Tolkien, *Letters*, 406).

7 *LOTR*, 1–16

8 J. R. R. Tolkien, *The Hobbit* (Boston: Houghton Mifflin, 2001), 312.

9   See Xinzhong Yao, *Confucianism and Christianity: A Comparative Study of* Jen *and* Agape (Brighton: Sussex Academic Press, 1996), 206; and Philip J. Ivanhoe, *Ethics in the Confucian Tradition: The Thought of Mengzi and Wang Yangming*, second edition (Indianapolis, IN: Hackett, 2002). In the Western tradition we might call such transmission a liberal education. "Why, then, do we educate our children in the liberal studies?" asks Seneca. "It is not because they can bestow virtue, but because they prepare the soul for the reception of virtue" (*Epistle* 88).

10   *The Epic of Gilgamesh*, trans. E.A. Speiser (Princeton, NJ: Princeton University Press, 1969).

11   *LOTR*, 901.

2: HUMILITY

1   *The Hobbit*, 4.

2   Echoed, for example, in Genesis 18 and Job 10:19. See Douglas Kindschi, "Coming from the earth: humus, humanity, humility," *Interfaith Insight* (9 Sept 2017), B1.

3   *Epic of Gilgamesh*, Tablet I. This is the tyrannical behavior that Samuel predicts will happen if the Israelites get their wish of having a king rule over them like other nations: see I Samuel 8.

4   Homer, *The Iliad*, trans. by Robert Fagles (New York: Penguin, 1998), Book 2, ll. 285-316.

5   See "Thersites: An Unbridled Tongue," *Kosmos* (2016): https://kosmossociety.chs.harvard.edu/?p=23541.

6   Aristotle, *Nicomachean Ethics* 4.3.

7   Matthew 5:3-11. *New Revised Standard Version, Catholic Edition* (San Francisco: HarperCollins, 2007). Cf. Luke 6:20–26.

8   Augustine, *Letters* 118:22.

9   Aquinas, *Summa Theologiae* II-II.161.1, ad. 1. Aquinas is here commenting on the definition of Isidore of Seville (560–636). See Craig A. Boyd, "*Nolo Heroizari*: Tolkien and Aquinas on the Humble Journey of Master Samwise," *Christianity & Literature* (2019), https://doi.org/10.1177/0148333119827022.

10   Aquinas, *Summa*, II-II.161.1. See Laura Garcia, "Pride and Humility in *The Hobbit*," in Bassham and Bronson (eds.), *'The Hobbit' and Philosophy*, 74–89 (83).

11   Lewis, "The Necessity of Chivalry," in C. S. Lewis, *Present Concerns* (London: Harcourt, 1986), 13–16.

12   Malory, *Morte D'Arthur*, book 21, chap. 12. For further discussion, see Chapter Nine below.

13   Tolkien, "*Beowulf*: The Monsters and the Critics," 118.

14   A divergence from the text—and, in my, opinion, a misstep—that Peter Jackson makes in his *Hobbit* films. In Tolkien's book, Bilbo only fights spiders (to save the Dwarves) and is knocked unconscious during the Battle of the Five Armies before seeing combat.

15   *The Hobbit*, 246. See the warning of Paul in Philippians 2: "Do nothing out of selfish ambition or vain conceit. Rather, in humility value others above yourselves, not looking to your own interests but each of you to the interests of the others."

16   Tolkien, *Letters*, 327.

17   Boyd, "*Nolo Heroizari*," 2.

18   Boyd, "*Nolo Heroizari*," 3.

19   Ralph C. Wood, "Review Essay: Following the Many Roads of Recent Tolkien Scholarship," *Christianity and Literature* 54, no. 4 (Summer 2005): 587–608 (601).

20   Especially in *The Anti-Christ* (*Der Antichrist*, 1888) and the essay "The Will to Power" (first published in 1901 from the author's notes 1883–88).

3: COURAGE

1   For a discussion of virtue ethics in the military, see Peter Olsthoorn, "Courage in the Military: Physical and Moral," *Journal of Military Ethics* 6, no. 4 (2007): 270–279, DOI: 10.1080/15027570701755471.

2   See Andrew Michael Flescher, *Heroes, Saints, and Ordinary Morality* (Washington, DC: Georgetown University Press, 2003); and Andrei G. Zavaliy and Michael Aristidou, "Courage: A Modern Look at an Ancient Virtue," *Journal of Military Ethics* 13, no. 2 (2014): 174–189, DOI: 10.1080/15027570.2014.943037.

3   For discussion of broader definitions of courage, see the essays in Barbara Darling-Smith, ed., *Courage* (Notre Dame, IN: University of Notre Dame Press, 2002).

4   See Geoffrey Hill, "Courage in Shakespeare," in Darling-Smith, ed., *Courage*, 54–64.

5   See Jonathan Shay, *Achilles in Vietnam: Combat Trauma and the Undoing of Character* (New York: Atheneum Books, 1994); Philip J. Ivanhoe, "The Virtue of Courage in the *Mencius*," in Darling-Smith, ed., *Courage*, 65–79; and Barbara Graziosi and Johannes Haubold, "Homeric Masculinity: ΗΝΟΡΕΗ and ΑΓΗΝΟΡΙΗ," *The Journal of Hellenic Studies* 123 (2003): 60-76. doi:10.2307/3246260. Both Odysseus and Penelope, however, also display another kind of courage we might term endurance or the will to resist: see W. Thomas Schmid, "The Socratic Conception of Courage," *History of Philosophy Quarterly* 2, no. 2 (1985): 113–29.

6   Alasdair MacIntyre, *After Virtue*, 3rd edition (Notre Dame, IN: University of Notre Dame Press, 2015), 122–24.

7   This distinction is made in Plato's *Laches*, where Socrates (who had fought heroically at the Battle of Delium) is cast as the true image of the harmony of both physical and moral courage. Like the Greek *andreia*, the Chinese word *yong* can describe either physical or moral courage. The Confucian thinker Mengzi, however, distinguishes between "petty courage" (*xiao yong*), such as protecting one's personal honor, and "great courage" (*da yong*), the cultivation of a moral or spiritual energy that helps one to pursue the Good. See Ivanhoe, "The Virtue," 67–68.

8   Other types of courage that have been posited include political, spiritual, and psychological. See Daniel Putman, "Psychological Courage," *Philosophy, Psychiatry, & Psychology* 4, no. 1 (March 1997): 1–11.

9   Plato, *Protagoras*, 360d; idem., *The Republic*, Book 4, 429–30, 440–42; idem., *Laches*, 194e–195a. For Plato, "weakness of will" (*akrasia*) is to act contrary to wisdom and the inability to act as one thinks right. For discussion, see Linda R. Rabieh, *Plato and the Virtue of Courage* (Baltimore, MD: Johns Hopkins University Press, 2006); and Josh Wilburn, "Courage and the Spirited Part of the Soul in Plato's *Republic*," *Philosopher's Imprint* 15, no. 26 (October 2015): 1–21.

10   Aristotle, *Nicomachean Ethics*, 2.5, 3.6–7.

11   Jamie Carlin Watson, "Out of the Frying Pan: Courage and Decision Making in Wilderland," in Bassham and Bronson, 218–34.

12   Laura Garcia, "Pride and Humility in *The Hobbit*," in Bassham and Bronson, 74–89 (74).

13   *The Hobbit*, 40.

14   *The Hobbit*, 170–74. "He felt a different person, and much fiercer and bolder in spite of an empty stomach, as he wiped his sword on the grass and put it back in its sheath" (170).

15   *The Hobbit*, 233.

16   Flescher, *Heroes*, 172.

17   See Garcia, "Pride and Humility," 87 n5.

18   *LOTR*, 24.

19   *LOTR*, 62. "I should like to save the Shire, if I could. . . ."

20   *LOTR*, 324–25.

21   *LOTR*, 777.

22   *LOTR*, 755–56.

23   *LOTR*, 270.

24   *LOTR*, 735, 901. The Ring tempts Sam here to be "Hero of the Age, striding with a flaming sword across the darkened land," commanding armies that could win him rule of Mordor, whence he would turn the whole valley into a garden of flowers and fruit-bearing trees. Love of his master and "plain hobbit-sense" save him from these illusions.

25   *LOTR*, 941.

26   Written on April 16, 1956, to H. Cotton Minchin. See, for commentary, John Garth, "Sam Gamgee and Tolkien's batmen," https://johngarth.wordpress.com/2014/02/13/sam-gamgee-and-tolkiens-batmen/ (posted February 13, 2014): "the fear, the resourcefulness, the demoralisation, the courage, the sorrow, the innocent laughter in the face of dreadful odds: all these things he had known, and he infused his fiction with them."

27   See, for example, George Kateb, "Courage as a Virtue," *Social Research* 71, no. 1 (Spring 2004): 39–72: "Courage is an impossible subject" (39).

28   Aquinas, *Summa*, 2a2ae, 128, 6.

29   J. R. R. Tolkien, "*Beowulf*: The Monsters and the Critics," 103–30 (114–15), reprinted in Seamus Heaney (trans.), *Beowulf*.

30   Tolkien, "*Beowulf*," 117. See also Tom Shippey, "Tolkien and 'that great northern spirit,'" in Catherine McIlwaine, *Tolkien: Maker of Middle-earth* (Oxford: Bodleian Library, 2018), 58–69.

31   Ker, *The Dark Ages*, 57.

32   For discussion of the virtues of Éowyn and Éomer, Aragorn and Faramir, see chapter nine.

33   See Christopher Tolkien's conjecture about his father's plans for the narrative in J. R. R. Tolkien, *The Fall of Arthur*, Christopher Tolkien, ed. (Boston: Houghton Mifflin, 2013).

34   Tolkien, "*Beowulf*," 115. See Michael D.C. Drout, "A Spliced Old English Quotation in 'Beowulf: The Monsters and the Critics,'" *Tolkien Studies 3* (2006): 149–52.

35   Tolkien, "*Beowulf*," 115, 119.

36   Ralph C. Wood, "Review Essay: Following the Many Roads of Recent Tolkien Scholarship," *Christianity and Literature* 54, no. 4 (Summer 2005): 587–608 (594).

37   Letter to his son Christopher (29 November 1943): Tolkien, *Letters*, 74.

38   C. S. Lewis, *Mere Christianity* (London: Fontana, 1955), 68–69. This is fairly consistent with Socrates's view in Plato's *Republic*. For discussion of the social good of private virtue, see Christine Swanton, *Virtue Ethics: A Pluralistic View* (Oxford: Oxford University Press, 2003), 66–68.

39   John Garth, *Tolkien and the Great War: The Threshold of Middle-earth* (Boston: Houghton Mifflin, 2003), 304.

4: FELLOWSHIP

1   Lilian Whiting, *The World Beautiful* (New York: Little, Brown, 1901).

2   Because in the movie the saying is inscribed in a copy of Mark Twain's *The Adventures of Tom Sawyer* (1876), it is often attributed to Twain, but Jimmy Stewart, who played George, remembers the source being director Frank Capra.

3   See Mary Carita O'Brien, "*Koinonia* from Classical to Christian Times" (Dissertation, Loyola University Chicago, 1966), 42.

4   See Lorraine Smith Pangle, *Aristotle and the Philosophy of Friendship* (Cambridge: Cambridge University Press, 2003).

5   Aristotle, *Politics* 1280b38–39; 1295b23–25; idem., *Nicomachean Ethics* Books VIII and IX. For commentary, see Eleni Leontsini, "The Motive of Society: Aristotle on Civic Friendship, Justice, and Concord." *Res Publica* 19, no. 1 (2013): 21–35.

6   Aristotle, *Nicomachean Ethics* 1155b21; idem. *Eudemian Ethics* 1236a32.

7   Aristotle, *Nicomachean Ethics* 1145a–1156b.

8   Aristotle, *Politics* II.1.1261a18; III.1.1275b20.

9   Seneca, *De Beneficiis* 4.18.2–3.

10   E.g., 2 Corinthians 9:13; Philippians 3:10.

11   1 John 1:3, 6–7.

12   O'Brien, 375.

13   My emphasis. For discussion, see Casey, *Pagan Virtue*, 183–94.

14   Aquinas, *Summa Theologiae*, 1a2ae, 28, 2.

15   John Casey, *Pagan Virtue: An Essay in Ethics* (Oxford: Clarendon Press, 1990), 186.

16   Apart from a brief hiatus, from 1902–3: see John Garth, "A Brief Biography," in Stuart Lee, ed., *A Companion to J.R.R. Tolkien* (Oxford: Wiley Blackwell, 2014), 7–23.

17   Humphrey Carpenter, *J.R.R. Tolkien: A Biography* (Boston: Houghton Mifflin, 2000), 53.

18   Philip and Carol Zaleski, *The Fellowship: The Literary Lives of the Inklings* (New York: Farrar, Straus and Giroux, 2016), 26.

19   Tolkien, *Letters*, 10.

20   Tolkien, *Letters*, 8–10.

21   See Humphrey Carpenter, *The Inklings* (London: HarperCollins, 1997); and Philip and Carol Zaleski, *The Fellowship: The Literary Lives of the Inklings* (New York: Farrar, Straus and Giroux, 2016). Tolkien himself attempted a parody of Inklings gatherings in his unfinished 1945 novel, *The Notion Club Papers*.

22   Nevill Coghill, "The Approach to English," in Jocelyn Gibb, ed., *Light on C.S. Lewis* (New York: Harcourt, 1965), 54–55.

23   Tolkien, *Letters*, 36, 67, 76, 126, and 388.

24   *The Collected Letters of C.S. Lewis*, ed. by Walter Hooper, Vol. II (San Francisco: HarperCollins, 2005), 501.

25   Letter to Dr. Firor (12 March 1948), C.S. Lewis Papers, Bodleian Library, Oxford. All but Cecil listed their rank in the British armed services.

26   *The Hobbit*, 294.

27   *The Hobbit*, 298–99.

28   *The Hobbit*, 312.

29   *The Hobbit*, 316.

30   *The Hobbit*, 327.

31   *LOTR*, 170, 172.

32   See Tolkien, *Letters*, 170–71; Wayne G. Hammond and Christina Scull, *'The Lord of the Rings': A Reader's Companion* (Boston: Houghton Mifflin, 2005), xxxiii.

33   *LOTR*, 276.

34   *LOTR*, 355, 357.

35   *LOTR*, 419.

36   *LOTR*, 970

37   *LOTR*, 981.

38   *LOTR*, 1030.

39   See Richard W. Kaeuper, *Chivalry and Violence in Medieval Europe* (Oxford: Oxford University Press, 2006). Kaeuper shows (31–33) that knights did indeed read (or at least listen to readings of) chivalric biography, *chansons de geste*, vernacular manuals of chivalry, and Arthurian romances.

40   Tolkien, *Letters*, 144. For the possible meanings of this enigmatic statement, see Snyder, *Making of Middle-earth*, 75ff.

41   For Tolkien's Arthurian influences, see Snyder, *Making of Middle-earth*, 72–83; and Sørina Higgins, ed., *The Inklings and King Arthur* (Berkeley, CA: Apocryphile Press, 2017).

42   Meriadoc is a name born by both a Welsh saint (6th century) and the knight-hero of the Arthurian romance *Mériadeuc*, or *The Knight of the Two Swords* (13th century). See Hammond and Scull, 42.

43   Lewis, *Collected Letters*, Vol. II, 16.

44   Tolkien, *Letters*, 341.

45   Tolkien, *Letters*, 341.

46   Ibid.; Carpenter, *Tolkien*, 52.

47   Lewis, *Four Loves*, 61.

48   Ibid., 72.

49   Plato, *Epistles*, 3.318E.

5: GOOD CHEER: FOOD, DRINK, AND LAUGHTER

1   James Davidson, *Courtesans & Fishcakes: The Consuming Passions of Classical Athens* (New York: HarperCollins, 1997), 26.

2   Though this may only be Socrates testing a premise: see J.P. Sullivan, "The Hedonism in Plato's *Protagoras*," *Phronesis* 6, no. 1 (1961): 10–28.

3   For a good discussion of these in the context of ancient virtue ethics, see Annas, *The Morality of Happiness*, 227–44.

4   Annas, *The Morality of Happiness*, 227.

5   Diogenes II 6, fr. 51 in Aristippus (IV A) in Giannantoni, *Socratis Reliquiae*, vol 2 (Naples: Bibliopolis, 1990).

6   *Vatican Sayings* 77.

7   *Eudemian Ethics* 2.3.1221b.

8   Trans. by William Hansen, in idem., *The Book of Greek and Roman Folktales, Legends, and Myths* (Princeton, NJ, and Oxford: Princeton University Press, 2017), 382. Hansen quotes a similar story from Euboulos, in which Dionysius claims the first cup is for health, the second for sexual pleasure, and the third for sleep, "which wise men drink up and [then] go home."

9   See Susan E. Hill, *Eating to Excess: The Meaning of Gluttony and the Fat Body in the Ancient World* (Oxford: Praeger, 2011), 4–9.

10 *Babylonian Talmud*, Megillah 7b. Maimonides's interpretation: "One should eat meat and prepare as nice a meal as one can afford and drink wine until one becomes drunk and falls asleep from drunkenness." See *Laws of Maimonides*, Megillah 2:15.

11 Hill, *Eating to Excess*, 13: "The fat body articulates a cultural tension between desired abundance that celebrates life and unwanted excess that overwhelms and leads to death."

12 See N. El-Guebaly and A. el-Guebaly, "Alcohol Abuse in Ancient Egypt: The Recorded Evidence," *International Journal of the Addictions* 16, no. 7 (1981): 1207–1221, DOI: 10.3109/10826088109039174.

13 See, for example, Deuteronomy 21:18–21; Proverbs 23:20–21 and 28:7.

14 Drunkenness at the courts of the early caliphates are described in the *khamriyyat*, or "odes to wine," written by the Arab poet Abu Nuwas (757–814).

15 E.g., Romans 16:17–20 and Philippians 3:17–20. See Hill, *Eating to Excess*, 38–39.

16 See Davidson, *Courtesans*, 43–49.

17 Ibid., 49.

18 Max Harris, "The Feast of Fools," in *Oxford Bibliographies*, last modified 29 October 2013, DOI: 10.1093/OBO/9780195396584-0078.

19 Aperitivi, tapas, pinxos, mezzas . . . the Madrileños are particularly adept at running one meal into another, but always with great cheer and fellowship.

20 *The Hobbit*, 4; *LOTR*, 1–2, 6.

21 *LOTR*, 8–9.

22 *The Hobbit*, 160. Dorwinion, an agricultural land northwest of the Sea of Rhûn, was famed for its wines in *The Silmarillion*.

23 *The Hobbit*, 48.

24 *LOTR*, 270.

25 *The Hobbit*, 68–71.

26 *The Hobbit*, 138–40. For the influence of medieval elf/fairy traditions like that of *Sir Orfeo* on Tolkien's depiction of the Wood-elves, see Rateliff, *A Brief History*, 232.

27 *LOTR*, 42.

28 *LOTR*, 68.

29 *LOTR*, 70.

30 *LOTR*, 125.

31   *LOTR*, 290.

32   *LOTR*, 369–70.

33   *LOTR*, 622.

34   *LOTR*, 653-54.

35   *LOTR*, 723.

36   *LOTR*, 724.

37   *The Hobbit*, 46.

38   *LOTR*, 951–52.

39   F.H. Buckley, *The Morality of Laughter* (Ann Arbor, MI: University of Michigan Press, 2003).

40   Buckley, *The Morality*, 102.

41   Tolkien, *Letters*, 129.

42   These continued until shortly after Lewis's death in 1963, though they became less frequent after the early 1950s. Tolkien and Lewis also met on Monday mornings, just the two of them, at the Eagle and Child for several years. Tolkien called this "the pleasantest spot" of his week.

43   Tolkien, *Letters*, 68.

44   Tolkien, *Letters*, 128.

45   Davidson, *Courtesans*, 37.

6: TELLING STORIES AND SINGING SONGS

1   Classicist William Hansen defines more than twenty types of ancient tales in his taxonomy: see Hansen, *The Book of Greek and Roman Folktales, Legends, and Myths*, 7–37.

2   See Anne Pellowski, *The World of Storytelling*, exp. and rev. ed. (New York: The H.W. Wilson Company, 1990), 18: ". . . oral narration of stories in verse and/or prose . . . performed or read by one person before a live audience; the narration may be spoken, chanted, or sung, with or without musical [or] pictorial accompaniment . . . [for] entertainment or delight and it must have at least a small element of spontaneity. . . ."

3   M. Aubert et al., "Pleistocene cave art from Sulawesi, Indonesia," *Nature* 514 (9 October 2014): 223–27.

4   Jo Marchant, "A Journey to the Oldest Cave Paintings in the World," *Smithsonian* (January 2016): https://www.smithsonianmag.com/history/journey-oldest-cave-paintings-world-180957685/#szEUTxLTPgFhdM33.99.

5   Aesop's historicity is not certain. See Christos A. Zafiropoulos, *Ethics in Aesop's Fables: The 'Augustana' Collection* (Leiden: Brill, 2001), 10–11.

6   Zafiropoulos, *Ethics*, 1.

7   Quintilian, *Institutio Oratoria* (Cambridge, MA: Harvard University Press, 1986), Book I, ch. 9, pt. 2. Trans. by Harold Edgeworth Butler.

8   Euripides, *Heracles* (Chicago: University of Chicago Press, 2013), lines 99-100. Trans. by William Arrowsmith.

9   Pellowski, *World of Storytelling*, 6–7.

10   For a detailed breakdown of these arguments, see Charles L. Griswald, "Plato on Rhetoric and Poetry" in *The Stanford Encyclopedia of Philosophy*: https://plato.stanford.edu/entries/plato-rhetoric/.

11   See Pellowski, *World of Storytelling*, 3–5.

12   The distinction need not mean that the *aoidos* created while the *rhapsode* merely performed: see José M. González, *The Epic Rhapsode and His Craft: Homeric Performance in a Diachronic Perspective*, Hellenic Studies Series 47 (Washington, DC: Center for Hellenic Studies, 2013). http://nrs.harvard.edu/urn-3:hul.ebook:CHS _GonzalezJ.The_Epic_Rhapsode_and_his_Craft.2013.

13   See Michael Richter, *The Formation of the Medieval West: Studies in the Oral Culture of the Barbarians* (New York: St. Martin's Press, 1994).

14   See the anonymously published review by C. S. Lewis of *The Hobbit* in *The Times Literary Supplement* (October 2, 1937), 714.

15   *The Hobbit*, 8.

16   *The Hobbit*, 16.

17   *The Hobbit*, 17.

18   *The Hobbit*, 19.

19   *The Hobbit*, 58.

20   See J. R. R. Tolkien, "Enigmata Saxonica Nuper Inventa Duo," in *A Northern Venture: verses by members of the Leeds University English School Association* (Leeds: The Swan Press, 1923), reprinted in *The Annotated Hobbit*, 124–125 n.19; Tolkien's reply to a reader in the *Observer* (January 16, 1938) regarding the sources for his riddles in Tolkien, *Letters*, 32; and Marie Nelson, "Time and J.R.R. Tolkien's 'Riddles in the Dark'" *Mythlore* 27, no. 1 (Fall/Winter 2008).

21   *LOTR*, 1.

22   *LOTR*, 21.

23   *LOTR*, 24.

24   *LOTR*, 30.

25   *LOTR*, 43.

26   *LOTR*, 77–78.

27   *LOTR*, 81.

28   *LOTR*, 101.

29   *LOTR*, 106, 112.

30   *LOTR*, 122–23.

31   *LOTR*, 129.

32   *LOTR*, 157–60. The rhyme dates back at least to the 16th century, and Tolkien first published the *LOTR* version in *The Cat and The Fiddle: A Nursery-Rhyme Undone and its Scandalous Secret Unlocked* (1923), renaming it "The Man in the Moon Stayed Up Too Late" for *The Adventures of Tom Bombadil* (1962): see Hammond and Scull, 156.

33   *LOTR*, 170. Tolkien's verse is a nod to Chaucer, Spenser, and Shakespeare and contains the prophecy of Aragorn claiming his kingship: see Hammond and Scull, 160.

34   *LOTR*, 191–93, 184, and 206–8.

35   *LOTR*, 230–31.

36   *LOTR*, 279.

37   *LOTR*, 847.

38   *LOTR*, 434.
39   *LOTR*, 464–77, 85.
40   *LOTR*, 597–98.
41   *LOTR*, 620, 628.
42   *LOTR*, 711–12.
43   *LOTR*, 849, 953.
44   *LOTR*, 956, 963.
45   Wood, "Review Essay," 603.
46   Cicero, *De Natura Deorum*, 1.34.
47   See Hansen, *Greek and Roman Folktales*, 36.
48   J. R. R. Tolkien, "On Fairy-Stories," in C. S. Lewis, ed., *Essays Presented to Charles Williams* (1947). Reprinted in J. R. R. Tolkien, *Tree and Leaf* (London: Allen and Unwin, 1964); and idem., *The Tolkien Reader* (New York: Ballantine, 1966). See also Verlyn Flieger and Douglas A. Anderson, eds., *Tolkien on Fairy-Stories* (London: HarperCollins, 2014).
49   Tolkien, *The Tolkien Reader*, 86.
50   Tolkien, *Letters*, 78.
51   *LOTR*, 273.

7: SERVICE, SELFLESSNESS, AND SELF-SACRIFICE

1   See, for example, Tolkien, *Letters*, 54–55.
2   John Ronald and Edith's eldest son, John Francis, became a priest. See Christina Scull and Wayne G. Hammond, *The J.R.R. Tolkien Companion and Guide: Reader's Guide* (Boston: Houghton Mifflin, 2000), 1017–22.
3   Tolkien, *Letters*, 55, 75–76.
4   For the historiography on Roman slavery, see Moses I. Finley, *Ancient Slavery and Modern Ideology*, Brent D. Shaw, ed. (Princeton, NJ: Markus Wiener, 1998).
5   For the sources and commentary, see Brent D. Shaw, ed. and trans., *Spartacus and the Slave Wars: A Brief History with Documents* (Boston: Bedford/St. Martin's, 2001).
6   See account by Florus (2nd cent. B.C.E.) in Shaw, ed., *Spartacus*, 153–55.
7   Cf. I Timothy 6:1–2; I Peter 2:18; and Titus 2:9–10.
8   Aristotle, *Politics*, Bk 1, Chs 4–7. See also Nicholas D. Smith, "Aristotle's Theory of Natural Slavery," *Phoenix* 37, no. 2 (1983): 109–22; and Malcolm Heath, "Aristotle on Natural Slavery," *Phronesis* 53, no. 3 (2008): 243–70.
9   Timothy P. Jackson, *Love Disconsoled: Meditations on Christian Charity* (Cambridge: Cambridge University Press, 1999), xi.
10   See, for example, Nietzsche, *Genealogy of Morals*, 1:7.
11   Roberta Bondi, *To Love as God Loves* (Philadelphia: Fortress Press, 1989), 9.
12   See Margaret Mary, "Slavery in the Writings of St. Augustine," *The Classical Journal* 49, no. 8 (1954): 363–69; and Susanna Elm, "Sold to Sin Through *Origo*: Augustine of Hippo and the late Roman Slave Trade," *Studia Patristica* 98 (2017): 1–21.

13 Augustine, *Civitas Dei*, ch. 15 (trans. Marcus Dods). Cf. John Chrysostom (ca. 345–407): "Slavery is the fruit of covetousness, of extravagance, of insatiable greediness."

14 Roman law by this time forbade any freeborn man or woman to sell themselves or their children into slavery. This did not prohibit slave raiders from grabbing Roman citizens and selling them as slaves in the provinces or outside the empire, as happened to Patrick.

15 The status of these free tenant farmers is clarified in the *Theodosian Code* 5.17.

16 With the exception of Islamic piracy and Viking raids of the eighth and ninth centuries, which supplied wealthy households with domestic slaves, servile field workers in Scandinavia, and even slave armies in Spain.

17 Aquinas, *Summa Theologiae*, 2a2ae.58.

18 Aristotle, *Nicomachean Ethics*, 1169a17–29. See Marcia L. Homiak, "Virtue and Self-Love in Aristotle's Ethics," *Canadian Journal of Philosophy* 11, no. 4 (1981): 633–51; and Héctor Zagal Arreguín, "The Role of *Philautia* in Aristotle's Ethics," *Acta Philosophica* 2, no. 18 (2009): 381–90.

19 Exodus 20:3; Deuteronomy 6:4–5; Jeremiah 31:3.

20 Leviticus 19:18.

21 As is illustrated in the parable of the Good Samaritan. See Jackson, *Love Disconsoled*, 3–4.

22 Jackson, *Love Disconsoled*, 9.

23 Aquinas, *Summa Theologiae*, II-II, quest. 23, art. 7. See Appendix B below. The Vulgate bible substitutes the Latin *caritas* for the Greek *agape*, while English translations variously use both "charity" and "love."

24 For a discussion of the origins and historical practices, see Amy Singer, *Charity in Islamic Societies* (Cambridge: Cambridge University Press, 2009).

25 See, for example, Qur'an sura, 107.

26 Singer, *Charity*, 18–21.

27 See, for example, *Rigveda* Book 10, Hymn 117; *Brihadaranyaka Upanishad* V.ii.3; and *The Bhagavad Gita* Book 17.

28 Xinzhong Yao, *Confucianism and Christianity: A Comparative Study of Jen and Agape* (Brighton: Sussex Academic Press, 1996), 23.

29 Sir John Templeton, *Agape Love: A Tradition Found in Eight World Religions* (Philadelphia: Templeton Foundation Press, 1999), 4.

30 Terry Eagleton, *Radical Sacrifice* (New Haven, CT: Yale University Press, 2018), 1.

31 Ibid., 2.

32 Many ancient peoples, like the Scythians and Gauls, cut off the heads of enemy combatants and displayed them as war trophies. Heads and scalps were also collected in this way by the indigenous peoples of the Americas. Rome itself was not above the practice of the sacrifice or ritual murder of barbarians.

33 See Moshe Halbertal, *On Sacrifice* (Princeton, NJ: Princeton University Press, 2012), 7ff.

34 Ibid., 11.

35 Jackson, *Love Disconsoled*, 179.

36 The Jewish ritual of sacrifice ended abruptly with the destruction of the Second Temple by the Romans in AD 70. See Halbertal, *On Sacrifice*, 7.

37 Eagleton, *Radical Sacrifice*, 31.

38 Ali's note on Sura 3:92.

39   See the pioneering scholarship of Peter Brown, e.g., Brown, *Society and the Holy in Late Antiquity* (Los Angeles: University of California Press, 1989); and idem, *Authority and the Sacred* (Cambridge: Cambridge University Press, 1997).

40   See "Rules of Monastic Restraint" in Edward Conze, trans., *Buddhist Scriptures* (New York: Penguin, 1959), 73–77.

41   Alfred, Lord Tennyson, *Idylls of the King* (New York: Signet, 1961), 242.

42   Reinhold Niebuhr, *The Nature and Destiny of Man*, 2 vols (New York: Charles Scribner's Sons, 1949), 2:72.

43   *The Hobbit*, 13.

44   *The Hobbit*, 133.

45   *LOTR*, 63–64.

46   *LOTR*, 728.

47   *LOTR*, 899.

48   *LOTR*, 940–41.

49   *LOTR*, 755–56.

50   *LOTR*, 777.

51   *LOTR*, 687.

52   *LOTR*, 944.

53   *LOTR*, 947.

54   *The Hobbit*, 210.

55   *The Hobbit*, 294.

56   *LOTR*, 652.

57   Rozema, "*The Lord of the Rings*," 444.

58   Benedict XVI, *Charity in Truth (*Caritas in Veritate*)*, Encyclical Letter, (San Francisco: Ignatius Press, 2009), 7. Pope Benedict also equates love and Grace: "Charity is love received and given. It is 'grace' (*cháris*). Its source is the wellspring of the Father's love for the Son, in the Holy Spirit" (11).

59   Boyd, "*Nolo Heroizari*," 7; Laura Garcia, "Pride and Humility in *The Hobbit*," in Bassham and Bronson, 74–89.

60   *LOTR*, 1023.

61   *LOTR*, 1025.

62   *LOTR*, 1026.

63   See J. R. R. Tolkien, *The Homecoming of Beorhtnoth Beorhthelm's Son*, in idem., *The Tolkien Reader* (New York: Ballantine Books, 1965), 5; and p. 29 above.

64   Conze, trans., *Buddhist Scriptures*, 78.

65   Tolkien, *Letters*, p. 54. The whole letter to admirer H. Cotton Minchin has now been photographed and transcribed online: see http://tolkiengateway.net/wiki/H._Cotton_Minchin_16_April_1956.

66   See John Garth, "Sam Gamgee and Tolkien's batmen" (https://johngarth.wordpress.com/2014/02/13/sam-gamgee-and-tolkiens-batmen/).

67   Ibid.

68   Eagleton, *Radical Sacrifice*, 3.

69   E.O. Wilson, *Sociobiology: The New Synthesis* (Cambridge, MA: Harvard University Press, 1975), 547.

70   Michael Boylan, *The Good, the True and the Beautiful* (New York: Continuum, 2008), 30.

71   See Elliott Sober and David Sloan Wilson, *Unto Others: The Evolution and Psychology of Unselfish Behavior* (Cambridge, MA: Harvard University Press, 1998).

72   Thomas J. Lasley, *Teaching Peace: Toward Cultural Selflessness* (London: Bergin & Garvey, 1994), xix.

73   *The Hobbit*, 4.

8: MERCY

1   Wood, "Tolkien and Postmodernism," in idem, ed., *Tolkien Among the Moderns*, 247–77 (270).

2   Kreeft, *The Philosophy of Tolkien*, 217.

3   See Adrian Fortescue, "Kyrie Eleison," *The Catholic Encyclopedia*, vol. 8. (New York: Robert Appleton Company, 1910), December 18, 2019 http://www.newadvent.org/cathen/08714a.htm.

4   Homer, *The Iliad*, translated by Robert Fagle (New York: Penguin, 1998), Book 24, ll. 559–91.

5   Rachel Hall Sternberg, "The Nature of Pity," in idem, ed., *Pity and Power in Ancient Athens* (New York: Cambridge University Press, 2005), 15–47.

6   Dana LaCourse Munteanu, *Tragic Pathos: Pity and Fear in Greek Philosophy and Tragedy* (New York: Cambridge University Press, 2012).

7   Aristotle, *The Poetics*, chs. 6, 13, and 14.

8   Aristotle, *The Rhetoric*, 2.8. See Alan Brinton, "Pathos and the 'Appeal to Emotion': An Aristotelian Analysis," *History of Philosophy Quarterly* 5, no. 3 (1988): 207–19, www.jstor.org/stable/27743856.

9   Augustus, *Res Gestae* 3 and 34.

10   Tacitus, *Annals* 12.37.

11   See Andrew Wallace-Hadrill, "The Emperor and His Virtues," *Historia: Zeitschrift Für Alte Geschichte* 30, no. 3 (1981): 298–323, www.jstor.org/stable/4435768.

12   Seneca, *De Clementia*, 2.3.1. See discussion in Malcolm Bull, *On Mercy* (Princeton, NJ: Princeton University Press, 2019), 10–12.

13   Eagleton, *Radical Sacrifice*, 31.

14   Mahatma Gandhi, *Mahatma, II, Young India* (August 11, 1920, and April 2, 1931).

15   *Rig Veda*, 7.89.

16   John Milton, *Paradise Lost*, Book X, Line 77.

17   Aquinas, *Summa Theologiae* I, q. 21, a. 3.

18   See Matthew Strickland, *War and Chivalry: The Conduct and Perception of War in England and Normandy 1066–1217* (Cambridge: Cambridge University Press, 1996); and Craig Taylor, *Chivalry and the Ideals of Knighthood in France during the Hundred Years' War* (Cambridge: Cambridge University Press, 2013).

19   Jeffrie G. Murphy and Jean Hampton, *Forgiveness and Mercy* (New York: Cambridge University Press, 1988), 20.

20   Christine de Pizan, *Epistre Othéa*, 212–13. See Taylor, *Chivalry*, 179.

21   Dante, *Inferno*, line 65.

22   Machiavelli, *The Prince*, ch. 8. Compare to ch. 17, where Machiavelli suggests that too much mercy can be of greater harm than a few public acts of cruelty. See Bull, *On Mercy*, 22–25.

23 See Mary Villeponteaux, *The Queen's Mercy: Gender and Judgments in Representations of Elizabeth* (New York: Palgrave Macmillan, 2014), ch. 2.

24 William Shakespeare, *The Merchant of Venice*, Act IV, Scene I.

25 *The Hobbit*, 81.

26 *The Hobbit*, 88–92.

27 *The Hobbit*, 96.

28 Louis Markos, *On the Shoulders of Hobbits: The Road to Virtue with Tolkien and Lewis* (Chicago: Moody Publishers, 2012), 136.

29 *The Hobbit*, 287.

30 *LOTR*, 54.

31 *LOTR*, 59.

32 *LOTR*, 615.

33 *LOTR*, 695–96.

34 Markos, *On the Shoulders*, 139.

35 Kreeft, *Philosophy of Tolkien*, 217.

36 Sheldon Vanauken, *A Severe Mercy* (New York: Harper & Rowe, 1977), 210.

37 Tolkien, *Letters*, 234.

38 Sr Joan Chittester, *God's Tender Mercy: Reflections on Forgiveness* (New London, CT: Twenty-Third Publications, 2010), 10.

39 *LOTR*, 583, 983–84. Gandalf says that Saruman is "pitiable" and offers him freedom, despite his betrayal.

40 *LOTR*, 1019.

41 *LOTR*, 1020.

42 Tolkien, *Letters*, 326.

43 See discussion in Jeffrie G. Murphy and Jean Hampton, *Forgiveness and Mercy* (New York: Cambridge University Press, 1988), 2–10.

44 *LOTR*, 366.

45 Peter M. Candler, Jr., "Tolkien or Nietzsche; Philology and Nihilism," in Wood, ed., *Tolkien Among the Moderns*, 95–130 (113).

9: VIRTUE AND VICE IN MIDDLE-EARTH

1 Henry Giroux, "Militant Hope in the Age of the Politics of the Disconnect," *Counter Punch* (23 Dec 2016), https://www.counterpunch.org/2016/12/23militant-hope-in-the-age-of-the-politics-of-the-disconnect/.

2 *LOTR*, 270. The wording I use here is from the Peter Jackson film *The Fellowship of the Ring* (2000).

3 *LOTR*, 365.

4 Aristotle, *Nicomachean Ethics*, IV.3, 1123b5–8 and 1124a3–5.

5 Ibid., IV.3, 1124a5–6, 19.

6 Robin W. Lovin, *Christian Ethics: An Essential Guide* (Nashville: Abingdon Press, 2000), 67.

7 *Nicomachean Ethics*, IV.3, 1124b23–28.

8   *LOTR*, 463–64.
9   *LOTR*, 465.
10   *Nicomachean Ethics*, IV.3, 1124a13–17.
11   Lovin, *Christian Ethics*, 67.
12   *LOTR*, 472.
13   *LOTR*, 670.
14   Rozema, "*The Lord of the Rings*," 437ff.
15   *LOTR*, 330.
16   *LOTR*, 670–71.
17   *LOTR*, 758.
18   *LOTR*, 813.
19   *LOTR*, 742.
20   Rozema, "*The Lord of the Rings*," 438.
21   *LOTR*, 473.
22   *LOTR*, 578–84.
23   *The Hobbit*, 51.
24   *LOTR*, 268, 1085. Gil-galad gave his ring to Elrond before he died, while Cirdan later surrendered his to Mithrandir (Gandalf).
25   *LOTR*, 356.
26   *LOTR*, 357.
27   *LOTR*, 365.
28   *LOTR*, 370–76.
29   *LOTR*, 348.
30   *LOTR*, 356.
31   *LOTR*, 376.
32   *LOTR*, 229.
33   *LOTR*, 1076–77.
34   *LOTR*, 356.
35   *LOTR*, 376.
36   *The Hobbit*, 214.
37   *The Hobbit*, 218.
38   *The Hobbit*, 272.
39   *LOTR*, 430.
40   *LOTR*, 757.
41   *LOTR*, 810.
42   *LOTR*, 672.
43   *LOTR*, 681.
44   *LOTR*, 681.
45   Tolkien, *Letters*, 323.

46 *LOTR*, 812–13.

47 Peter Brown, "The Saint as Exemplar in Late Antiquity," in John Stratton Hawley, ed., *Saints and Virtues* (Berkeley, CA: University of California Press, 1987), 4–14 (5). My emphasis added.

48 *LOTR*, 964.

49 Tolkien, *Letters*, 324.

50 Sir Thomas Malory, *Morte D'Arthur*, translated by Dorsey Armstrong (Anderson, SC: Parlor Press, 2009), 635–36.

51 Boyd, "*Nolo Heroizari*," 14.

52 Daniel Rozema, "*The Lord of the Rings*: Tolkien, Jackson, and 'The Core of the Original,'" *Christian Scholar's Review* 37, no. 4 (2008): 427–445.

53 *The Return of the King* won all eleven Academy Awards for which it was nominated.

54 Kreeft, *The Philosophy of Tolkien*, 44.

55 The criticism does not hold for the posthumously published *Silmarillion*, *Children of Húrin*, *Fall of Arthur*, *Legend of Sigurd*, and *Beren and Lúthien*. These works show that Tolkien was interested in romance and sexual relationships, women as rulers, motherhood, and other gendered circumstances.

56 This is the film's version of the dialog, which is more sparse and dramatic. See *LOTR*, 841.

57 Tolkien, *Letters*, 323.

58 In the *Republic*, for example, women can receive the same education as men and be members of the Guardian class, while Aristotle argues in the *Politics* for the inferiority of women. See, however, Thomas M. Robinson, "*Arete* and Gender-Differentiation in Socrates/Plato and Aristotle," *Areté* 11, nos. 1-2 (1999), 71-81.

59 *LOTR*, 784.

60 *LOTR*, 964.

61 *LOTR*, 539.

62 *LOTR*, 267, 289.

63 Evagrius, *On the Eight Principal Vices*: "There are eight tempting thoughts (*logismoi*). . . . The first is that of gluttony; and with it, sexual immorality; third, love of money; fourth, sadness; fifth, anger; sixth, acedia; seventh, vainglory; and eighth, pride." In Buddhism there are five deadly sins: killing one's mother, killing one's father, killing an *Arhat* (saint), causing dissension in the Order, and deliberately causing a Buddha's blood to flow.

64 Charles W. Nelson argues that in *LOTR* Tolkien composed, in part, a moral scheme based on the Seven Deadly Sins, with Dwarves exemplifying greed, Men pride, Elves envy, Ents sloth, Hobbits gluttony, Wormtongue lechery, and orcs anger. See Charles W. Nelson, "The Sins of Middle-earth: Tolkien's Use of Medieval Allegory," in George Clark and Daniel Timmons, eds., *J.R.R. Tolkien and his Literary Resonances* (Westport, CT: Greenwood Press, 2000), 83–94.

65 Tolkien, "*Beowulf*," 114.

66 Michael C. Brannigan, "'The Road Goes Ever On': A Hobbit's Tao," in Bassham and Bronson, 20–31.

67 *The Hobbit*, 328.

68 *LOTR*, 54.

69 *LOTR*, 55.

70   Aristotle, *Nicomachean Ethics* 4.3, 1124a.
71   Aquinas, *Summa Theologiae*, II–II, Question 161, a.1.
72   Garcia, "Pride and Humility," 83–84.
73   *LOTR*, 48.
74   Tolkien, *Letters*, 151, 178, 191, 287. Tolkien notes (*Letters*, 90) that there is a difference in this regard in the Primary and Secondary worlds: "There are no genuine Uruks [in the Primary world], that is folk made bad by the intentions of their maker; and not many who are so corrupted as to be irredeemable. . . ."
75   See Richard W. Kaeuper, *Chivalry and Violence in Medieval Europe* (Oxford: Oxford University Press, 2006), 22–23.
76   *LOTR*, 400–401.
77   *LOTR*, 538–39.
78   Tolkien, *Letters*, 54.
79   *LOTR*, 49.
80   Tolkien, *Letters*, 76.
81   Tolkien, *Letters*, 82.
82   See Tolkien's comments in *Letters*, 241.
83   Rick Szostak, *Unifying Ethics* (Lanham, MD: University Press of America, 2005), vii.
84   Thomas J. Lasley, *Teaching Peace: Toward Cultural Selflessness* (London: Bergin & Garvey, 1994), xix–xx.
85   *LOTR*, 24.
86   *LOTR*, 438.

10: BEING SMALL IN A BIG WORLD
1   Benedict XVI, *Charity in Truth*, 18.
2   Tolkien, *Letters*, 111.
3   *The Hobbit*, 330.
4   Aquinas, *Summa Theologiae*, II–II.161.1, ad3.
5   Boyd, "*Nolo Heroizari*," 9.
6   Robert Merrihew Adams, *A Theory of Virtue: Excellence in Being for the Good* (Oxford: Clarendon Press, 2006), 169.
7   Aristotle loved to walk in a wooded sanctuary outside the walls of Athens while he taught his students, with the result that he and his followers are called the Peripatetic school of philosophy, from *peripatoi* ("walks").
8   See Hilary Tolkien, *Black and White Ogre Country: The Lost Tales of Hilary Tolkien* (Moreton-in-Marsh: ADC Publications, 2009).
9   *LOTR*, 33.
10   *LOTR*, 5.
11   *LOTR*, 14.
12   *LOTR*, 14.
13   In Peter Jackson's films, these oaths are more explicit: all the Companions make oaths at the Council of Elrond, and Sam says, after nearly drowning going after Frodo at the end of *The Fellowship*: "I made a promise to Gandalf, to not leave you, Mr. Frodo, and I don't mean to break my promise. I don't mean to."

14 *LOTR*, 730.
15 *LOTR*, 664, 671.
16 *LOTR*, 681.
17 Aristotle, *Nicomachean Ethics* 4.3.
18 See Carlon A. Barton, *Roman Honor: The Fire in the Bones* (Berkeley: University of California Press, 2001), 11.
19 Tolkien, *Letters* (January 14, 1956), 232.
20 Tolkien, *Letters* (December 24, 1944), 105. Frodo's ultimate fate, described this way, is very similar to that of Sir Galahad on the Grail quest.
21 Stanley Hauerwas and Charles Pinches, *Christians among the Virtues: Theological Conversations with Ancient and Modern Ethics* (Notre Dame, IN: University of Notre Dame Press, 1997), xii. Their list of essential Christian, or "hopeful," virtues: Faith, Hope, and Charity (the Theological Virtues), Love (*agape*), Friendship (*filia*), Forgiveness, Suffering (or "Endurance that allows us to rejoice in our suffering"), Character ("we attain character not by our constant effort to reach an ideal but by discovery, as we look back on our lives and, by God's forgiveness, claim them as our own"), Obedience (to God), Courage, Prudence, and Patience.
22 *LOTR*, 1062–63.
23 Plato, *Protagoras* 352C.
24 See C. Emlyn-Jones, "Socrates, Plato, and Piety," *Mediterranean Studies* 2 (1990): 21–28, www .jstor.org/stable/41163976.
25 At least in *The Hobbit* and *LOTR*. In *The Silmarillion* there is a divine Creator (Ilúvatar), greater spirits (the Valar), and lesser spirits (the Maiar), and the Elves display great reverence and piety toward them, on occasion.
26 Tolkien, "*Beowulf*," 120.
27 Shippey, *Road to Middle-earth*, 202.
28 Wood, "Review Essay," 600.
29 Tolkien, "Letter to H. Cotton Minchin," (16 April 1956).
30 Mother Theresa, *A Call to Mercy: Hearts to Love, Hands to Serve*, (New York: Penguin, 2016), xiii–xiv.
31 Dennis Knepp, "Bilbo Baggins: The Cosmopolitan Hobbit," in Bassham and Bronson, 45–58.
32 Diogenes Laertius VI 63.
33 Garcia, "Pride and Humility," 88 n11, quoting from Tolkien, "The Quest of Erebor," in *Unfinished Tales*, 332–33.
34 *LOTR*, 269.
35 *LOTR*, 270.
36 "Heroic Endeavour," *Times Literary Supplement* (27 Aug 1954), 541. See Hammond and Scull, xxxxv.
37 Plato, *Protagoras* 329C–334C, 349B–360E. For critique of this unity theory, see Gregory Vlastos, "The Unity of the Virtues in the "Protagoras," *Review of Metaphysics* 25, no. 3 (1972): 415-58; and Adams, *A Theory of Virtue*, 171ff.
38 E.g., in Aristotle, *Metaphysics* 12.7, 9, 10. See Stephen Menn, "Aristotle and Plato on God as Nous and as the Good," *The Review of Metaphysics* 45, no. 3 (March 1992): 543–73: *nous* is "the goal or model in imitation of which all good things, including the world-order, are produced" (573).
39 Hauerwas and Pinches, *Christians among the Virtues*, 17.
40 Augustine, *Against the Manichees and the Donatists*, ch. 15.

41   E.g., Aquinas, *Summa*, II–II q.23 a.1. For discussion, see Raphael Joshua Christianson OP, "A Thomistic Model of Friendship with God as Deification," *New Blackfriars* DOI:10.1111/nbfr.12398; and Hauerwas and Pinches, *Christians among the Virtues*, xi.

42   See Kevin Ryan, "Foreword," in Lasley, *Teaching Peace*, xiii: both values clarification and cognitive development theory have "had a positive message" and "were highly promoted in the educational literature and the popular educational press," but both ignored the classical approach of "having the young study virtues such as responsibility, courage, kindness and, yes, selflessness."

43   Allan Bloom, *The Closing of the American Mind* (New York: Simon and Schuster, 1987), 27, 61.

44   Richard Eldridge, "What Was Liberal Education?" *LA Review of Books* (21 Jan 2018): https://lareviewofbooks. org/?p=255908&post_type=article&preview=1&_%20ppp=4175dead77#!

45   "William Caxton's Preface," in Malory, *Morte D'Arthur*, translated by Dorsey Armstrong, 1–2.

46   Tolkien, *Letters*, 144.

47   Tolkien, *Letters*, 194 (September 1954): "I would claim, if I did not think it presumptuous in one so ill-instructed, to have as one object the elucidation of truth, and the encouragement of good morals in this real world, by the ancient device of exemplifying them in unfamiliar embodiments. . . ."

48   *LOTR*, 972.

APPENDIX C: VIRTUES EAST AND WEST, ANCIENT AND MEDIEVAL

1   MacIntyre, *After Virtue*, 122–23.

2   For a brief discussion relevant to modern identity politics, see Andre Archie, review of Francis Fukuyama, *Identity: The Demand for Dignity and the Politics of Resentment* (New York: Farrar, Straus and Giroux, 2019), in *Modern Age* (Spring 2019), 67–72.

3   See John Casey, *Pagan Virtue: An Essay in Ethics* (Oxford: Clarendon Press, 1990), v.

4   John 15:9,12

5   *Catechism of the Catholic Church*, Part III, Section I, Chapter I, Article VII, 2.1814. http://www .vatican.va/archive/ccc_css/archive/catechism/p3s1c1a7.htm.

6   Ibid., 2.1817.

7   Ibid., 1.1807.

8   Keen, *Chivalry*, 2.

9   Kaeuper, *Chivalry*, 194.

10   James Hankins, "The Forgotten Virtue: Humanitas is the Cure for Incivility," *First Things* (Dec 2018): https://www.firstthings.com/article/2018/12/the-forgotten-virtue?utm_source=Intercollegiate+Studies +Institute+Subscribers&utm_campaign=d377400a8a-Intercollegiate+Review+December+6+2018&utm _medium=email&utm_term=0_3ab42370fb-d377400a8a-93113877&goal=0_3ab42370fb-d377400a8a -93113877&mc_cid=d377400a8a&mc_eid=3ff943e654.

11   See Geoffrey Hill, "Courage in Shakespeare," in Darling-Smith, ed., *Courage*, 55.

INDEX

A

Abel, 97
Abraham, 97–98
Achilles, 11, 16
Adalbero of Leon, Bishop, 92
Adams, Robert, 161
advertising, xvii
Aeschylus, 27
Aesop, 71
Agamemnon, 11
agape, 95, 96, 99, 107
agrarian imagery, 8
alcohol, 55–58; *see also* drink
Aldhelm of Malmesbury, 57
Alexander the Great, 12, 13, 55, 174
Allegory of the Cave, 72
altruism, 93–96, 110–112
amor amicitiae, 37
Analects (Confucius), xv
anarchy, 31
ancient Egypt, 55–56, 97
ancient Greece, 53, 55, 71, 73–74, 88, 97, 116, 171, 181–182
ancient Rome, 8, 11–13, 14–15, 22–23, 53, 74, 88–89, 91, 97, 99, 117–118, 167, 171, 173
anger, 156
Anglo-Saxons, 29, 30, 31, 38, 47, 74, 76, 109, 143, 156

Annas, Julia, xviii
Apuleius, 83
Aquinas, Thomas, xvii, 15, 19, 28, 36–37, 92, 95, 119, 155, 161, 175, 176, 184
Aragorn Elfstone, 5, 18, 42, 43–44, 143, 146, 150–152, 159, 167, 169, 180
archaeology, xvii
Archilochus, 73
Aristippus, 54
Aristophanes, 58
Aristotle, xiv–xv, xvii, xviii, 5, 7, 8, 12, 22, 23, 30, 52, 86, 133, 152, 175, 178; on friendship, 35, 36–37; on honor, 167; on love, 93; *megalopsychos* of, 133–135, 155, 182; on moderation, 54, 56; moral virtues of, 181–182; on pity, 117; on slavery, 90; on wisdom, 171
Armies of the Dead, 156
Arthurian legend, xvii, 46–47, 100, 146–147, 149, 156
ascetics, 57
Athena, 170
Athenians, 11–12; *see also* ancient Greece
Augustine, Saint, xvii, 15, 91, 176
authenticity, 28

B

Bacchus, 99
banquets, 58–59
Bard the Bowman, 142–143
bards, 73–75
Barfield, Owen, 39
Barth, Karl, 101
batman, 108–109
Battle of Maldon, 29, 31, 109
Beatitudes, 13
beer, 55–56, 57; *see also* drink
Benedict (pope), 107, 160
Beorn, 62, 102
Beowulf, 17, 30, 74, 153, 156, 172
"*Beowulf*: The Monsters and the Critics" (Tolkien), 29, 31
Bhagavad Gita, The, 12
Bible, 56, 73, 115
Bilbo Baggins, xv–xvi, 10, 60–62, 76–77; country walks by, 163; courage of, 23–25, 123; desire for adventure of, 3; fellowship and, 41–42; garden of, 2; good cheer and, 54; humility of, 16–17, 161; mercy by, 122–123; pride of, 155; sacrifices by, 105–106; service of, 102; songs by, 80; storytelling by, 77–78
Bird and Baby, 66–68
Black Riders, 26, 78, 156